Life in a Cambodian Orphanage

Rutgers Series in Childhood Studies

The Rutgers Series in Childhood Studies is dedicated to increasing our understanding of children and childhoods throughout the world, reflecting a perspective that highlights cultural dimensions of the human experience. The books in this series are intended for students, scholars, practitioners, and those who formulate policies that affect children's everyday lives and futures.

For a list of all the titles in the series, please see the last page of the book.

Life in a Cambodian Orphanage

A Childhood Journey for New Opportunities

KATHIE CARPENTER

RUTGERS UNIVERSITY PRESS

NEW BRUNSWICK, CAMDEN, AND NEWARK, NEW JERSEY, AND LONDON

LIBRARY OF CONGRESS CATALOGING-IN-PUBLICATION DATA

Names: Carpenter, Kathie Lou, author.
Title: Life in a Cambodian orphanage: a childhood journey for new opportunities / Kathie Carpenter.
Description: New Brunswick: Rutgers University Press, [2021] | Series: Rutgers series in childhood studies | Includes bibliographical references and index.
Identifiers: LCCN 2020035571 | ISBN 9781978804845 (paperback) | ISBN 9781978804852 (hardcover) | ISBN 9781978804869 (epub) | ISBN 9781978804876 (mobi) | ISBN 9781978804883 (pdf)
Subjects: LCSH: Orphanages—Cambodia. | Orphans—Cambodia—Social conditions.
Classification: LCC HV1300.3 .C48 2021 | DDC 362.73/2—dc23
LC record available at https://lccn.loc.gov/2020035571

A British Cataloging-in-Publication record for this book is available from the British Library.

♾ The paper used in this publication meets the requirements of the American National Standard for Information Sciences—Permanence of Paper for Printed Library Materials, ANSI Z39.48-1992.

www.rutgersuniversitypress.org

Manufactured in the United States of America

For my daughter, Delpha, who grew up alongside this project, and helped me understand what I was seeing through the eyes of a kid.

CONTENTS

Life in a Cambodian Orphanage

1

Introduction

One Morning at the Orphanage

Sovay howled, and his facial expressions ranged from stunned to furious. It was his first week at the orphanage, and he was grieving. His mother was dead, and his father, a soldier on the Thai-Cambodia border, was overwhelmed with the tensions that had heated up with Thailand over an ancient temple on their shared border. Those tensions would erupt a few weeks later in shootings, deaths, and evacuations of villagers from their homes. If Sovay had stayed, he would have been evacuated along with them, except that it's not clear who would have carried him.[1] His grandparents had been out of the picture for a long time already, and his father had requested help in finding somewhere safe for him where he would be able to receive the medical care he needed and go to school the following year. He was brought to the Children's Opportunity Center (COC), an orphanage in a small village about thirty kilometers from the city of Siem Reap, and he was currently adjusting to life as the youngest child in a new family with thirty-nine brothers and sisters. When Sovay's wailing did not stop, the adults who were working in the kitchen briefly looked his way, then called out to a group of older children playing in the nearby playground. One of them, a girl of nine, rushed over and scooped him up; he molded to her hip and immediately quieted. She carried him back to the other children, and he laughed as she bounced him up and down on the seesaw.

This brief episode illustrates many of the issues that drive the controversy around the so-called orphanage boom of Cambodia. Sovay wasn't "really" an orphan, according to those who insist on a definition that requires both parents of the child to be deceased, but he was struggling with challenges that required consistent attention from a parent who was simply unable to provide it. His home village was unsafe. The anecdote further illustrates how the adults, absorbed with the business of running the kitchen, were aware of his distress but did not rush to comfort him, instead delegating another child, who carried, comforted, entertained, and defended him. Much of the responsibility for the daily tasks needed to keep things going smoothly in Cambodian orphanages falls on the children themselves. At the orphanage, Sovay receives his medicines regularly, something that was difficult to ensure when he stayed with his father. When he is older, he will accompany the other children to the public school, an easy walk down the road, and he will have help with his homework. While his alternating tears, rage, and withdrawal are checklist indicators of "institutionalization," they all got better, not worse, the longer he lived in the orphanage. Five years later, when I last saw him, he was doing fine, and if I hadn't happened to be there when he first entered the orphanage, I would never have suspected that his desolate wailing and blank-faced withdrawal had even existed, let alone improved the longer he was living there in the orphanage.

Overview of This Book

The issues raised in Sovay's story are the focus of this book, and they are vexing, complicated, and weighty. In this book readers will find a detailed description of life as it unfolded in one orphanage in Cambodia, documenting and offering insight into one historical moment in Cambodia's rich history. The description is based on my own observations as well as the reflections of twenty-two of the children who lived there, speaking after they left and went to live in the community, although one point that I make is that the orphanage itself *is* part of the community. My purpose is to present both a portrait and an argument; the portrait is of the daily life of the children in residence, and the argument is that practices are what matter, not category labels, and furthermore that practices, unlike category labels, vary widely. Orphanages should not be dismissed out of hand as inevitably harmful to children, to their families, or to the communities in which they are located without a deeper understanding of the practices that take place within them. How children's needs are met is local and contingent and need not be implemented in the same way everywhere.

I primarily show what life in one orphanage is like, but I also make comparisons with other orphanages I have visited in order to show how varied the range is in terms of possible solutions to the same challenges. I show that there are legitimate alternatives to the narrative of orphanages as the bleak institutions widespread in stereotype and fiction and replace assumptions and pop-culture tropes with descriptions of real orphanages and the real children who live there. Despite the popular perception that a "good enough" orphanage is an oxymoron, I show that this assumption is not always supported by the evidence and that the dichotomies assumed to exist between community-based care and orphanage care are blurry and possibly misleading.

The structure of this book is as follows: In this introduction I present some background into my own engagement with this topic, followed by a summary of research on orphanage care, especially the controversies surrounding its effects on children. I also survey research into the emotive power of words and tropes associated with orphans and how they impact the orphanage controversy, as well as some discussion of the significance of this topic in the realms of research and policy. Chapter 2 is a detailed study of the history of orphanage care in Cambodia, followed by a discussion in chapter 3 of the rise of what has been called orphanage tourism and the anti-orphanage-tourism campaign that was mobilized to combat it. Chapter 4 describes my research methods, and chapter 5 portrays daily life in the COC, showing the rhythms of daily routines and interactions. Chapters 6 and 7 present the results of follow-up interviews I conducted with former residents after the orphanage closed in 2019, and finally in chapter 8 I discuss how the information and insights gained through this research can shed light on prevailing controversies. I draw some conclusions about orphanages and suggest recommendations that have relevance for policy and for improving care for children in a variety of circumstances.

Since I began this project, the forced removals of children from their families along the U.S. southern border have horrified the world, and rightly so. What you will not find in this book, therefore, is a justification for forced or fraudulent family separations, or the claim that institutional care is always a good idea. Orphanage care benefitted the children in the COC partly because they were *not* placed there fraudulently or through force, and the positive outcomes I describe are not to be taken as evidence that taking children from their parents and putting them in cages is ever justifiable. Having studied the COC in depth, I am qualified to speak of good residential care and to recognize all the ways that cages on our southern border constitute bad, very bad, residential care.

While the precise number of unparented children around the world is contested and estimates vary widely, the truth is that even if there were just one, for instance Sovay, we would still be challenged by the need to figure out the best solution for him. Multiply this by thousands of Sovays, and the challenges inherent in finding the best solutions for all of them jump to a daunting level. While perfect solutions exist in the realm of abstract principles, best solutions can exist only in the real world, given local conditions and constraints, and even a principled prioritizing of the child's best interests must necessarily be followed by an unspoken "best interests . . . here, for this child, now, not last year or five years from now." The problem for children is that they don't stay the same age while the adults around them are figuring out the optimal way to improve public schools or to create a viable foster care system in the face of a dire shortage of social workers. Although these are both solutions that have been proposed as alternatives to orphanages in Cambodia, current orphanage residents are likely to be grown with children of their own before they are fully implemented.

Orphanages have been adopted and rejected before as a solution to the widespread social challenge of unparented children, and yet they keep reappearing because in particular circumstances for particular children, orphanages still strike many adults as the best option available relative to the alternatives. In Cambodia the conversation around children's best interests is further complicated by the way that orphanage proliferation has been fueled by foreign donations and what has been termed orphanage tourism. My own role in this controversy is as both an observer and a participant, since I started out as an "orphanage tourist" myself and remain deeply ambivalent about my experience. My first trip to Cambodia was in 2008, on a visit arranged by an award-winning socially responsible travel company that had been working with my university to provide students with travel opportunities to Southeast Asia. I accompanied the group on the entire itinerary, including a visit to an orphanage. The visit seemed to us at the time to be a good thing—after touring the city garbage dump where many of the children had previously lived and worked, the dozen or so of us arrived at the orphanage that was providing the children with an alternative to the garbage-picking life. The children came rushing toward us in an enthusiastic, boisterous crowd, and we were each assigned a "little sister" or "little brother" for the day. My little sister tugged my hand and led me to her classroom, proudly posing in front of the map of Cambodia on the wall. She waved over to the sleeping quarters, but when I started in that direction she dropped my hand and shook her head. An adult staff person gave us an introduction to the project, and then we all boarded a chartered bus for a day at a Phnom Penh water park. We paid admission fees for all the resident children and the orphanage staff and treated them to lunch. At the water park, the children were wild with excitement, but the orphanage staff were able to enjoy a quiet afternoon and a picnic respite, while the college students earned the adoration of the children by swimming and playing with them inexhaustibly for hours. I towed my little sister around and around the pool while she reclined on an inner tube, a blissful expression on her face. I remember a couple of the children were frightened of the waterfalls, but they were otherwise open to the experience and to us, especially all the splashing and horsing around with the students. After fried chicken and ice cream, we all rode back on the bus, dropped them off, and went back to our guest house, located right across the street from the Tuol Sleng genocide museum, which provided, we told ourselves, the backstory to "our" orphans' current lives.

This anecdote also illustrates dilemmas and complexities of orphanage life in Cambodia. In the 1990s and throughout much of the 2000s many tours, *especially* the socially responsible ones, featured a visit to an orphanage, invariably referred to as a volunteer experience. We all trooped along, eager and unquestioning. It is unlikely that any of the children could ever have gone to the water park or eaten such a luxurious meal without our contributions, and it is unlikely that the staff could have either paid for or safely supervised such a large number of children without the extra help. They certainly would not have been able to enjoy themselves as much as they were able to while we entertained the children. However, and contrary to my expectations, that is not to say that the children or their environment appeared deprived. The orphanage itself was plain but not grim. It was clean and well maintained, and the on-site school was a tremendous source of pride for the children. Nor did the children appear to be neglected or lacking in supervision or attention. Although we took them off the premises, the staff were always right there with us, and at the orphanage the children were careful not to go anywhere with us that was off-limits or out of their caretakers' sight. Although we were just playing with the children, and certainly having as much fun as they were, we were also speaking English with them and keeping them safe in the water so that the staff got a relaxing day off while the children got some English practice, which everyone clearly appreciated. Although I was anticipating indicators of institutionalization such as indiscriminate affection or blunted affect, these children were initially shy but interested and warmed up to the group as the day wore on. My fellow travelers were all teens and early twentysomethings, and their energy and youth were a tonic for the children, who were starstruck by them in the way that young children are always starstruck by youth of that age. For these young travelers, their subsequent social media posts indicated that the day counted among the peak experiences, not just of the trip, but of their lives.

In 2010 I returned to Cambodia with a different organization that also prided itself on socially responsible principles and practices. This itinerary also featured a short orphanage volunteer experience, which consisted of a trip to the local market to buy food that we then cooked and ate together with the children and staff. There was a tour of the premises and a performance of Khmer dancing by the children, who at this orphanage also appeared to be healthy and happy and in general faring well, thriving even. Although both visits raised many issues that I will discuss in more detail later in this book, what struck me most after those visits was the contradiction between these real orphanages filled with real children and the expectations I had come with about what orphanages were supposed to be like. I was surprised and intrigued. My expectations had been shaped first by Oliver Twist–style folk tropes and then by the news stories about the horrors revealed in Romania's orphanages after the fall of Ceausescu. More recently I had read academic papers on institutionalization and attachment in intercountry adoptions. I knew about "institutionalization syndrome," for example, and had expected to see the constellation of observable characteristics it is widely assumed to entail—aggression, indiscriminate affection, blunted affect, social withdrawal, developmental delays, inability to focus, and/or apathy, among others.[2] But I simply hadn't seen anything like what I "knew" I would see, and I wanted to understand why. When I turned to the literature, I discovered that I was not alone. For example, in 2005, Holt Children's Services surveyed 204 residential centers in all regions of Cambodia and reported that "most children (88%) were considered to be healthy and developing typically, a finding that was surprising because children with developmental delays are typically over represented in institutional care."[3]

Why was I, along with many other visitors to Cambodian orphanages during the 2000s, surprised to find children in orphanages who seemed to be doing so well? The academic consensus complements the popular construction of orphanages as bleak, overly regimented, and poorly resourced institutions that are invariably and inherently harmful for children. However, orphanages have not always everywhere been viewed as inevitably harmful or as the worst alternative for vulnerable and unparented children. At that time in Cambodia, they appeared to many Cambodians, as well as many foreigners, to be a reasonable and realistic solution for children left unparented by social disruption, disease, and other challenges. A few years later though, despite the fact that the children in many Cambodian orphanages appeared to be doing well, both the abovementioned tour organizations halted all orphanage visits in response to the negative attention that orphanage tourism was increasingly receiving.

The Trouble with Orphanages

As vilified as orphanages are now, it is hard to believe that they were once considered a progressive solution, both in Cambodia and in the United States, although their respective periods in favor were separated by about a century. In the 1980s and 1990s orphanages were seen as an acceptable, if not wholly desirable, humanitarian response to Cambodia's crises of war and refugees; in the 1880s and 1890s, orphanages in the United States were considered to be a humanitarian response to the problem of the poorhouse, in which children were warehoused alongside adults and vulnerable to their "corrupting influence."[4] Orphanages, referred to as "orphan asylums" in the United States beginning in 1729 when the first one was founded, have played a large role in the history of child welfare in North America and Europe, and the similarities with the orphanage scene in Cambodia are rather striking.[5] Then as now, the generalized term obscured differences among institutions that represented an enormous range of purposes, philosophies, and practices.[6]

In the nineteenth-century United States, orphanages were seen by many as a way to support families, especially by providing respite to single mothers. Although they served children from a range of circumstances, then as well as now, orphanages were frequently home to children with a living parent. In contrast to today though, this did not necessarily cause them to be considered "fake orphanages."[7] Often relatives placed children in orphanages as a way to invest in the entire family's long-term success; the education and training they received could enable children to contribute to their family's well-being when they were reunited. For many poor families in the nineteenth century, just as for many poor families in the twenty-first, orphanages were deployed strategically as resources to improve, not undermine, the long-term prospects of families. Ironically, then as now, while reformers viewed family care as superior because only a child's family could have the child's best interests at heart, the families themselves often thought that it was in the child's best interests to reside in an orphanage.

While orphanages were originally meant as a compassionate alternative to the horrible conditions of workhouses and poorhouses, they soon came under fire themselves, and in the United States by the 1950s most were closed or closing. The practitioner and scholarly consensus continues to maintain that institutional care is invariably and inherently harmful for children, but the framing has shifted and the dominant reasons now are somewhat different.[8] In the twentieth century critics expressed a more generalized progressive distaste for regimentation, along with the belief that families were superior because they have the child's best interests at heart, whereas now a rights discourse dominates, which holds that children have a right to grow up in a family because of developmentalist paradigms such as attachment theory. In other words, family care was previously assumed to be superior because of characteristics intrinsic to families, while today it is assumed to be inherent in the child's identity as a rights-bearing human being with an intrinsic need for a particular kind of relationship. The orphanage literature almost universally presumes that "children exposed to institutional care do not receive the type of nurturing and stimulating environment needed for normal growth and healthy psychological development," due to the "structural neglect" that typifies most of them.[9] Even when the material conditions of an orphanage are good and the children are well fed, well cared for, and well educated, it is presumed that "even children growing up in 'good' orphanages will be at high risk of developing clinical personality disorders, growth and speech delays, and an impaired ability to re-enter society later in life."[10]

These tensions might seem to lend themselves to empirical resolution, but their ideological dimensions make them difficult to resolve satisfactorily. While both historically and currently, objections to orphanages have been grounded in dominant beliefs about the superiority of family care, it is striking that ideologies of the family are fluid and contested and have changed in the intervening time. The stakes are high because a privileging of family-based care can lead to a bias to return children even to families that do not want them or when it is unsafe to do so. While deinstitutionalization of children in orphanages in favor of foster care sounds like an improvement, a shortage of foster families in the

United States, for example, has sometimes meant that children "ended up in improper facilities, such as detention centers, reformatories and state hospitals."[11] These institutions are even less suitable for meeting children's needs than orphanages are. When intentional and regulated institutions become unavailable, children sometimes end up in ad hoc and even potentially hazardous ones.

One uniquely modern aspect of the controversy is the centrality of attachment theory in modern critiques of orphanages. The potential for disrupted attachment and attachment disorders began its ascendance as a dominant concern in child development in the 1950s when Bowlby derived the foundations of his theory from studies of children who had been separated from their parents after World War II.[12] It is frequently invoked as a major consequence of institutionalization by professionals and laypeople alike, as can be seen in the following excerpts from a media report about a visit to a Cambodian orphanage:

> Short-term engagement with vulnerable children causes serious attachment problems. The country's orphanages are brimming, but along with brighter opportunities for poor kids come signs of long-lasting attachment issues. There is formal evidence for the concern. Children in residential centers are vulnerable to psychological and developmental disorders. Studies have found that children raised in institutions can develop Reactive Attachment Disorder. With the confusion of forming and breaking so many relationships with volunteers, the kids can become indiscriminate in affection. We saw it at SCAO in children like Seyma: We were only there an hour before he started hugging us and holding our hands.[13]

Even though widely regarded as an objective, universal, and evidence-based principle of child development, attachment theory took shape under the influence of a particular model of the ideal family that was shaped as much by ideology as by objective standards for what children need.[14] Despite the *many* difficulties faced by the children Bowlby studied, his conclusion was that the root cause of their trauma was that they had lacked maternal care. Within the dominant narratives of that time, it was less salient that they had also lacked paternal care and had endured a barrage of physical and psychological stresses prior to their placement in institutions. The quality of care provided by institutions was also not deemed relevant. Bowlby's conclusions based on traumatic separations led him to condemn even good-quality day care for children living in stable families. While attachment theory has undergone refinement and revision, Bowlby's core theories have been influential for popular lay ideas of parenting as well as clinical family practice, despite the fact that offshoots such as attachment parenting are not supported by research.[15] An acquaintance of mine who returned to work after her child was born was informed by their family therapist that her son had attachment disorder because of her "abandonment" of him to go to work, an overextension of the term that shows how pervasive and ideologically motivated it has become. Attachment disorders are a tempting villain and therefore much invoked in the Cambodian orphanage controversy, particularly because many orphanages there do see a steady stream of short-term visitors and volunteers coming and going. However, attachment is actually not even relevant because Cambodian children typically enter orphanages at an average age of eight. This is well after the age window that is affected, according to even very strong versions of attachment theory, which maintain that inconsistent or insufficient caretaking relationships by age three at the very latest cause attachment disorders. Scholarly beliefs about attachment are less conclusive than one might assume based on the somewhat oversimplified way it is invoked in the orphanage controversy. Attachment theory, "like most theories, is not a unified monolith built on a scholarly consensus, but is really a complex of observations, hypotheses and ongoing research, and many major areas of dispute are recognized as needing further research and refinement."[16]

The high age at placement typical of Cambodian orphanages is one example of how orphanages function as culturally embedded institutions, distinctive to each social environment in which they are found. Rather than being considered a confounding variable, contextual variation should be viewed as one of the host of factors that can work together to affect outcomes, and which therefore need to be documented and understood.[17] Orphanages in Cambodia are mostly for school-age children and older because one of their primary purposes is to provide educational access. Thus, the whole cultural ecology of orphanages in Cambodia is quite different from that of either the United States in the early twentieth century or Eastern Europe in the 1980s. The fact that most children in Cambodian orphanages are older also means that when younger children enter care, they have a very different experience from what they might have had if they had been just one infant or toddler among many.

UNICEF is one of the leaders in the pivot away from residential care, strongly promoting the position that residential care is only a last resort, and an unacceptable one at that. Reasons given include high child-to-staff ratios that exacerbate a care deficit; high staff turnover rates; chronic lack of resources, particularly in nutrition and health care; stigma; inadequate controls for preventing the abuse of resident children; and lack of stimulation due to an overly austere environment, both physically and in terms of human interaction. Difficulties in reintegration during early adulthood, due in part to community stigma and in part to inadequate preparation, failure to respond adequately to the psychological needs of children, higher costs compared to community-based care, lack of government standards and monitoring, and overall worse outcomes physically and mentally for children living in residential care facilities have also been noted in the research cited, especially in Eastern Europe.[18] Another widespread concern is that institutional care may perpetuate a cycle of inadequate caregiving because children without parental care may lack the opportunity to learn appropriate parenting skills, thus possibly passing on patterns of neglect or abuse to the next generation.

It is important to examine these concerns critically however. None are necessarily inherent to residential care. Each could simply be considered an indicator of poor-quality care, rather than an inevitable feature of all residential care, both good and bad.[19] Furthermore, all of these problems can be found in family-based care as well. In order to ascertain whether family care is always better than institutional care, two questions must be asked: Can an orphanage never provide the things that children need to thrive? And do families always provide those things? It is common to compare good family care with poor orphanage care; rarely is good orphanage care compared with poor family care, even though the circumstances under which many children are relinquished are often marked by extreme neglect or violence.[20]

Often condemnations of orphanages do not take into account the actual alternatives available. The hierarchy of preferred options reflects choices that are, in principle at least, available in the wealthier countries from which most critics hail. For example, home visitation, the currently ascendant best practice in supporting vulnerable children and their families, faces staff shortages and high turnover even in the United States, making it difficult to see how the personnel and infrastructure for an effective home visitation program could be mobilized quickly enough to benefit the current cohort of Cambodian children in residential care, although of course it is a desirable long-term solution to aim for.[21] There are also pragmatic concerns that must be weighed. Orphanages may realistically be the most feasible option in some situations, and there is by no means unanimity in the scholarly literature about whether there is truly no place at all for orphanages in the child care repertoire of a community. Why is it so difficult to achieve consensus on the right answer as to whether orphanages are good or bad?

One reason is that the ideological nature of beliefs about childhood base questions of good or bad implicitly but not always consciously on values rather than universal and unambiguous principles of child development.[22] There is no consensus position on what the ideal outcome of childhood should be. What someone considers a good or bad childhood depends crucially on what they think a good or a bad adult is and how much they believe childhood experiences contribute to shaping this ideal adult. This subjectivity is amplified when it comes to questions about childhood because of the ideological weight that childhood bears, leading to moral panics, hidden agendas, and the pendulum swings of a "scandal-reform" approach to designing child welfare policies.[23]

More Recent Reexaminations

While most media coverage still focuses on the scandalous nature of orphanage excesses, research is already moving toward a more nuanced approach. Despite widespread criticisms, orphanages continue to proliferate, in Cambodia as well as in other less wealthy countries, and not all research on orphanages in these settings has painted so bleak a picture. Zimmerman found that in the orphanage she studied in Malawi the children not only were better off materially than children in foster care but had a broader concept of their future potential.[24] She described a local strategy to combat stigma by providing the orphanage with attractive play equipment that encouraged local children to befriend the orphans, first so they could share the facilities, but later, once stigma had been overcome, real friendships developed. She also found that orphans in orphanages had more free time to play than did orphans in foster care and that looking after younger children was their main responsibility, in contrast to the sometimes heavier burden of chores that children usually assumed in families. Likewise, Gibbons found that some Egyptian orphanages provided children with considerable emotional and practical support.[25] She found stigma was deliberately countered by development of orphanage schools that were superior to the local public schools and that girls in orphanages were less affected by gender bias than those in their natal families. While concern is often raised about the inadequate care resulting from high staff-to-child ratios, Neimetz, in detailed observations of a Chinese orphanage, observed that children frequently and effectively provided care for each other.[26] So did Emond, who also found that, in contrast to the pervasive assumption that children in orphanages are desperate to leave and live in a family, many of the Cambodian children she interviewed considered themselves lucky to be living in an orphanage.[27] They explained that orphanage placement opened up future possibilities that would have been unimaginable to them had they remained with their families.

Whetten and colleagues' large cross-sectional study in Cambodia, as well as Tanzania, Kenya, Ethiopia, and India, generated controversy with evidence showing that orphans and separated children living in orphanages often fared as well as, and sometimes even better than, orphans and separated children in family care in their natal communities.[28] In explicitly arguing against the assumption that orphanages are invariably damaging, their conclusion was that orphanage care may be "not so bad" and should be considered one viable option among the suite of choices a community has for caring for vulnerable children. Whetten et al. also presented evidence that there was more variation across orphanages, and across family-based care situations, than there was between orphanages and family-based care. They proposed that more research should target concrete aspects of care situations that may be leading to better or worse outcomes rather than lumping all orphanages together under the assumption that they are inevitably harmful.[29]

Subsequent work has continued to bolster the conclusion that orphanages can have a more positive effect on children's lives than many of the alternatives available to them and that careful attention must be paid to attributes of care situations, rather than terms used to refer to them.[30] Yendork and Somhlaba found that orphanage-dwelling children in Ghana reported stronger support from friends than did their counterparts living in families and that peer support is a protective factor against adverse effects.[31] They found no significant differences in the self-efficacy and resilience of orphanage-dwelling versus family-dwelling children. Gayapersad et al. documented how care centers in Kenya reproduce kinship connections in ways that helped residents feel that they were still part of a family.[32] Whetten et al.'s follow-up study of family-dwelling and institution-dwelling orphaned and separated children showed that overall "differences between institution- and family-based children and the differences in changes over time were substantively negligible when compared to the variation between children within settings."[33] Gray et al. found that orphaned and separated children living in institutions experienced fewer potentially traumatic events, including abuse, than did similar children living with families in five countries in Africa and Asia, including Cambodia.[34] Likewise, Mishra and Sondhi found that going to live in an orphanage promoted resilience and positive life changes for orphaned adolescents in India, and Hong et al. found that AIDS orphans in orphanages and group homes in rural China fared better than AIDS orphans in kinship care.[35] Xia and Lam found that residential care provided a sense of security and stability to children with incarcerated parents in China and that placement came as a relief even for those previously living with relatives because they often felt unwanted and stigmatized.[36] Thus, a recent body of research, using a range of methods and investigating an array of indicators and outcomes in a broad swath of societies, has found that residential care can be, at the very least, as good as family care, and in some respects even better.

While a frequent argument used against orphanages in developing countries is that they have already been shuttered in wealthy Western countries because they were found to be harmful, in fact residential care continues to be practiced in the United States and other wealthier countries, although the label "orphanage" is rarely used. Now, because it is seen as a last resort rather than a desirable option, residential congregate care is usually reserved for children who have already undergone failed foster care placements and, almost invariably, adverse experiences.[37] This leads to a policy conundrum: the least-favored care option is reserved for the children who need high-quality care the most. It also highlights the fact that despite the rhetoric, family-based care does *not* always work out well for children.

As Gordon has pointed out, current research supports the position that orphanages are not "inevitably and necessarily bad; the truth is that they have always been so regularly underfunded that they never got a fair trial."[38] However, Cambodia presents a contrast to the chronic underfunding of residential care. A distinctive feature of Cambodian orphanages is that foreigners enthusiastically make donations to them, more willingly than to other care arrangements, because of the emotive power of the words "orphan" and "orphanage."

Orphan Semantics and Tropes

One factor leading to the complex and sometimes contradictory positions with respect to orphans and orphanages stems from the semantics and cultural schemata associated with the words themselves. Although the words are used to refer to a broad array of distinct phenomena, people often treat the terms "orphan" and "orphanage" as though they have unvarying core meanings that link all residential care with a common set of characteristics. This nominalist fallacy leads to the erroneous assumption that what is true of some orphanages is true of all orphanages because they are the same thing. Naming is not explaining, however, and this tendency to sort all orphanages into a black box category rather than look at specific care practices follows inevitably but subliminally from the complex definitions and powerful connotations of the words "orphan" and "orphanage" and dominant orphan tropes in the Western imagination as seen in literature and popular culture.

Simple lack of translational equivalency leads to many of the confusions. There is rarely a precise one-to-one mapping of words across languages, and this is especially true of a term like "orphan," which references culture-specific notions of kinship and responsibility, not just the objective fact of whether a given set of parents is dead or alive. *Kamprea*, the Khmer word that most commonly translates as "orphan," is appropriately used to refer to any child lacking parental care, not just one whose parents are both dead. It is not necessarily disingenuous when Cambodians translate *kamprea* into English as "orphan" to refer to children who have a living parent or two. While much of the criticism of Cambodian orphanages revolves around the two-thirds to three-fourths of children in them who have at least one living parent, there isn't necessarily intentional deception taking place.[39] Children whose parents are alive can legitimately be real *kamprea*. Most Khmer-English dictionaries translate *kamprea* as "orphan," so referring to a residential center as an "orphanage" is often done in complete good faith.

In fact, in most languages, including English, "orphan" has never meant just "child whose parents are both dead."[40] Cultural constructions of vulnerability and family structure have never been simple, and it has always been recognized that while, on the one hand, a child with two dead parents may thrive in the care of extended kin, on the other hand, a child with one or two living parents may still be vulnerable to abuse or neglect. The meaning of "orphan" has been broad and complicated for a very long time. The root is ancient; the Proto-Indo-European form *orbh-* meant "to change allegiance, to pass from one status to another," leading to *orbho-* meaning "bereft of father," and also "deprived of free status." "Orphan" is cognate with the Sanskrit word for "weak" and "child" and the Ancient Greek root *orphanos* was used to mean "destitute" or "bereft" in general, including but not limited to "fatherless" in addition to "parentless."[41] In Latin the cognate *orbus* meant "deprived of benefits" or "destitute," not just "lacking parents." The Arabic translation of "orphan" means "fatherless," whereas in Quechua "orphan" and "poor" are the same word. In other words, many societies have long recognized that death of both parents is not the only important reason that children may need a special label to indicate their vulnerability and lack of affiliation. Definitions reveal cultural assumptions about what kinds of children belong or lack belonging, and what kinds of factors are significant in making them vulnerable. In English, the word "orphan" has been used historically for anyone bereaved of kin, including parentless children, the widowed, and even the childless.[42] Most of the U.S. "orphan asylums" of the nineteenth century in fact were designed for and mainly accepted what are now sometimes termed "half orphans," the children of single mothers, who often were required to apply for their child's admission, which depended on judgments of their relatives' character. Orphanage placement was an opportunity intended for the "worthy but unfortunate," rather than the truly desperate.

To further complicate matters, organizations and entities may adopt their own usage conventions and may even use different definitions depending on the particular goals at hand. For example, UNICEF and global partners define an orphan as "a child under 18 years of age who has lost one or both parents to any cause of death."[43] If both parents are dead, the term "double orphan" is used. The Cambodian government, in its Policy on Alternative Care, defines "orphan" as "a child who has lost one or both parents"; it does not specify that a parent must have been lost through death. At the same time however, UNICEF policy documents contain some of the strongest criticism of the Cambodian orphanages that house children who are not "real" orphans because they have at least one living parent. As the press relays this message, statements such as "UNICEF suggests 75% of children in Cambodian orphanages actually are not even orphans" and "UNICEF: Cambodia's orphans not really orphans" further confuse the situation and reinforce the perception that intentional fraud is being committed, even though such claims are contradictory to both UNICEF's and the Cambodian government's own definitions.[44]

While it is not so surprising that colloquial usage of the word "orphan" is complex and contested, one might expect to find more consistency in domains that require precision, such as the language of the law. However, legal definitions have also long been contested. In an 1852 case, the Georgia State Supreme Court ruled "it will be impossible to conclude that, when the Legislature speaks of an orphan, it meant to designate alone a minor whose parents are dead."[45] Likewise, in a document detailing the mandate of the Philadelphia Orphans' Court Division, it is stated that the court "serves to protect the personal and property rights of all persons and entities who are otherwise incapable of managing their own affairs. The name 'Orphans' in the name of the Court is derived from the general definition of 'orphan' as one lacking protection, not the common association of a child deprived by the death of his or her parents."[46]

Even within the very specific domain of eligibility for an orphan visa, the meaning of the word "orphan" depends on factors entirely external to the child and their parents, namely whether the country of residence is party to the Hague Convention or not. If a child is adopted under the Hague Convention, eligibility criteria say nothing about orphan status and the word is not used anywhere in them. Adopting from non-Hague countries requires that the child be an orphan, but that is defined as a child under sixteen who either "does not have any parents because of the death or disappearance of, abandonment or desertion by, or separation or loss from, both parents" or "has a sole or surviving parent who is unable to care for the child, consistent with the local standards of the foreign sending country, and who has, in writing, irrevocably released the child for emigration and adoption."[47] In other words, even in the very constrained context of determining eligibility for ethical adoption, a child can legally and legitimately be considered an orphan even if one or both parents are living and their identities and whereabouts are known.

It can be seen from this brief overview that meanings of the word "orphan" are already complex and can shift according to context. One response, recognizing that many children need special assistance and support, not just those with deceased parents, is the term "orphans and vulnerable children" (OVC). Using OVC highlights the rights and needs of all vulnerable children, not just those without parents who are privileged by the power of the orphan trope. However, while OVC has been useful in policy documents circulated among specialists, the acronym and its rationale are not widely known among the general public. Equally importantly, it lacks the powerful connotations of the words "orphan" and "orphanage," and so is far less useful for mobilizing concern and fundraising.[48] Another solution, retaining the emotive power of the term "orphan," has been to increase transparency through use of the term "social orphan," referring to children whose living parents are estranged or unable or unwilling to care for them.

While connotations are not formalized in dictionaries or legal codes, they can have profound consequences for perceptions and therefore policies. Connotations lend the words "orphan" and "orphanage" considerable power and highlight interesting tensions inherent in our perceptions and constructions of orphans themselves. On the one hand, we pity and fear the plight of orphans; on the other hand, their independence fascinates and attracts us.[49] This ambivalence is evident in the literary and popular culture tropes that rely on orphans to move the plot forward in comfortingly familiar but thrillingly risky ways and leads to a recycling of the theme of plucky orphans surmounting insurmountable challenges and transforming the adults around them for the better.

A few years ago, headlines in the *Telegraph* blared "Harry Potter was inspired by Oliver Twist."[50] One might legitimately wonder why this is even news. The orphan is an archetype, informing not just the imagined worlds of Oliver Twist and Harry Potter, but our own responses to these fictional characters as well as to orphans we might encounter in the real world. Cambodia's orphanage boom is able to rely on foreign donors and volunteers partly because it piggybacks on a foundation of Western cultural schemata and visceral responses to what it means to be an orphan and our desire to participate in orphans' lives, a desire that is shaped partly by our own curiosity and ambivalence about how it would feel to lose a parent.

Even though average life expectancy has lengthened so that the death of parents with still-dependent children is relatively rare in modern wealthy societies, orphans remain disproportionately important in story arcs and as characters, not just in literature and film, but even in more current media such as gaming.[51] Most of us have little other experience with orphans. Children surviving the deaths of their parents remain salient in wildly popular works such as the Harry Potter series as well as the seemingly endless remakes of *Anne of Green Gables*. These present-day forms reinforce the patterns of parentless children in traditional literature, created when parental, especially maternal, deaths were far more common and when the real lived variety of the orphan experience led to orphan tropes that were much more complicated than simple constructions of innocence or vulnerability would suggest. Orphans are objects of fascination and anxiety, envy as well as pity, and the net effect of these seemingly contradictory constructions gives them great power alongside their surface vulnerability. The ambivalent emotions are complementary rather than competing and provide ready-made plot arcs in which, by saving orphans, irredeemable adults are able to save themselves because orphans effect transformation upon those around them. From Luke Skywalker's redemption of Darth Vader through Lilo's transformation of Stitch from unsentient genetic experiment to devoted family member, orphans transduce conflicting emotions into spiritual transformation.[52] While consciously most adults would deny that we envy orphans, the "Orphan Emancipation Fantasy" of a commitment-free childhood is irresistible in fiction and permits orphaned characters to have adventures unencumbered by family ties.[53] Orphans play an important discursive role because their quest for their parents, sometimes to avenge their deaths, other times to unravel the mystery of their own origins, provides a conventional but nonetheless gripping plot, while at the same time orphans' parentless status allows them to forge new, unconventional relationships.

Another appeal of the orphan trope, and one that especially resonates with the young travelers who visit Cambodian orphanages, is that rather than inheriting a family, orphans have the option of creating their own family, something that young foreign volunteers want to be a part of.[54] These Western orphan tropes inevitably affect the emotive, often unconscious response that foreigners have to Cambodian orphanages, especially their desire to volunteer and make donations, which gives them entrée into the plotline of the plucky, heartwarming orphan who performs the emotional work of helping adults to appreciate their own lives and so become better people. This expectation certainly forms part of the allure for the many foreign travelers who visit, volunteer in, and make donations to orphanages.

Although orphanages have fallen out of favor among Western child welfare professionals, the "saving the orphanage" plot remains common in popular culture and serves rhetorically to juxtapose pure evil against pure good.[55] In pop-culture portrayals, orphanages either are nurturing places, filled with adorable orphans cared for by dedicated loving adults in the face of foreclosure by unscrupulous landlords and lenders, or are dark and scary, full of frightened children and frightening adults, a portrayal especially common in horror movies. Either way, the children in orphanages need and deserve the help of well-intentioned adults.

The power of these orphan tropes also helps to explain why messages to support family preservation programs or schools in remote rural areas are not as effective for fundraising as orphanages are, and why many residential children's centers were slow to change their names to "shelter" or "boarding school," even though that might better reflect their role in Cambodian society and could make them the target of less criticism. Other institutions can't generate the same transformative effects that firsthand contact with orphans is believed to. Fundraisers struggle with this dilemma because while they probably realize when children are not the kind of orphans whom donors believe them to be, they also understand that orphan tropes make fundraising to help orphans much easier than fundraising for other causes. These complexities appear to be deliberately harvested by some fundraisers and probably explain why UNICEF, for example, uses different definitions in different kinds of materials.

Significance and Theoretical Framing

The lens provided by an in-depth study of one particular orphanage can elucidate the causes and consequences of Cambodia's orphanage boom. This study is situated at a unique historical confluence of postconflict social disruption, neoliberal economic excesses, and mass tourism, all colluding to make orphanages

salient as a solution to the problem of large numbers of children who, for whatever reason, are outside parental care. The importance of this topic, though,
lies not just in objective policy implications but also in the visceral way it resonates with most of us, even as adults. The topic is inherently riveting because
the idea of losing one's parents touches most of us in a profound, and deeply
ambivalent, way; the notion of orphanhood is both devastating and alluring.

The topic of orphanages in Cambodia is timely, important, and unique, and
yet at the same time timeless, unremarkable, and universal. According to UNICEF,
there are almost 140 million children around the world who can be considered
orphans.[56] Controversy surrounds all solutions for their care, particularly in
communities that have been hardest hit, such as postconflict societies and
those heavily affected by HIV/AIDS. Even at its peak of some one thousand
orphanages in the United States in 1900, the density of orphanages never
matched that of Cambodia, and the controversy surrounding orphanage care in
Cambodia is proportionately that much more vexing.[57] Despite blanket condemnations and a near consensus that holds all orphanage care to be undesirable,
or in the words of Pamela Kruger, a journalist focusing on parenting issues, "an
orphanage is an orphanage is an orphanage," a more nuanced approach is
needed now.[58] Tolstoy wrote that all happy families are alike; the same cannot
be said for all orphanages, even the happy ones. All orphanages are not the same,
and it is important to look closely at specific features of actual, particular care
arrangements, especially outside of the United States and Eastern Europe, which
have inspired the bulk of conclusions and policy decisions. Policy making needs
to be responsive to local conditions; just as not all orphanages are the same, not
all social, cultural, and economic conditions are the same across all communities in which orphanages are located. If an orphanage, such as the COC, has
found ways to mitigate harms to children, then documenting and reporting the
strategies it uses can be a valuable contribution to the well-being of all children,
regardless of where they live.

The controversy over orphanages in Cambodia is informed by broader controversies over the nature of childhood, and so the theoretical frames provided
by childhood studies are especially valuable for contextualizing this research.
In particular, the work of David Lancy, who shows how particularistic ideas about
appropriate ways for adults to interact with children become globalized as an
"exportable social good," provides an insightful framework for reconciling differing approaches to the nature of childhood.[59] Are children most insightfully
viewed as "developing beings who are vulnerable and in need of protection," or
do we gain more by emphasizing how they are "in possession of agency, capable
and able to make interpretations of their worlds and act on them"?[60] While these
positions are in principle complementary, tension can arise between the two
approaches and their proponents.[61] Children are indisputably biologically
immature, developing entities, but they are also indisputably social actors in

their own right who must adapt to and function in present realities and not just future possibilities.

The tensions, and the intellectual excitement, inherent in the simultaneous consideration of different beliefs about the very purpose of childhood and the ideal adult-child relationship come into focus particularly around the flow of resources across generations. The conceptual framework of this research therefore also draws inspiration notably from Viviana Zelizer, whose analysis of children's shift from economically useful to economically marginalized but affectively priceless helps explain some of the tensions between the attitudes of various of the partisans in the orphanage controversy.[62]

Because childhood is so symbolically charged with ideas such as innocence and the future, debates about children often take on a vehemence that is rooted as much in ideology as in actual well-being or lack thereof. Cross-cultural research on children is complexified by the ways that childhood can be viewed as a metaphorical space as well as a biological stage, and so in this research I strive to "resist universal definitions of children and childhood" and to be skeptical of the "bright line dividing childhood from adulthood solely on the basis of years lived."[63] I also strive therefore to be richly descriptive and to allow ample opportunities for the children's own experiences to take center stage, both while they were living in the orphanage as well as later, after they have gone to live elsewhere. None of the ideas about orphanages that I took with me on my first trip to Cambodia prepared me for the richness and variety of the lived experience of the children living in the COC. To understand why, it is first necessary to examine the historical and social setting in which the COC was created, a topic that I discuss in detail in chapters 2 and 3.

2

History of Orphanages in Cambodia

The modern history of Cambodia is a history of the resilience of the Cambodian family. But this resilience can be understood only in juxtaposition with a history marred by the corrosion of the Cambodian family, sometimes unintended but too often intentional. Colonialism, the U.S. bombings, the Khmer Rouge children's camps, civil war, and years of refugees languishing in camps all foreshadow and exacerbate new challenges such as increasing inequality and labor migration of parents who are forbidden by law from taking their children with them.[1] Although an entire generation has now grown up in peacetime, the orphanage boom can be understood only in the context of the preceding decades of turmoil because one of the most serious criticisms levied against orphanages regards not just their consequences to individual children but the ways they may be provoking one more insult to the Cambodian family and to Cambodian society more broadly. Surprisingly though, upon closer examination orphanages can also be viewed as resources to be deployed by families in times of transition or vulnerability, affording a safety net that strengthens rather than undermines the long-term prospects not just of individual children but of the entire family. This seeming paradox can be understood only in the context of the history of out-of-family residential care for children in Cambodia, which is the topic of this chapter.

The structure of this chapter is as follows: I begin with some description of traditional out-of-family care arrangements in Cambodia. Next, I turn to an explanation of the rise and proliferation of orphanages, initially triggered by the U.S. bombing beginning in 1969. The resulting destruction necessitated emergency shelter for the many children who were separated from their caretakers through death, hunger, and displacement. Then, the further disruptions to families during the Khmer Rouge period 1975 to 1979 are discussed, followed by some discussion of the proliferation of orphanages in the refugee camps along the Thai border during the civil war years that followed. Finally, I describe the growth of orphanages after the repatriation began in the early 1990s. This history continues in chapter 3, which shows how the rise of mass tourism was pivotal in making orphanages such a common feature of today's Cambodian child welfare landscape.

Out-of-Parental-Care Arrangements in the Past

While the title of this chapter focuses it on the history of orphanages, it is in fact a history more generally of out-of-family care for children, from which the history of orphanages develops in a continuous rather than disjunctive manner. While orphanages were until recently uncommon in Cambodia, it has never been unheard of or pathologized for Cambodian children to live apart from their parents. Out-of-family residence has been seen as a way to improve children's spiritual or material life prospects in ways that can also improve prospects for the entire family.

The warmth and closeness between Cambodian parents and their children is striking, and yet it is also expected that children will regularly spend much of their time in the company of others, often without much parental interaction or supervision.[2] One practice that has been especially important for the meaning that Cambodians assign to orphanage care is boys leaving their families to live with Buddhist monks as temple boys. Throughout Theravada Southeast Asia, pagodas have long sheltered poor and orphaned boys as well as those whose villages lacked schools and also those who posed discipline challenges to their parents.[3] Temple boys often, but not always, are ordained as novice monks, and boys as young as seven have been ordained in order to make merit for their parents as well as for access to educational opportunities.[4] Thus Khmer Buddhism, followed by over 95 percent of Cambodians, has long provided a valuable indigenous safety net, as temple boys usually receive room, board, and access to education in exchange for performing chores for the monks. Sending one's son to live apart in this way has not been viewed as a rejection; rather, it has conveyed very real advantages to boys and their families.[5] The director of the NGO that manages the COC himself was sent to live with another family after his father's death and ordained as a novice monk after finishing primary school so that he could continue studying.

Because historically living at the pagoda was not an option for girls, child circulation for them was more likely to take the form of living with and serving wealthier relatives or nonfamily members who were childless.[6] Whether in households or in pagodas, the workload could be heavy for children residing outside of parental care, but the arrangement was nonetheless recognized as a reciprocal exchange in which children learned useful skills and widened their families' and their own social networks and future life prospects, for instance by helping them to secure a more advantageous marriage. Sometimes the work that drew children into living outside of parental care was even prestigious and highly skilled, most notably for girls who lived in residential dance troupes, often under the auspices of governors, local nobility, or the royal family.

For a very long time dance has been central to Khmer self-expression, aesthetics, and religion and an avenue for out-of-family residence. Inscriptions from as early as the seventh century indicate that dancers were presented as offerings to temples.[7] In addition to their centrality to religious ritual and mediation between the human and the spiritual realms, dance troupes are also a longstanding response to the social challenge of unparented children. The earliest known reference to the role of dance in enriching the lives of orphans comes from a twelfth-century stele found at Angkor Thom, the last capital of the Khmer empire. The inscriptions refer to Queen Jayarajadevi, who during her husband's long absence on a military campaign "wept, prayed and then found solace in Buddhist practices. [As she] . . . realized the benefits of Buddhism, she charged her own dancers to perform and to give representations drawn from the Jatakas. . . . Having taken, as her own daughters, a miserable troupe of a hundred young women abandoned by their mothers, she increased the renown of a village named Dharmakirti for its virtue, happiness and prosperity."[8]

This passage describes phenomena that continue to be important today. It is the earliest known reference to the use of a residential dance troupe as a way to support both unparented children as well as children whose parents might still be living but no longer provide care for them. It references a way that orphans' dance is used as a symbol to effect transformation in adults, in this case to mobilize support for a new state religion. And it alludes to the way that support for vulnerable children can be celebrated as a respected way for the more fortunate to make merit by supporting the residential care of vulnerable children. These aspects of orphanage dance shows continue to be relevant today, even as they have become a lightning rod drawing attention to everything that is wrong with Cambodian orphanages, as will be seen in the discussion of orphanage tourism in the next chapter.

Dance troupes were in many ways similar to present-day orphanages. They could include dozens or even hundreds of dancers and housed even children whose still-living parents had relinquished them, often at a very young age because it was widely believed that dance training should begin at age eight or younger.[9] This resulted in a kind of social orphaning of even very young children, because "children presented to the king were usually about six years old and in many cases would never see their parents again."[10] Residential dance troupes also served as a social safety net for children who lacked adequate care because children could also offer themselves to the king.

The similarities between residential dance troupes and present-day orphanages highlight important continuities between modern orphanages and more-established cultural practices. Because orphanages are not perceived as a radical departure from traditional patterns of child circulation, there are ways for Cambodians to make sense of orphanages other than through the Oliver Twist tropes that predominate in Western interpretations. Children living apart from their relatives are not necessarily considered estranged or deprived. Instead, separate residence can be a valuable opportunity for upward mobility for children and an important avenue for strengthening social networks, making merit, or relieving pressures on their families.

Care arrangements such as child circulation, temple boys, residential dance troupes, fostering, adoption, and orphanages may all seem to be distinct today, but in practice they shade into one another and form a continuum. This is especially clear from a historical perspective. When institutional bureaucracies did not intrude as rigidly into the family sphere, kinship was not necessarily completely revoked when children circulated in traditional patterns of care, meaning that these practices did not need to be mutually exclusive or clearly distinguished. The relative porousness of the boundaries between these various phenomena undermines the rigid approaches to the controversies surrounding them that are prevalent today.

Modern History

Cambodia became a French protectorate in 1863 and remained a colony until independence in 1953. During the colonial period and prior to the escalation of war in the late 1960s, most children whose parents passed away were able to remain in extended family care and Cambodia had few orphanages. Institutional orphanages based on the European model were established on a limited basis with an explicitly racist agenda. Rather than accepting children whose parents could not provide care, colonial orphanages targeted the children of French fathers and Cambodian mothers, as part of a deliberate campaign to "make them French," in a campaign similar to the forced removal of the Stolen Generation of Australian Aboriginal children. Taking children from their families outright and housing them in orphanages continued until well into the 1960s.[11] Thus, until the U.S. war in Southeast Asia overtook Cambodia's neutrality in the late 1960s, orphanages remained an unnecessary, marginal, and usually abhorrent option.

There is evidence also that residential dance troupes remained available as a resource for providing care to unparented children. Dancer and teacher Chheng Phon, who later served as minister of culture from 1981 through 1989, explained, "Before the war my wife and I had three children and 13 orphans whom I looked after, I brought them up to be artists."[12] While the overthrow of King Sihanouk in 1970 meant that dance no longer officially served as mediator between the king and the spirit world, "the notion of the dance as embodying a transcendent essence of the nation remained powerful."[13] This power would make it an inviting target when the Khmer Rouge later took control of the country, leading to its suppression during their rule from 1975 through 1979, and animating the revitalization of dance during and after the refugee camp years of 1979 through 1991, which also had consequences for the orphanage tourism phenomenon of the 1990s and early 2000s.

In March 1969 the United States began its devastating four-year carpet-bombing campaign of the Cambodian countryside, killing thousands of civilians and displacing over one million. This massively increased the number of vulnerable children in Cambodia, straining extended family care networks and magnifying the need for other kinds of solutions. Orphanages, both private and state-run, proliferated to shelter the increasing numbers of children whose parents were unable to care for them due to death, disability, or other forms of disruption. All were overwhelmed by "desperate parents—starving and fearing for their lives . . . the babies would not stop coming."[14] Dance teacher Chheng Phon, quoted above, describes the war's effects on his residential dance troupe; after the bombing, he "had an orphanage with more than 100 children."[15]

This is the turning point in Cambodia's history when orphanages became normalized as a way to care for children in extenuating circumstances. The perceived need for this model of care, combined with the deteriorating conditions within Cambodia, spurred well-intentioned aid workers to open even more orphanages, which quickly filled as well. For example, Eloise Charet traveled to Cambodia in 1975 to volunteer in an orphanage and saw how "one of the rooms had all these children that were left to die. . . . You could see ants crawling all over their bodies, flies, everything, devouring them while they were still alive."[16] In response, she and her sister started their own orphanage, which quickly filled. "Babies were sometimes left on the front steps," she later recalled, describing how soldiers would also bring them children they had found abandoned in ransacked villages.

The Khmer Rouge Period

The 1975 defeat of the U.S.-backed Khmer Republic by the Khmer Rouge led to a radical restructuring of every aspect of Cambodian society, including an abasement of traditionally powerful and meaningful institutions, such as the family and the arts, under the new leaders' idiosyncratic version of traditional peasant culture.[17] Even though the Khmer family would be a central reference point in any plausible version of traditional rural life, family was viewed as a threat to the exclusive authority of the regime, which called itself Angka, the organization. According to one of the slogans used to reinforce doctrine and control, children were the property of Angka because "Angka is the mother and father of all young children, as well as all adolescent boys and girls."[18] Efforts to intentionally dismantle the family included forced separation of family members to different work camps and conscription to mobile labor or military details. Forced marriage in "impersonal mass ceremonies" was "systematic and widespread."[19] Children as young as six or seven were sent to live and work in children's camps, often far from their parents; by eleven or twelve they joined children's roving work brigades. The Khmer Rouge leadership maintained that separating children from their parents was necessary to counter the tendency of family bonds and "old thinking" to corrupt the revolutionary spirit of children, who were held to be ideologically pure and uncorrupted by past counterrevolutionary and foreign influences. However, the Khmer Rouge also made a practice of arresting and often executing children of political prisoners; the slogan "when you pull out a weed, you must pull out all the roots" reinforced the drive to prevent the families of those imprisoned, tortured, and executed from growing up to seek revenge.[20] This extension of punishment to other family members facilitated another strategy for further undermining family bonds, which was that children were encouraged to spy and inform on their parents, rewarding children for turning on their parents and further eroding trust among family members.

These measures had their intended effect; as historian and journalist Henri Locard testified at the Extraordinary Chambers in the Courts of Cambodia, "They did not eliminate the family, it was more like they blew it up, exploded it."[21] These practices caused tremendous suffering and demoralized Cambodian people, with lingering consequences that are especially relevant to the current discussion on orphanages and that color the conversation about them, even today, nearly a half century later. In the context of the family disruption caused by conflict and deliberate policy decisions, orphanages today are perceived by some as part of a recurring pattern, as history repeating itself in yet another separation of children from their families that comes too soon after the separations enforced by the Khmer Rouge.[22] Large numbers of children residing separately from their families with other, unrelated children and few adults is too eerily reminiscent of the Khmer Rouge children's camps, lowering some people's tolerance for residential care in general, and contributing to the vehemence of some of the discussion surrounding orphanages. There is also widespread concern that the generation of Cambodians who were raising their children in the 1990s and 2000s may have had their own ability to parent compromised by their experiences of violence and family rupture.

Like the family, the performing arts, particularly court dance traditions, came similarly close to annihilation. Although independence from France in 1953 ushered in a host of changes in order to realign dance traditions to better fit the needs of a modern nation-state, dancers had still been "revered as a living symbol of the kingdom."[23] The symbolic power of classical dance was made clear during this time in the way that the Khmer Rouge suppressed it. Dance provided a powerful connection to the past and to the institution of the monarchy, placing it in explicit conflict with the Khmer Rouge anti-monarchical ideology and their attempts to stamp out "old thinking." Even popular and folk dances, which had been central to village celebrations, were banned and replaced by "public displays of revolutionary songs and dances," despite the Khmer Rouge's nominal commitment to traditional rural culture.[24] Dancers and musicians were singled out for special persecution and execution, and it has been reported that "close to 90 per cent of Cambodia's professional artists . . . perished" during this time.[25]

The Khmer Rouge era, 1975–1979, was objectively short, but the consequences have been vast and profound, especially in light of the long years of conflict that preceded and followed it. As is common in postconflict communities, Cambodia has a high level of domestic violence, and the use of "harsh, often abusive disciplinary practices (e.g. hitting and berating) by parents has grown to epidemic proportions."[26] While the severity of the lingering effects is exacerbated by the extreme nature of the social disruptions imposed by the Khmer Rouge, too often in discussions of Cambodia, attention is focused disproportionately on the sensational nature of the Khmer Rouge to the neglect of the inherently disruptive effects of war itself, such as the massive internal displacement before 1975 and swelling of refugee camps along the Thai border afterward. The refugee camp years, spanning 1979 through mid-1993, when repatriation was finally completed, were profoundly affecting as well.

1979–1993: The Refugee Camp Years

By 1979, when the Vietnamese drove the Khmer Rouge out of power and into the forest, many traditions that had provided meaning and continuity throughout Cambodia's history, particularly the family and the performing arts, had suffered severe disruption. As refugees, dispirited if not terrified and often near starvation, began to seek sanctuary along the Thai border, these sources of emotional well-being and identity were therefore often denied them. The solutions in the camps to both of these deprivations would have consequences for the proliferation and profile of orphanages in the refugee camps throughout the 1980s, and in Cambodia after the repatriation in the 1990s.

Among the refugees who massed along the Thai-Cambodia border were several thousand children who either arrived unaccompanied or suffered the loss of parental care after arriving in a refugee camp.[27] Orphanages sprang up, as what was seen then to be the most humane, or at least the most feasible, way to provide care for them.[28] The reasons children lacked parental care were numerous and knotty. In addition to children whose parents had died, the social disruption caused by the camp experience itself meant that "babies were abandoned frequently, at the rate of one every three days."[29] Sexual abuse by guards and soldiers was rampant, and pregnancy of even very young girls sometimes resulted in banishment by their families or abandonment of the infant. Domestic violence drove some children to flee their families, and after divorce, if a new spouse rejected the children of the first marriage, there was sometimes no alternative but relinquishment to an orphanage. Abandoned or abused children sometimes were detained when they turned to theft in order to survive, and if nobody came to retrieve them from the police station, they were "shipped to an orphanage."[30]

In the context of widespread crime and abuse throughout the camps, many residents came to idealize the advantages they saw orphans receiving, and in one case, not unique, as many as fifty-eight out of seventy children in centers for unaccompanied children actually had relatives living in the camp, whose existence they had been instructed to deny because camp residents "commonly believed that unaccompanied children would receive better care and would eventually be resettled to Western nations."[31]

The number of orphanages in the camps climbed steadily. There were several large children's centers (100–150 children) in Site II, the largest camp with almost 200,000 refugees, and Jan Williamson's memoir of working in Khao I Dang, population 160,000, mentions five, with need for sixteen more.[32] Sometimes centers that had been created for entirely different purposes were inadvertently transformed into orphanages because so many shelterless children materialized. For example, Nuon Phaly, founder of the Future Light Orphanage, originally had started a mental health center for women suffering from depression, but reported that "the space quickly filled with children."[33] As expressed by one volunteer at the time, "If you're not careful, all the children in Cambodia could end up in orphanages. . . . Khmers feel that such a facility, especially if run by foreigners, is an educational opportunity not to be missed."[34]

Although some aid workers expressed feeling "offended by this casual attitude of parents toward their child," others recognized that family-based care was not always ideal and that it could even foreclose desirable opportunities.[35] Sometimes orphans were invited to live in families only because of the work they could be expected to perform, as described in the following observation by anthropologist Josephine Reynell, who conducted participant-observation research in the refugee camps while working as a researcher at the Refugee Studies Centre of University of Oxford: "Child labour is extremely useful, particularly to households without male adults. . . . The particularly vulnerable children are the orphans, who often live with poor households to provide an extra pair of hands. Normally they work rather than going to school, and the KWA [Khmer Women's Association] reports that they often receive less food than other children in the household."[36]

Orphanages were not just numerous, they were salient, and a focal point of humanitarian aid and public and media attention. In the 1980s, this "crisis of Western conscience" inspired many foreigners to volunteer in the camps, including in the orphanages, a historical and conceptual precedent for volunteering in orphanages located inside Cambodia after repatriation.[37] While volunteer tourism is often presented as a new development in tourism, Shapiro-Phim reports that camp residents often referred to themselves as animals in a zoo, "especially with reference to the large numbers of visitors the camp hosted fairly regularly—journalists, government or United Nations officials, and 'tourists.'"[38]

Despite the extreme hardship of refugee camp life, there were continuities with respect to attitudes about residential care before and after the war. While some aid workers expressed concern about the large numbers of children in out-of-family care, many of the reasons children ended up in residential care in the camps continue to be significant today. Some Cambodian camp residents viewed out-of-family residence as not necessarily harmful, and they reckoned that the educational and material benefits of orphanages could outweigh the disadvantages, especially in the context of domestic violence, spousal rejection, or unsafe or unhealthy living conditions. At the time, a sizable portion of Westerners agreed, or at least pragmatically recognized that orphanages were better than any of the realistic alternatives. Both Westerners and resident Cambodians, therefore, saw orphanages as an acceptable, albeit imperfect, solution to the overwhelming challenges of refugee camp life, rather than as a problem space in their own right. Structurally as well, some precedents were set that are typical of the Cambodian-run, but not necessarily the foreigner-run, orphanages today, regarding how the orphanages would be configured and their connection to the wider community. Integration and openness were typical. The facilities were usually not closed, and while special enrichment activities such as dance were offered in them, the children usually attended school outside the center with the rest of the children in the camp, after the Thai government's "humane deterrence" policy, which initially forbid formal education, was lifted.[39]

Although it was the powerful media images of starving Cambodians staggering across the border that had seized the world's attention, the ensuing flood of donations and volunteers meant that before long, material conditions inside the camps exceeded the living conditions of many Cambodians who remained inside Cambodia, and the "most insidious problem, which is to be found inside even the most physically comfortable camp, is that of boredom and enforced idleness. . . . Refugees stood in line endlessly" and "the air of desperation was palpable."[40] The challenge for camp residents and aid workers alike became to devise ways to counter the boredom and desperation. The losses endured by the refugees were legion, and the devastation of the performing arts, aligned with the need for physical activity and emotional purpose, was heightened by an overarching "anxiety that the Khmer as a people will cease to exist."[41] Dance training and performance emerged as an especially inviting focal point for efforts to address at least a few of the refugees' losses. Because dance had been central to Cambodian self-expression for so long, an emphasis on dance seemed to be a rare solution in the midst of intractable problems. Cambodian culture could be supported simply by enjoying it. By attending a dance performance, visitors could feel as though they were doing something both "cathartic and beautiful," providing dancers with not just physical activity and entertainment, but "the return of their dignity, their humanness."[42] Foreign aid workers transduced the affective value of performance into concrete advantages such as invitations to perform in Thailand or abroad, and even preferential opportunities for resettlement. Therefore, at the same time that orphanages were proliferating due to the sheer overwhelming number of children without parental care, dance was becoming popular as a way to benefit individuals and to preserve Khmer cultural traditions. Teaching children to dance seemed particularly urgent because of the disruption in transmission caused by conflict and exile, and the idea of extending privileged knowledge to the most marginalized members of society was especially compelling. Orphans' dance classes and dance performances became popular in the camps. In some cases orphanage dance classes were opened to non-orphanage children, a strategy that continues to be used today in order to defuse resentment about the material benefits that children in orphanages often received then and continue to receive today.

Children's center founder and teacher Benoît Duchâteau-Arminjon writes in his memoir how performing arts, in contrast to other possible activities to occupy children's time in the camps, not just provided a way to prevent boredom and inactivity, but served to integrate them back into the society from which they had been estranged through loss of kinship ties. Linking to tradition through dance was a way to compensate for the loss of other kinds of social linkages, and he writes in his memoir of how dance provided a bridge back to their rightful place in their own society: "When the cultural activity is linked to tradition, this gives the child identity and dignity; it makes him feel that he fits in. With a newfound identity, the child's dignity is restored and he becomes capable of fitting in with his own country."[43]

In the refugee camps, performing for audiences of foreign adults was regarded as an appropriate way to encourage or show gratitude for donations. Traditional dance performances seemed like an obvious win-win enrichment activity, which boosted the morale of the resident children and also provided them with special privileges, improved living conditions, or spending money. Dance was recognized as an effective fundraising tool, and donors and officials from aid organizations were usually treated to a dance show, often by children from an orphanage. The fact that the audience was composed of foreigners was considered to be especially validating for them, as Duchâteau-Arminjon describes in his memoir about a performance given for European diplomats. At the end, the children "are most impressed to be applauded by an audience of foreigners. Such ovations help them grow in self-confidence, something they desperately lack."[44] Dance performances by the children graced visits of VIPs, such as Joan Baez, who toured the camps with Amnesty International and who was inspired to write a song about her experience. The affective power of the orphan trope made it irresistible for journalists, who highlighted orphaning even in articles that were about different topics entirely, because the juxtaposition of the grace under duress with the horrors of their life stories lent an additional layer of momentousness.

Meanwhile, inside Cambodia, as the civil war and Vietnamese occupation continued, orphanages also proliferated; Phnom Penh had at least six government orphanages by 1991.[45] As in the refugee camps, dance inside Cambodia also took on a powerful symbolic and nationalist value.[46] The few Westerners who were able to visit Cambodia at that time were also beguiled by the symbolic power of orphans as the vessels through which to relay dance traditions to future generations, and reacted with approval to the dance rehearsals and performances they viewed. As one aid worker recounts in an interview from the period, after basic needs were met, the next priority was to "give them back their culture" through dance.[47] The possibility of reconciling two irreconcilable symbols—the ugliness of war and the beauty of art—was transcendent, and when dancers were also orphans, that fact was explicitly noted by most writers during the period. Orphan dancers made the performances not just enjoyable entertainment but a symbol of hope for the future, precisely the kind of transformative emotional work that orphans provide for adults in Western orphanage schemata, as Volkman described after a visit to Phnom Penh in the 1980s: "At the School of Fine Arts, young orphans of the Pol Pot period are trained to be the new generation of dancers. . . . Watching these survivors turn into lovely little apsaras or leaping Hanumans, even the most jaded cynic cannot but feel that there is hope."[48]

Repatriation

The Paris Peace Accords, signed in 1991, opened the door for Cambodians to return home. As camps closed, entire orphanages sometimes repatriated en masse back into Cambodia. Throughout the 1990s, refugees returned to a challenged and challenging society. The Cambodian landscape and society had been devastated by two decades of war, and the remnants of the Khmer Rouge did not formally surrender until 1998. The "fierce and uncertain scramble for livelihood" was daunting especially for children.[49] Fifty percent of the returnees were younger than fifteen, with little to no memory of life outside the refugee camps.[50] The number of street children increased dramatically, and more orphanages were formed during this time.[51] For example, the Cambodian Light Children Association (CLCA) was founded in 1995 by a restaurant owner who started an orphanage because, as he stated in a newspaper interview at the time, "many street children came to my restaurant begging."[52]

The social and economic disruptions caused by war were exacerbated by HIV/AIDS, which also fueled the post-repatriation growth in orphanages. The first diagnosed case of HIV/AIDS in Cambodia was in 1991, the same year that the Paris Peace Accords were signed, and the incidence of infection quickly rose in 1998 to 2 percent, the highest in Asia.[53] At the turn of the century there were large numbers of children losing parental care through death or incapacitation or who were HIV-positive themselves. The death rate did not start to diminish until 2003, when free antiretroviral (ARV) treatment became widely available, and today Cambodia is widely considered to be a success story in the fight against HIV/AIDS; virtual elimination is projected by 2025.[54] However, the lack of availability of ARV treatments until the early 2000s contributed to the distinctive profile of Cambodia's orphanage residents. The common family pattern was that both parents and the youngest child, who had been infected prenatally, would die, leaving the older siblings as survivors, one reason why children tended to enter Cambodian orphanages at a later age, and often in sibling groups.[55]

Another phenomenon that impacted the growth of orphanages in Cambodia was the rise and fall of transnational adoption from Cambodia. In the second half of the 1990s, the numbers of children adopted internationally from Cambodia "began to climb dramatically."[56] From the start, adoption from Cambodia was plagued with well-documented cases of corruption including questionable practices such as payments to birth parents, deceptive or coercive agreements and even abductions, as well as pervasive bribery of government officials. Many orphanages at this time were reportedly little more than transit centers for children destined for adoption abroad.[57] In 2001 the United States, among other countries, responded to the widespread corruption by suspending their processing of adoption petitions. The numbers of infants in orphanages dropped after the start of the moratorium, but they were soon replaced by larger numbers of older children.[58]

Cambodia entered the twenty-first century with over 1,100 children under the age of fifteen not living with either of their parents; by 2005, the year the COC was founded, Holt International Children's Services reported that there were 8,270 Cambodian children in residential care.[59]

History of the COC

The history of the COC flows naturally out of this more general history and is typical of many orphanages that arose after the turn of the century. It was shaped by the confluence of European charity and the socially engaged Buddhism that surged in Cambodia after the decades of conflict. The COC provides a focused lens through which to view the broader trends that characterize orphanage phenomena in Cambodia, including the orphanage boom, the rise of volunteer tourism and orphanage tourism, the anti-orphanage-tourism campaign and the response to the campaign, and the eventual move away from reliance on orphanages and focus on other care and fundraising solutions. This study of the COC is a way to understand the human dimension of these broader and more abstract society-wide trends and to translate them into the lived experiences of Cambodian children growing up during these times.

The COC was founded by a European traveler who, like so many other visitors in the mid-1990s, traveled to Cambodia to visit the temples but was touched by the poverty she witnessed in the context of the recent, tragic history that confronted her.[60] In 1997 she founded a charity that supported local children's initiatives with funds she gathered from donors in Europe. In 2001 the charity changed its approach to more direct action by providing conditional cash transfers to struggling single mothers, with the main condition being that children attended school regularly. As she came to more closely know the families and the social context in which they struggled, the founder observed that giving money directly to parents did not necessarily always improve the circumstances that many of the children faced. Four years later, in 2005, she purchased property for an orphanage about thirty kilometers outside Siem Reap. The center was quickly filled with children she had encountered who needed care, and within a few years the original six children had grown to forty-three.

Meanwhile, in the early 2000s, as the HIV/AIDS crisis was accelerating, a Buddhist pagoda in Siem Reap, along with many others, opened its grounds as both shelter and hospice for HIV/AIDS-affected people who came to the city to seek care or who had lost their livelihood and homes due to illness and stigma. Sometimes children were left there, other times children stayed on after their parents' deaths, and an orphanage organically sprang up on the pagoda grounds in order to shelter and care for them. In 2004, the monks founded an NGO focused on education and poverty alleviation, and in 2006, management of the COC was transferred to them, although the European charity continued to be their main donor. The two organizations' different notions of best practices for vulnerable children sometimes clashed. While united in sincere concern for the children, especially their access to education, differing outlooks made different issues more salient and different responses more intuitively available. Tensions built for four years, and then the European charity cut off funding in 2010.

An anxious and uncertain period of program cuts followed the 2010 halt in funding. During the period between the cessation of funding and the securing of new sources, which was about a year, dance classes and other enrichment activities were eliminated and the children did homework by shared candlelight because electricity was less essential than food and school fees. The COC concluded that their ties to other donors and volunteers had been the only thing that kept them afloat. While a large source of tension had been their willingness to allow a wider array of foreign visitors than the founder was comfortable with, they continued to actively cultivate these relationships because they believed they were "maybe not so good, but necessary," as one staff member explained to me.

The time that I spent most intensively engaged in regular observations over-lapped with the funding crisis and with the identification of new funding sources, so that I witnessed both the shortages, including the candlelight home-work sessions, and later the reinstatement of dance classes and admissions of new children. The fallout from the funding crisis, and the subsequent replace-ment of funding from other sources, illustrates the benefits as well as the vul-nerabilities inherent in reliance on foreign donations. Donors can be quite generous, and the material conditions of children in the COC, as well as many other orphanages, were considerably better than conditions under which many Cambodian families live. However, funding that is subject to the whims of donors is unpredictable and relying on it is precarious, and this kind of funding crisis has also occurred in several other very well-respected children's centers. The vul-nerabilities inherent in reliance on a single large source of support can be buff-ered by building a larger network of donors, which the COC worked hard to do, but this inevitably meant that the management needed to put more time into cultivating new donor networks. Donors understandably want to meet the children they are supporting, so more donors meant more visitors whom staff needed to greet, feed, and keep an eye on.

Inevitably, the reliance on foreign donations meant that the sequence of events between making donations and visiting the orphanage got reversed; rather than welcoming donors who wished to meet the children they were sup-porting, the orphanage welcomed visitors in the hope that they would be moved to make donations in the future. Thus was born the phenomenon that has come to be called orphanage tourism.[61] In the next chapter, I discuss how yet another kind of foreign invasion in Cambodia's history, namely mass tourism, joined with orphanages' dependence on foreign donations to stimulate the proliferation of orphanages and the growth of orphanage tourism, and contributed to the back-lash against orphanages in Cambodia.

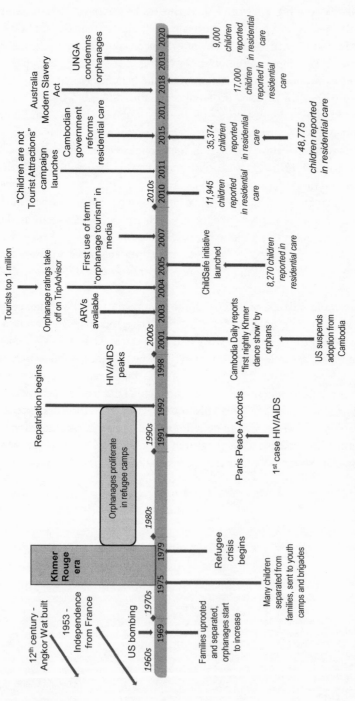

FIGURE 1 Timeline of milestones in the history of Cambodian orphanages.

Sources: Khadka and Sem, "Caring for Children Left Behind in Residential Care during COVID-19"; Mauney, "Cambodia Orphanage Survey"; MoSVY, "Mapping of Residential Care Facilities"; MoSVY, "Statistical Profile of Child Protection in Cambodia"; Stark et al., "National Estimation of Children in Residential Care Institutions in Cambodia"; UNICEF, "Cambodia Launches the 'Strong Family Campaign.'"

3

Orphanage Tourism and the Anti-Orphanage-Tourism Campaign

Ennew has written that "despite the rhetoric of kindness and concern about orphans, no one wants to pay the cost of their upbringing," but the truth is that foreigners have been clamoring to pay the costs of bringing up Cambodia's orphans.[1] As Cambodia emerged from the devastating decades of war, the tourism industry also expanded, quite extraordinarily in fact. Tourism arrivals to Cambodia in 1993 were just over 118,000.[2] They first topped one million in 2004 and have increased consistently every year thereafter until 2019.[3] Most tourists are drawn by the UNESCO-listed Angkor Archaeological Park, but because throughout the 2000s the dominant Western narrative of Cambodia cast it as a site for humanitarian concern, many visitors supplement tours of monuments by visiting or volunteering for aid projects, including orphanages. The money that visitors bring with them, or that they send after returning home, provides ongoing support for many of the orphanages in Siem Reap and the rest of Cambodia, and the COC's reliance on foreign volunteers and donors was typical rather than unusual among the orphanages of Cambodia.[4] This reliance led to increased visibility of orphanages and gave even casual short-term visitors open access, so that visiting an orphanage came to be viewed as simply one more thing to see and do in Cambodia.

Figure 1 shows the main events and milestones in the history of orphanages in Cambodia, introduced in chapter 2 and continued in this chapter. The COC's own history is integrally tied to these phenomena. It was founded in 2005, the year that worries about increasing numbers of volunteers and visitors led to the launch of the ChildSafe Initiative to educate both tourists and workers in the hospitality sector about threats to children's well-being. It closed in 2019, the year that the United Nations General Assembly officially condemned orphanages. The lives of the resident children likewise span important milestones in this history. The oldest, Prak, was born in 1991, the year that the Paris Peace

Accords were signed, and the youngest, Sovay, was born in 2007, the year the term "orphanage tourism" was coined in the media.

Voluntourism in Cambodia

Beginning in the late 1990s and accelerating throughout the 2000s, the rise of voluntourism, a blend of the two words "volunteer" and "tourism," has been a global phenomenon, but it found especially fertile ground in Cambodia.[5] Cambodia's unique confluence of several separate but interrelated trends—mass tourism, the narrative of Cambodia as a site for humanitarian concern, baby boomer guilt about the bombing, postconflict demographics marked by large numbers of children and relatively fewer older adults, disrupted educational system in a society that highly values education—all combined to give the worldwide rise in voluntourism a special salience and consequence in Cambodia. The steep rise in tourism arrivals to Cambodia before the country really had tourism infrastructure to handle those large numbers, combined with Westerners' relative lack of knowledge about Cambodia, was also a factor. In the late 1990s the Tuol Sleng genocide museum had not been much changed after the Khmer Rouge deserted it when they fled the Vietnamese military, and there was little explanatory signage. Hughes interviewed visitors after their shocked encounters with bloodstained floors and casually abandoned torture instruments.[6] She argues that the raw conditions and the paucity of interpretive materials provoked visitors into interpreting their experience as an act of bearing witness rather than one of education or even entertainment, stimulating an orientation toward Cambodia distinct from consumption in the conventional sense. Hughes's interviewees spoke of a "moral imperative" to visit unpleasant sites, framing their relationship to Cambodia in terms of "duty," often as a prelude to "the shuttling from a tourist subjectivity to that of a humanitarian actor."[7] This reorientation encouraged many visitors to seek volunteer opportunities in sites such as orphanages and recast touristic voyeurism into a kind of testimonial, bridging the gap between visiting traditional touristic sites, such as temples, and visiting sites of others' misfortune, such as orphanages.[8] The shock of tourists' unmediated experience of the horrors of Tuol Sleng and similar sites was amplified by the fact that for younger visitors, it was usually the first time they ever heard of the Cambodian genocide, the U.S. bombing that preceded it, or the civil war that followed it. Their horror was magnified by distress that they could have remained ignorant of such unsettling events, and for young Americans, the fact that their country was implicated in the chain of atrocities further fueled their distress and their resolve to give back in some way.

An epiphany that inspires one generation may become a static default framing for subsequent ones, and many of the insights experienced firsthand by Hughes's interviewees in the 1990s later became fossilized as the conventional perception of Cambodia as a great place to volunteer, a change that has been accompanied by a proliferation of both volunteer agencies and NGOs, including orphanages, and intense competition for visitors and their dollars. And the visitors just kept coming. While a moral imperative may have inspired the earliest cohorts of tourists to act rather than to just consume, some visitors who followed transformed the act of volunteering itself into an act of consumption. Volunteering has become not only a necessary credential for academic and employment prospects, but a taken-for-granted experience and even a rite of passage for young people coming of age in the West today, much as backpacking through Europe or following the "hippie trail" across continents to India was a defining experience for baby boomers.[9] As such, it was a site of solidarity and peer bonding through a common defining experience, and from the perspective of volunteers themselves, a way to connect with people, both local as well as other foreigners, and to move beyond a superficial, monetized engagement with the visited-upon society.

While some orphanage visitors came for a brief look, just an hour or so, others came for as long as a year or more, either in one continuous stay or in regular visits once or twice a year for several years running. Some orphanages in Siem Reap have semipermanent volunteers, often retirees from Western countries who confided to me that opportunities for feeling useful combined with a low cost of living, especially for medical care, make Siem Reap an appealing retirement destination. These older volunteers can contribute professional skills such as accounting, teaching, fundraising, and managing other, more short-term volunteers. Their age and skills fill gaps left by the high mortality rates and disrupted education during the conflict decades. Regularly, an entire group of visitors from a school or club will donate materials for a building project like a bathroom or a playground, and then come together and pitch in with the work.

The primacy of the quest for intimacy as Conran describes it means that firsthand interactions with local people, particularly children, are especially prized, over other possible tasks that are arguably equally important such as maintaining records, writing reports, or corresponding with donors abroad, all tasks that are vital but tend not to be as highly sought after by volunteers.[10] Even donors who don't volunteer often consider it their right to interact with children, sometimes even to tell staff how to use their donations and how to run their programs, and to "help" (or, too often, to get in the way) on projects for which they have no skills, such as construction.

By far the most common orphanage volunteer activities revolved around the teaching and learning of English. Although most of the volunteers who taught English have no training or experience in language teaching, English is such a highly sought-after skill that English classes fill to capacity when orphanages open them to neighborhood children, as I observed firsthand at four orphanages in Siem Reap that allowed nonresident children into the classes. The national curriculum requires foreign language instruction beginning in grade 7, but English proficiency is so prized that most orphanages start instruction much earlier. Volunteers often use English while playing games or doing activities with the children, so that from their perspective, just hanging out with the kids constitutes a kind of immersion English lesson. Volunteers are also appreciated for providing a glimpse into, and for stimulating curiosity about, the wider world or for modeling fresh perspectives about social issues such as gender roles.[11] Because Siem Reap is a tourist town, many staff believe that the tourism and hospitality industries present promising career opportunities for children, and so encourage interaction with foreigners.

In 2011, only one orphanage in Siem Reap did not take volunteers, but even so it was completely funded by foreign donors, who were encouraged to visit. It still allows walk-in visitors to take a guided tour of the premises in the hope that they will become donors, because donations for orphanages, especially smaller locally run ones, come most consistently after visitors have established a personal connection. Larger, foreign-run orphanages are less reliant on visitors because they have access to international networks and often professional fundraisers, putting smaller, locally run orphanages at a disadvantage. This increases the pressure on locally run orphanages to allow frequent volunteers or to develop other ways to attract donors, such as dance performances.

The most consequential, as well as the most controversial, result of this steady stream of well-intentioned visitors is that their contributions have encouraged Cambodians to open more orphanages and to bring more children to live in them.[12] Not all orphanages were opened with just a profit motive in mind, but orphanages have come to be seen as an entrepreneurial niche in a country where many people are still struggling to make ends meet. While volunteers and visitors treasure the memories of their interactions with the children, from the perspective of the orphanage staff even volunteers without sought-after skills may be most appreciated as potential donors. Enough visitors donate cash, either when visiting or after returning home, that it makes up a significant, unrestricted, and often undocumented revenue stream that can make orphanages quite profitable. While major donors have always exercised the prerogative to visit sites that receive their donations and judge how their money is being spent, the situation in Cambodia granted this prerogative to even very small-scale donors. While equalizing the privileges that had been previously granted only to the very wealthy, the net effect for the children was that many, many visitors now had access to them.

The expectation for donations became increasingly explicit and insistent. By 2011 most orphanages had a guest book, with the expected columns for name, country of origin, and comments and an additional one labeled "amount," in which visitors were expected to put the size of the donation they made. While this served as a record-keeping system, it also put powerful pressure on visitors to give money, so that donations came to feel like the price of admission for an attraction, rather than a voluntary and spontaneous gift. The online lore shared among volunteers maintained that they should not arrive empty-handed, but at the same time they should be wary of adult staff who might skim off donations for themselves. Some foreign visitors also resist the feeling that coming with cash in hand is crass, preferring to make contributions that could be construed as a kind of hostess gift, recognizing that they are visiting with the children in their home. Many visitors therefore bring food or supplies when they come, although there are numerous reports of orphanage staff simply reselling bags of rice or other donations back to the market for cash after the visitors leave. While visitors complain about the way the push for donations has monetized a relationship that they enter into precisely because they are seeking "new spaces of engagement that exist in not-fully capitalist relations," donations also serve to at least partially compensate staff for their time, since visitors are met, often toured around the premises, and usually accompanied so they are not left alone with children.[13] However, wording such as "visits are free for current donors and sponsors" invites the impression that visitors pay admission to tour the orphanage, reinforcing the perception of orphanage visits as touristic.[14] One very famous and generally well-regarded orphanage now simply refuses to open their gate to visitors who don't give a minimum donation of fifty dollars.

From the perspective of many Cambodian adults, the foreign visitors who were so eager to donate their time and resources seemed to be an ideal solution to a problem that most societies struggle with, namely the chronic underfunding of social services, especially services for children. Why not let tourists pay for them? Tourism brings with it a host of economic issues—it drives up local prices, crowds out other livelihoods and sources of employment, and strains the natural and built environment. Orphanage donations to many initially appeared to be a legitimate, voluntary "tourist tax," and Cambodia seemed to have found an original, maybe even sustainable solution to the predicament of supporting child well-being and education. However, as in all cases where there is a substantial amount of money changing hands, at some point, for some adults, the temptations began to outweigh the legitimate need. Not only did some staff begin to use donations for their own well-being instead of the children's, but the lure of easy money started to draw people into the orphanage sector simply because of its power to stimulate foreign donations.

The rising tide of visitors and volunteers was certainly one reason for the proliferation of orphanages in Cambodia, sparking the orphanage boom of the 2000s. Visitor donations encouraged the opening of new orphanages, and encouraged more children to be placed in them. The impact was amplified by the new media that flourished after the turn of the century, especially the rise of online travel forums. Online travel forums and reviews have come to dominate the way that travelers make their decisions about destinations and what they will do there, and thus it was no surprise that orphanages started to appear on them, with visitors sharing tips about how and where to volunteer. A vast amount of information about volunteer possibilities came to be communicated widely and nearly instantly, along with norms established among online communities that made volunteering simply one more experience to enjoy while visiting Cambodia. By early 2004, former and prospective volunteers were posting inquiries and information about Cambodian orphanages, inquiring about volunteer opportunities as well as logistical issues such as the best kinds of treats or school supplies to bring. Inevitably, they included assessments of which orphanages were the best sites for visiting. Because online comments tend to be spontaneous rather than prompted, they provide a valuable window onto prevailing public opinion regarding orphanage volunteer tourism. They show how public perceptions of volunteering rose and then fell, as doubts came increasingly to be expressed about whether volunteering, visiting, and making donations was truly benefitting the children they were intended to benefit.

Changing Perceptions

Throughout the 1990s and up until the mid-2000s, orphanages and their courting of foreign tourists for fundraising purposes retained a generally benign image. This emerged clearly when a scandal erupted in early 2005 because a corrupt official prevented an orphanage dance troupe from touring Japan and the United States by withholding their passports in order to extract a bribe. What was scandalous was the official's extortion rather than the orphans' performing for foreign audiences, and public sympathy for the children was conveyed in the headline "Official Accused of Extorting Orphan Dancers." The orphanage director who had arranged for the children's tour was portrayed as a patriot and was quoted sympathetically as saying, "It is a great loss for our country . . . the opportunity to promote our culture."[15] Likewise, in 1994 the children of Krousar Thmey, an orphanage that had repatriated en masse from Site II refugee camp in Thailand, garnered the official support of the royal family and of the prime minister when they performed for Cambodia's queen, who was "so moved to see the young orphan girls dance to the music played by the blind musicians that she stands to applaud them."[16] Performing in front of audiences was still seen as a tremendous opportunity for the children rather than an example of exploitation, and it was assumed that funds raised through ticket sales and donations were a legitimate way for the children to contribute to their own well-being.

Performances, open rehearsals, and images of dancing children came to be common ways to attract visitors to orphanages. Soon, restaurants and guest houses featured orphan dancers as a way to draw in customers more reliably than adult professional dancers could.[17] Through the mid-2000s, most orphanages had dance instruction and gave performances, modeled on the successful use of dance inside the refugee camps, and often supported by government ministries, NGOs, or foreign donors. The association of orphans with dance in Cambodia was so consistent that it became conventionalized, so the two were automatically linked in people's minds, and the schema of a Cambodian orphanage had come to include dance simply as an expected component of the programming. Centers' own materials were unselfconscious in their promotion of dance, and foreign audiences were encouraged to interpret skillful dancing as evidence of the good care that children were receiving—an indicator of a well-intentioned and responsible center. In her 2000 memoir, Geraldine Cox, founder of the Sunrise Children's Centres and one of the few foreigners to be granted Cambodian citizenship as recognition for her efforts to support Cambodian orphans, wrote explicitly about the benefits of dance and how she could leverage them for the center's and the children's advantage: "I envisage busloads of tourists coming to the centre to see the music and dance lessons in progress."[18] In 2001, the *Cambodia Daily* appreciatively reported on the "first nightly Khmer dance show since 1975," featuring children from an orphanage who performed in a restaurant, providing "the enthusiastic children a chance to perform" as well as "pretty much double the income of the charity." The only drawback expressed in the article was possible rivalry with other orphanages because "they expect similar shows to pop up to compete with them."[19] There was no mention in the article of any discomfort with the idea that dance could become a kind of ancillary entertainment for diners or that the children should not be performing in such a venue under such circumstances.

Around the mid-2000s, cautionary messages began to appear in online travel forums alongside more positive descriptions. Initially, these did not criticize orphanages per se, nor the fact that foreigners were allowed to pay short visits and interact with the children. Instead, they focused on specific orphanages that were accused of being "organized in an irresponsible, corrupt way, where more money goes to the organization than to the children," as described in a 2005 posting on the Lonely Planet Thorn Tree Forum.[20] The goal of posters was to share information about the trustworthiness of specific orphanages so that prospective volunteers could devote their time and resources to ones that deserved support. There was not yet an implication that it might be better not to volunteer at all or that the children and premises might be kept deliberately shabby so that visitors would be prompted to give more donations for corrupt staff to appropriate.

The perception of orphanages as a kind of tourist attraction was further cemented by the popularity of dance performances by resident children. Orphanage dance shows started to receive ratings and reviews on travel forums, making explicit their equivalence with other kinds of tourist attractions. One orphanage known for giving regular dance performances received an overall rating of 71 percent excellent, with reviews declaring, "Amazing . . . An evening to remember . . . Wonderful Khmer Dancing by nice Children."[21] Viewing orphanage dance performances, like visiting orphanages or volunteering in them, moved from being framed as intentional acts of bearing witness to simply being promoted as some of the local attractions, as Natanddrew on Lonely Planet's Thorn Tree Forum recommends: "Please go and see their performance, I am sure you will see the best traditional dance performance available in Siem Reap!"[22]

The schema that positioned dance performance as a way to enhance self-confidence and cultural connectedness remained dominant until the end of the decade, but a backlash about the entire orphanage volunteer enterprise, not just individual corrupt or poorly run orphanages, also began around 2007. While previously criticism had focused on whether or not a particular orphanage was a good one or a bad one, posts condemning the entire enterprise started to appear, as did more negative critiques of specific orphanages. Where once dilapidated and poorly maintained facilities were interpreted as evidence of need, they were coming to be seen instead as evidence of corruption, of adult staff who pocketed donations and intentionally kept premises in poor condition in order to elicit more sympathy and more donations. The travel forums were used as a way to spread information about the orphanages *not* to visit or support. One 2007 posting, for instance, warned about the "Cambodian Orphan Tourist Trade," cautioning that "more and more of these orphanages are popping up with the primary drive to cater to the tourist trade," pointing out how children have "become a valuable commodity to certain people," and explaining that "most of the time the children are not even orphans."[23]

Despite these criticisms, the orphanage boom was in full swing and orphanages were still increasing in both number and salience. But when posters remarked on the enjoyment, self-confidence, or other benefits that might accrue from performing dance, rebuttals inevitably appeared. Dance performances by orphans came increasingly to receive negative reviews instead of the positive ones quoted above, with characterizations such as "Untrustworthy . . . Do not Support: Child Tourism . . . SCAM: If you support this place you are supporting child abuse . . . zoo."[24]

The very fact of a foreign tourist gazing at a child, regardless of how much respect might be conveyed in that gaze, was susceptible to reinterpretation as exploitation, and in 2011 Natanddrew's review, quoted above, received this response, making the increasingly frequent comparison of the children to trained animals: "Why do people think it's commendable to . . . have them perform like dancing bears for tourists?"[25] Although many volunteers continued to note that the children they knew enjoyed and looked forward to performing, the tourist gaze was increasingly construed as inherently exploitative. The vulnerable child constructed by rights instruments as anyone under eighteen cannot give consent, and therefore it was irrelevant whether or not the children appeared to enjoy performing. By then, simply the fact of dancing for tourists had come to be considered inherently degrading.

Orphanage Tourism?

The rise of orphanage tourism and the subsequent backlash against it trailed by several years the rise of volunteer tourism more generally and the subsequent disenchantment with it. In contrast to "volunteer tourism," however, the term "orphanage tourism" had negative connotations from its first print usage, a March 2007 *Phnom Penh Post* headline: "Orphanage Tourism: A Questionable Industry."[26] The article described concerns raised by rights groups and child protection agencies regarding tourists brought directly to orphanages by tour guides and tuk-tuk drivers without regulation or monitoring. Although motivated by the growing position that "tourists should see the regular sights instead, and get over their delusions about any good they can do by visiting so called orphanages, especially when it's mostly to satisfy their selfish desire for a 'cute fuzzy moment,'" there was particular concern that children were encouraged to dance in order to solicit donations from tourists at the expense of their regular school attendance, made even more concerning by instances of children wandering tourist areas at night to promote their dance shows.[27] The scanty financial accountability and lack of screening or supervision of visitors were also worrisome.

By 2010, the terms "orphanage tourism" and "orphan tourism" had become widespread, and the first discussion in the scholarly literature appeared, with Richter and Norman defining "orphan tourism" as "travel to residential care facilities, volunteering for generally short periods of time as caregivers."[28] Subsequently, Guiney and Mostafanezhad refined the definition to refer to "the donation of money and goods, attending performances or volunteering on a short-term basis at orphanages as part of one's holiday."[29] In the scholarly literature, the requirement that the experience be short-term is criterial, although most authors discuss the hazards of short-term volunteering without specifying what duration counts as short-term or how long one would need to stay in order to be considered long-term. Reas is an exception in stipulating explicitly that "short-term" refers to experiences lasting less than six months, although there is no empirical or theoretical basis given for why that particular length of time is the cutoff.[30] The term "orphanage tourism" has come to replace many usages of the more neutral term "volunteer," especially short-term volunteering or volunteering by less skilled individuals. While visitors often label activities such as playing games or singing songs with children as "volunteering," critics refer to these experiences as "orphanage tourism."[31] The definition of "orphanage tourism" poses its own challenges, similar to the semantic complexities accompanying the terms "orphan" and "orphanage" discussed in chapter I, and with additional connotational baggage conveyed through the word "tourism."

While the referential meaning of the term "orphanage tourism" varies, uses are unified in their negative connotations, and most discussions in the scholarly literature are cautionary if not outright condemnatory.[32] Richter and Norman emphasize the risk of attachment disorders for children who interact with an ever-changing stream of transient volunteers, and Guiney stresses how commodification of children in orphanages leads to emotionally draining, potentially damaging interactions with foreign visitors.[33] Reas likewise focuses her critique on the commodification of Cambodian orphans even as orphanage tourism fails to address the "fundamental inequalities between the needy and the benevolent."[34] Wilson stresses the inadequate child protection policies and practices of many organizations that rely on volunteers, highlighting particularly the vulnerabilities that can be exacerbated by residential care. Focusing primarily on sex abuse, she points out that not only are most volunteers unfamiliar with appropriate ways to interact with children who are survivors of, or at risk for, abuse, but volunteers themselves can be abusers.[35] The most frequent and most serious concern is that the resources provided by foreigners are exacerbating rather than contributing to the overall long-term well-being of Cambodia's children because they function as pull factors that simply encourage Cambodians to open more unneeded orphanages. Implicit in this concern is the notion that orphanage care is inevitably and inherently undesirable, although explicit concerns also center on the possibility that families may be paid or deceived into relinquishing their children. As discussed in the introduction, for many the most troubling indicator of the problems inherent in Cambodia's orphanage boom is the fact that a majority of children in Cambodian orphanages, including Sovay, who was introduced at the very beginning of this book, have at least one living parent.[36]

Once the term "orphanage tourism" was available, critics who previously had been generally uneasy with the situation had a focal point toward which to target their unease, and a backlash was not long in coming. The term "orphanage tourism" is powerful for advocacy; it conveniently packs in all the negative connotations of the word "tourist" and all the tropes of vulnerability and innocence of the word "orphan." It both created and reflected the visceral, vague but dogged sense that something was terribly wrong in the orphanage scene in Cambodia, and it was only a matter of time until public opinion started to shift away from the view that visits and volunteering in orphanages were positive things to do. As travel photographer and blogger Kathryn Burrington summed up the chilling effects of the term "orphanage tourism," "Just the phrase sends shivers down your spine."[37]

The backlash was powerful and sweeping. At the same time that the term "orphanage tourism" was coming to be known in the academic literature, postings on travel forums were becoming more generally negative toward the entire enterprise, rather than specifically focused on individual corrupt or poorly managed orphanages. Concerned observers of the orphanage scene in Cambodia made a practice of monitoring travel forums and responding to inquiries about volunteering with explanations of why they considered it to be inappropriate in principle, even in forums that were no longer active. For example, the negative response, quoted above, to Natanddrew's 2008 post appeared in 2011. The following quote from jjack, a regular poster on the Thorn Tree Forum, is typical of the responses that started to appear whenever someone asked about volunteering in an orphanage: "There are no orphanages anywhere in SEA for you to volunteer at, that's why you're having such a hard time. Do orphanages in your own country let strangers on holiday pop in to play with the kids? Of course not. Donate your money but don't expect any contact with the kids. With a bit of luck this whole distasteful practice will be made illegal soon."[38]

The Anti-orphanage-Tourism Campaign

In 2011 concerns about orphanage tourism that had circulated informally online and in conversations within the foreigners' community in Cambodia coalesced into a formal campaign spearheaded by Friends International, known as Mith Samlanh in Khmer, a respected NGO that has been serving vulnerable children in Cambodia since 1994. Friends was founded by three travelers who, like so many visitors to Cambodia at that time, were moved by the extreme poverty they witnessed and stayed on to provide help. They started bringing food to a group of children they encountered sleeping on cardboard laid out on an unpaved footpath in Phnom Penh. Unlike many well-intentioned but inexperienced travelers who tried to provide assistance at that time, Friends responded to the expressed needs of the children they wanted to serve and adapted their programs accordingly. They have been enormously successful and remain in operation today. Friends began by supporting seventeen children and by 1999 was a registered NGO providing a host of services for the thousands of marginalized urban children and youth living and/or working on the streets. Most prominently and in contrast to many charities, they emphasize practical skills training that can lead to jobs, which the children and youth they worked with had voiced as their most pressing need.

As mass tourism increased, Cambodia's widespread poverty and weak enforcement gained it a reputation for sex tourism. For service providers such as Friends, therefore, in the early 2000s the most salient threat to children's well-being was not orphanages but rather child sexual exploitation, a pervasive concern that shaped the focus of Friends' 2005 ChildSafe initiative.[39] ChildSafe offered trainings for hotel staff, drivers, and others employed in tourism about ways to recognize and respond to child sexual exploitation and endangerment.[40]

After completing the training and pledging to follow best practices, participants received a bright blue shirt with the eye-catching ChildSafe thumbs-up logo prominently displayed, so that foreign visitors could easily recognize them and choose to patronize them. Volunteers and tourists were enlisted as allies in efforts to prevent child exploitation and endangerment and were educated to patronize only individuals and establishments that had made the ChildSafe commitment and to avoid people and places that did not display the ChildSafe logo. Orphanages and orphanage staff were not a focus, although orphanages were mentioned as a venue where it was especially easy for predators to gain access to children. ChildSafe also established an online presence with tips for travelers and foreign residents, which revealed the most prominent child well-being concerns of that time. For example, they advised, "Don't be foolish; don't take children home or in your room. Many tourists are put in critical situations for having taken a child to their room to give them a shower, some food, etc." and "Do not buy anything from children on the streets."[41]

Although in 2006 the government of Cambodia, in close collaboration with UNICEF, had issued a set of minimum standards for alternative care facilities, enforcement of the minimum standards had been inconsistent. Thus, as in so many instances in Cambodia, an NGO leaped in to fill the void left by the state, and in 2009 Friends launched its own alternative care project with the objectives of "reinforcing capacity of families to take care of children so as to reduce abandonment, developing traceability of children to avoid trafficking, support of orphanages for implementation of good practices and behavior change campaign towards Cambodians and foreigners."[42] Best practices in orphanage care, but not orphanages per se, were the focus of this campaign, and tourists were alerted that they needed to be allies in the effort to prevent abuse through a campaign targeting Cambodians and foreigners.

While volunteers and visitors still tended to see themselves as central to the solution, many resident aid workers had come to see them as central to the problem instead, and as the Friends alternative care campaign gathered momentum, the focus soon shifted from concerns about the potential for sexual exploitation in orphanages to concerns about orphanages per se. In 2011, Friends International enlarged the scope of ChildSafe and launched their "children are not tourist attractions" campaign, with a specific focus on discouraging orphanage tourism. This was the first organized effort aimed specifically at ending orphanage visits, rather than improving the behavior of visitors to orphanages or enlisting them as allies to combat other forms of exploitation. It consolidated and disseminated the many concerns that had been for some time circulating informally among the aid community or in online discussions. It drew on the children's rights-based framework that had been increasingly influential since the 1990s. It addressed not just sexual exploitation but the perceived violation of children's right to privacy and dignity seen to ensue when tourists visited orphanages.

After the Friends campaign started in 2011, a consensus quickly coalesced around the idea that orphanage tourism was inherently problematic in ways that attempts at best practices could not fix.[43] The term was generally used broadly to include most volunteering, but special scorn was usually reserved for dance performances. Positive reviews of orphanage performances on online travel forums slowed after 2011 and had stopped altogether by mid-2015; most orphanages today do not have dance shows.[44] Although the process was a gradual accretion of many separate changes that originated independently, they combined to support each other in a single, clear message, exemplified in the following advice that has replaced all the positive reviews that formerly appeared on the Travelfish forum: "One word of caution. Some orphanages offer Khmer dance shows, performed by the young children in their care. We can only advise, 'Don't do it!'"[45]

Responses and Consequences

The anti-orphanage-tourism campaign resonated both inside Cambodia and abroad and was readily picked up and quoted by the global media. It was timely, ingeniously and engagingly designed, and well supported with compelling information. It has had real, measurable consequences, seen not only in the cessation of orphan dance performances but also in the decreasing numbers of children in residential care in Cambodia. However, with such an emotion-laden topic, it is not surprising that accurate figures have been difficult to verify, and they can be off by as much as an order of magnitude. Total counts are affected by definitional and methodological inconsistencies, as well as logistical challenges such as the fact that so many Cambodian orphanages fly under the radar because they are not registered as orphanages with the government, often referring to themselves as shelters, homes, foster families, schools, or centers instead.[46] The discrepant numbers are themselves an indicator of the complexity and emotional valence of the situation, and the patterns are revealing.

The first systematic counting of children in residential care was in 2005 when the Ministry of Social Affairs, Veterans and Youth Rehabilitation (MoSVY) began compiling numbers of children they found living in centers in their annual inspections. In 2005, they found 6,254 children in residential care. That same year, Holt International Children's Services documented 8,270 children in orphanages. The discrepancy is largely due to the fact that the Holt team interviewed staff at unregistered as well as registered centers and included estimates for the numbers of children residing in centers that declined to participate in the survey, usually because they rejected the orphanage label even though they met all of the Holt team's criteria for inclusion.[47]

By 2010, the MoSVY inspection reports showed 11,945 children in residential care, an approximate 90 percent increase over their 2005 figure. From 2010 to 2016, the years when anti-orphanage and anti-orphanage-tourism sentiment became globally significant forces, MoSVY inspection reports showed a decline to 8,155 children living in residential care.[48] Concerns nonetheless continued about the rapid proliferation of care centers that were unregistered and therefore operating outside of MoSVY oversight. To determine how many children might be missed in its annual inspection of registered centers, MoSVY undertook a mapping of care centers in 2014 through early 2015 and identified a "staggering" 35,374 children and youth living in residential care—nearly 1 out of every 350 Cambodian children.[49] This survey covered a broader array of kinds of facilities than their inspection reports and included children as well as youth over eighteen living in group homes, boarding schools, and pagodas, in addition to the 16,579 children who were living in the kind of facility that MoSVY defined as an orphanage. Even this figure has been seen by some to be an underestimate. UNICEF reports over 26,000 children in what they defined as orphanage care in 2015.[50] In 2015 Stark et al., in collaboration with Cambodia's National Institute of Statistics, visited 122 care institutions in eleven of Cambodia's twenty-four provinces and extrapolated their careful counts of resident children to estimate that there were 48,775 children, or one percent of all Cambodia's children, living in residential care. Like the Holt study, their study included centers that were not registered with MoSVY as well as ones that were registered but had not been inspected by MoSVY the previous year; it did not include youth over the age of eighteen who were still living in care facilities.[51]

No matter which figures one accepts as accurate, all of them bolstered the concerns highlighted in the anti-orphanage and anti-orphanage-tourism campaigns and inspired changes of both attitude and behavior among many Cambodians and foreigners. In 2015 the Cambodian government initiated "sweeping reforms."[52] They set a target of reintegrating 30 percent of children in residential care back to their families and communities from the five most tourism-impacted provinces by the end of 2018.[53] In 2016 alone the government shut down fifty-six centers due to mismanagement or outright abuse, but the scale of the problem had turned out to be far more enormous than previously realized; the fifty-six shutterings represented just 9 percent of the total number of *registered* centers.

In late 2017, the Ministry of Social Affairs announced that they were not meeting their target, pointing out that the realities of reintegration were far more complex than the foreign-staffed NGOs seemed to realize. While government officials have been criticized for corruptly allowing unregistered or mismanaged orphanages to proliferate, they in turn report that NGOs have "improperly reintegrated" some children.[54] A Ministry of Social Affairs representative pointed out that as of 2015 the Cambodian government employed just fourteen social workers for the entire country. While they were prioritizing the rapid training of more social workers, hastily arranged and unmonitored reintegrations could jeopardize children if they were returned to unsafe family situations. According to some child welfare workers in Cambodia who were aiding in the reintegration process, the government had "openly acknowledged that they don't have the resources to deal with all of the social care issues the country has now," and some children had been "improperly reintegrated"; others stress that "reuniting families is a fickle, individualised process."[55] Nonetheless, the numbers continued to drop rapidly. In 2018, MoSVY reported 17,000 children in residential care facilities and in 2020 reported that 9,000 were still in residential care.[56]

Today there are fewer children in orphanages and fewer orphanages overall, and the government has instituted stricter regulation and oversight.[57] Also striking is the effect the campaign has had on the public face of orphanages themselves. In 2014 most still had a "volunteer with us" button on their websites and readily accepted volunteers. Just five years later, those volunteer buttons were scarce and most orphanage websites had been updated to state that they no longer accepted volunteers. Orphanages that did accept volunteers required background checks and specified a minimum length of stay. Fewer and fewer volunteer placement agencies offered volunteer experiences with orphanages, and many added warnings about volunteering in orphanages or explanations for why they didn't offer that option.[58] The anti-orphanage-tourism campaign expanded into a global movement, and responses rose all the way to the governmental level when Australia became the first nation in the world to legally recognize "trafficking and/or exploitation of children in orphanages" as a form of modern slavery in the Modern Slavery Act of 2018.[59] The COVID-19 pandemic caused the definitive end to orphanage tourism in Cambodia—visits to orphanages were suspended by the government in order to prevent transmission.

The complete reversal of public opinion toward residential care in Cambodia is in many ways extraordinary. Orphanages and orphanage volunteering arose organically and probably inevitably out of a situation of total devastation and were widely perceived as a legitimate and positive response for almost three decades. Then, in less than ten years, a global condemnation achieved a near consensus that was even written into the legal code of a large and influential nation-state.[60] As a model for self-regulation in the absence of effective government enforcement of minimum standards, Cambodia's anti-orphanage-tourism campaign has been quite influential, but it is vital to recognize how fundamentally the campaign relies on imported minority world ideas about childhood.[61] The near consensus took hold largely within the Western aid community and Western media; the voices of the Cambodian children themselves were largely missing from the pronouncements. What do they have to say about their experiences in residential care? In the next chapter, I discuss how I went about addressing this gap with a description of my methodologies, and in chapters 5, 6, and 7 I present my findings—observations of the daily lives of the children living in the Children's Opportunity Center, followed by their own reflections on their experiences, drawn from interviews with them.

4

Methods

This research draws upon evidence from a range of sources. Initially, I used a participant-observation methodology during four separate visits between 2008 and 2016, and followed up in 2019 with interviews with former residents. Popular and scholarly written materials, travelers' blogs and travel review sites, and policy and organizational reports were also consulted. Because scholarly constructions are necessarily informed by the worldviews ascendant at the time of their construction, research articles are sometimes used as primary data, rather than simply as secondary reports. Both participant observation and interview protocols were conducted according to the guidelines of, and with the approval of, the University of Oregon Institutional Review Board for the Protection of Human Subjects.

Participant Observation

In order to select a primary research site as well as to contextualize the observations with broader information about orphanage care in Cambodia more generally, I visited a total of thirty-two orphanages, each between one and three times, over three visits to Cambodia from winter 2008 through spring 2011. All but two of the orphanages were in Siem Reap; one was in Phnom Penh and one was in Kampot. Visits were unstructured and included a range of activities depending on circumstances and resident and staff preferences. They ranged from highly interactive activities such as teaching English and playing basketball, through moderately interactive tasks such as preparing and serving meals, all the way to simple observation or a tour of the premises. I have described elsewhere and in more detail the methods used to identify the primary research site.[1]

To complement the relatively briefer observations at many orphanages, the Children's Opportunity Center was chosen as the site for sustained participant-observation research, with regular visits over a period of two months during the winter of 2010–2011 and follow-up visits in 2014 and 2016. It was chosen for the following reasons: it was stable and had been in operation for five years; it was staffed by Cambodians and managed by a Cambodian NGO, although like most orphanages in Cambodia its funding came primarily from foreign donations; it was registered with the Cambodian government; with 40 children, it was mid-range in terms of the number of children served, which in Siem Reap's orphanages ranged from 7 to 138; it had an active volunteer program; and my initial visit revealed that it provided good-quality care, a judgment confirmed in subsequent visits. In other words, and very importantly, it did not make me feel uncomfortable to spend time there or cause me ethical dilemmas about whether there were circumstances I needed to intervene in or report. My assessment was corroborated by its 2010 rating of 84.88 percent compliance with MoSVY's minimum standards, which placed it good in terms of quality—it was neither exceptional in meeting the minimum standards, as were the two orphanages assigned a score of 98.83 percent compliance, nor failing, as were the nine orphanages that were deemed not sufficiently compliant. In addition, and crucially, program administration expressed interest in and support for my research.

The participant-observation methodology used in this study involved more observation than participation. Participation consisted mostly of using English while interacting with the children, because the managing NGO had prioritized education, especially English language education, and recognized that immersion language learning was effective and valuable. Participation also included, to a much lesser degree, cleaning and maintenance tasks like sweeping and picking up trash, helping out on construction and gardening projects, and food preparation. Mostly though, I sat in a quiet spot nearby the children's activities but not right among them, and took notes. I followed the residents' and staff members' lead when they initiated activities or interactions, although occasionally I intervened when I felt that the children's safety was at risk, such as once when they were climbing on the roof of a house. I sometimes brought art and writing supplies for them, although I let them take the lead on how to use them. The focus on language immersion allowed me a legitimate reason to be present and involved in most of the children's daily activities, and I spent time in all of the orphanage living spaces except for the inside of the children's sleeping quarters, which I visited a couple of times with staff escort but never otherwise entered. In fact, this turned out not to be a limitation, as traditional Cambodian architecture encourages most daily activities to take place outside or under the house.

My observations covered a range of settings and activities, including routine activities such as play, chores, meals, naps, homework/study sessions, and enrichment activities such as dance and music class and less routine activities such as off-site excursions and receiving visitors. I also accompanied the children to, and observed them at, the elementary and junior high schools they were attending, and spoke with teachers and administration members. One child was admitted during the study period, so I was able to observe his adjustment and the staff and other residents' reactions to him. I was not allowed to spend the night at the center, which limited my observations to the span of time from when they woke up to when the youngest ones retired to their houses for studying and quiet time before sleep. As I will discuss in the conclusions, I got to know the younger ones better than the older ones because the junior high school students had full-day rather than half-day school and often stayed late at school for activities.

Observations were complemented with unstructured interviews and informal conversations with staff, volunteers, and interested community members as well as visitors' and volunteers' comments on travel blogs, social media, and orphanages' and NGOs' websites.[2] The period of observations paralleled the orphanage boom in Cambodia, in which the number of centers providing residential care proliferated dramatically, as did their visibility and accessibility to foreign visitors. The initial purpose of the research was to document in detail the lived experience of children growing up in an orphanage, as a distinctive kind of childhood among the range and variety of different kinds of childhoods around the world. But as orphanages proliferated and became more and more controversial, an assessment of the children's perceptions of their own experiences became more evidently essential, and for that reason I also conducted follow-up interviews with former residents.

Interviews

In order to add the vital but often overlooked voice of the residents themselves, in fall 2019 I returned to Siem Reap for six weeks in order to speak with some of the young people who had previously lived in the COC and hear their memories of their experiences. The interviews had three separate but interlocking goals:

- To document outcomes, especially in education and employment
- To elicit stories and gather a finely grained portrait of the lived experience of growing up in an orphanage
- To gather opinions regarding what participants found to be positive and negative about residence in the COC

I was fortunate in this project to have the full support of the managing NGO because they were concerned about the quality of their programming, sincerely interested in what residents had to say, and receptive to the framing of it as a research project, giving me full autonomy regarding the questions I asked and the use of the results. Their support was essential, especially when it came to locating and contacting the former residents.[3] They also provided me with a research assistant, who conducted the interviews in Khmer and was invaluable in helping me to understand and contextualize some of the participants' comments. She is herself a former participant in one of their other programs. Although I had worried that some participants might hesitate to criticize the center because of her association with the NGO, this turned out not to be a problem. Some participants were very critical, either of particular aspects of the orphanage itself or of other programs run by the same organization. It turned out to be very helpful for the interviewer to be someone from a similar background as the former residents because of her ability to put them at ease. Research methods inevitably and eternally involve trade-offs, and in this case I prioritized the need to have someone the organization was willing to trust.

Starting with the original six children who came to live there at its creation in 2005, a total of fifty-one children have passed through the gates to live at the COC; two have since passed away. I was able to interview twenty-two of the remaining forty-nine. The managing NGO staff helped me enlist participation by reaching out to sixteen former residents and asking them if they wanted to meet with me; I contacted a further six of the twenty-two interviewees myself on Facebook. I was in touch with nine others, but we didn't have time to arrange a meeting before I had to leave Siem Reap. Two former residents have passed away, and I was unable to obtain contact information for the remaining eighteen. Clearly the twenty-two whom I interviewed do not form a random sample. They are the ones who have remained close enough to Siem Reap that I could reach them easily, and I interviewed only those who were eager to talk to me. I intentionally did not push anyone who didn't immediately express enthusiasm, but I am certain that much of the reluctance was shyness rather than lack of a desire to share their memories. Probably the group that I interviewed skews toward those who (1) are well-off enough to have access to technology; (2) are confident or proud enough of their lives today to want to share their stories; and (3) have remained in contact with staff, the managing NGO, and/or other residents. These three factors suggest that participants do not have overwhelmingly negative memories of their lives in the orphanage.[4] However, it is also possible that they wanted to talk (4) because they have an axe to grind or (5) because they are lonely. Unable to control for these possible sources of bias, I can only suggest that the first three factors are likely to balance if not outweigh the last two.

Interviews were also conducted with four former staff members. All spoke English well, but in order to grant them full expression of their opinions with nuance and comfort, three of these interviews were conducted in Khmer by an experienced Cambodian researcher and translator, who has no affiliation with the NGO, and I conducted one myself in English.

I framed the interviews by explaining that I wanted to write a book to help provide information and make recommendations about ways to care for vulnerable children, based on what the people who had actually lived and worked in an orphanage said about their experiences. I encouraged them by saying that they were the experts when it came to the experience of living in an orphanage. I pointed out that orphanages were an important part of this moment in Cambodia's history, and it was essential to record people's thoughts and feelings and experiences while they could still clearly remember them, in order to preserve the historical record for future generations.

This study is qualitative, although in discussing the results I sometimes report "all participants said . . ." or "only two participants believed. . . ." Indeed, one of my most important conclusions is the wide variation in participants' orphanage experiences. The interviews therefore did not need to be conducted in a uniform manner, and the need to be sensitive to the desires of the participants took priority. I followed their lead in terms of when and where we met. Thus, interview locations included a library, an NGO conference room, an outside veranda, a Pizza Hut, a trendy coworking space, a hotel lobby, and the garden in a pagoda compound. If participants wanted to meet one-on-one, we did that, and if they asked to be able to be interviewed along with a friend or two, we did that as well. One participant preferred to talk over the phone early on Sunday morning because they were home with a young child, and another preferred to talk for shorter periods of time over several days. Likewise, there was range in who conducted the interviews since I also gave participants the choice about what language they wished to be interviewed in. Sixteen participants were interviewed by my research assistant in Khmer, while I attended to the recording equipment. These were translated and transcribed by a professional translation company. One of the participants was interviewed by a male NGO staff member because my research assistant was not available at the time they needed to meet with us. I interviewed five participants in English.

Research must inevitably reflect the art of the possible rather than the attainment of the optimal.[5] Since the goal of this research was to encourage reflection and gather stories, not to conduct statistical analyses on quantifiable questions, it made sense to me to honor participants' preferences, and I remain extremely grateful for their grace and cooperation. The participants' lives reflect their developmental stage in the life cycle, and they were all very busy—studying, parenting young children, establishing careers, finding a life partner—so I was appreciative of any time that they were willing to give me.

Siem Reap is a small town, and the community of former orphanage residents and NGO staff is even smaller. For that reason, I have anonymized and aggregated the information they gave me as much as possible in order to spare participants' possible future discomfort. I avoid tagging quotes with identifying information, and in a couple of instances I have used more than one different name for a single participant, in order to further obscure identity. This is unfortunate but necessary; their stories are riveting and their reflections profound, and I would love to give them credit. A collection of the transcribed interviews alone would make a wonderful book and would be a valuable window onto a unique moment in Cambodia's history. On the other hand though, the participants are all at pivotal moments in their lives, starting families and careers, and I will leave it to them to decide what they wish to reveal to future children, life partners, in-laws, and employers.

The interviews were semistructured and designed to be as conversational as possible, with open-ended questions and follow-ups based on what participants themselves chose to talk about. Rather than sticking to the script, we asked for elaboration and examples based on what the participants brought up. I encouraged them to ask me questions as well, and I encouraged my research assistant to share her own experiences where she felt it was appropriate. Participants were able to talk for as short or as long a time as they wished, and interviews of solo participants ranged in length from twenty-three minutes to one hour and seventeen minutes. The longest interview was the one with three participants in a sort of mini focus group, and the shortest was one with two young and very shy participants. With a goal of three distinct kinds of information—outcomes, stories, and opinions—the interview questions were separated into these three categories and asked in roughly that order. As the conversations unfolded, participants' responses didn't always conform to that order, but we tried to keep the questions flowing in the direction from more objective and less personal to more evaluative and more personal. However, rather than follow a script, we followed up by encouraging specificity and elaboration (e.g., "Can you give an example?," "Then what happened?") while encouraging storytelling and letting them decide what was important to them.

My second methodological concern, in addition to ensuring participants' comfort throughout, was to avoid biasing responses through assumptions and presuppositions encoded in the questions, although the questions one chooses to ask are obviously always reflective of one's own biases and concerns. It was important to avoid both obvious leading questions (for example, "Did the constant stream of short-term visitors staring at you make you feel like an animal in a zoo?") as well as excessively open-ended prompts, which would have left especially the shyer participants struggling for an entry point into the topic (for example, "So, about the volunteers . . ."). I opted for a middle ground between these two extremes by explicitly asking for both positives and negatives, phrased as, for instance, "What was the best thing about the foreign volunteers? What was the worst thing about them?"

The questions we asked are listed below, but because we wished the process to be comfortable and conversational, the list is a guide, not a script. My goal was to know what *they* wanted to say about the COC.

1. Outcomes: What are you doing now? How many years has it been since you lived in COC? What have you done since then?
2. Telling their COC stories: How old were you when you went to live in COC? What do you remember about that day? What do you remember about your life before you lived in COC? Can you remember the day you left COC? What did you do? How did you feel? Tell me about an ordinary day that you remember from when you lived at COC. Tell me about your friends / school / the food / playtimes / the housemothers / your chores / the foreign volunteers. What if somebody were to ask you "What is it like to live in an orphanage?" What would you tell them? Imagine a few years from now when you have children of your own. When they ask you "What was it like to live in the COC?" what will you say to them?
3. Opinions about their COC experience: What was the best thing about living in COC? What was the worst thing about living in COC? How do you imagine your life would have been different if you had not gone to live in COC? What advice would you give to a child who is going to live at a children's center? If you could say anything you want to the adults who worked with COC while you were there, what would you say? Where do you see yourself and your life in ten years? Do you think it would look differently or the same if you had not lived in COC?
4. Perceptions of foreign volunteers: Do you remember any foreign volunteers? What do you remember about them? How did you feel about them? What was the best thing about the foreign volunteers? What was the worst thing about them?

Because each interview was unique, not all participants addressed every topic, and we strove to make each interview as conversational and spontaneous as possible. We accepted participants' parries away from topics that they may have found uncomfortable rather than probing deeper. In particular, we had originally planned to ask participants about their lives before going to the COC and the reasons why they had gone there. However, we found in our first two interviews that the questions about their life before their placement elicited such painful memories that we decided not to ask those questions again.[6] Despite our avoidance of the topic in the rest of the interviews, some participants volunteered information about it, and in that case, we followed up when it seemed appropriate to do so.

Characteristics of the Interviewees

While my primary goal was to hear what the former residents had to say about their own experiences, one can't help but be curious about how their lives have turned out so far in terms of some of the more objective criteria that have underlain many of the controversies surrounding orphanage care. Recall that I chose this orphanage after "auditioning" many others, and so I naturally wondered whether it really had provided better access to education and employment. Outcomes also turned out to be very important for the former residents' own appraisals of their experiences in the orphanage, and so are relevant for understanding and appreciating their perspectives. Table 1 shows the gender, current age, ages spent living at the orphanage, most recent level attained in school, employment status, and whether they are married or still single.

Most Recent Level of Schooling

Overall, the interviewees' educational attainment is above average for Cambodians of their generation; by way of comparison, 42.6 percent of Cambodians complete ninth grade, which is the highest level of compulsory schooling, and just 20.2 percent complete high school.[7] Given the difficult circumstances from which all of the COC residents originated, the results are even more impressive because educational attainment is lower for children from rural areas and for poor children. Importantly too, the pride expressed when speaking of high school graduation, which involves passing a national exam in addition to completing coursework, makes it an important achievement. Likewise, some university enrollment, even without graduating, is itself viewed as a success. Even a year or two of university enrollment can help some students find a satisfactory job without completing a degree. Students from less wealthy families often need to work while they attend university, and therefore it takes them longer than four years to complete a bachelor's degree. Sometimes they must also suspend studies for a year or more to save money or relieve the stresses of combining employment with enrollment.

Marital Status

The median age of marriage for women in Cambodia is 20.5, and for men it is 23.5.[8] Only one of the interviewees is married, and he married at the median age, as did his wife, who was not a COC resident. The seven other participants at or above the median ages are still unmarried; none below the median ages are married. Marriage is integral to Cambodian adult life, and I do not wish to imply that it is good or bad for anyone to marry at the age they choose to marry. However, the Cambodian government is making efforts to raise the average age of marriage partners. Although it is easy to circumvent age limits by simply not registering the marriage, lack of registration compounds the risks already associated with early marriage. There are fewer legal protections for partners and children in unregistered marriages, and it is easier to desert the marriage altogether. Early marriage also correlates with all the risks associated with adolescent pregnancy, and pregnancy-related complications are the second leading cause of death among fifteen- to nineteen-year-old girls in Cambodia; children

TABLE 1

Demographic Characteristics of Interview Participants

Name	Sex	Age	Years at COC	Education	Employment	Marital status
Achariya	F	17	11–15	In HS	Student	Single
Arunny	F	17	8–15	In HS	Student	Single
Ary	F	14	7–14	In HS	Student	Single
Bopha	F	16	4–15	In HS	Student	Single
Botum	F	16	2–16	In HS	Student	Single
Charaya	M	22	8–15	HS grad, some university	Office	Single
Chaya	F	16	8–15	In HS	Student	Single
Daevy	F	20	7–15	6th grade, vocational	Tailor	Single
Kolab	F	22	8–14	HS grad, some university	Student, works part-time	Single
Kosal	M	19	6–16	HS grad, some technical	Student, works part-time	Single
Mach	F	17	10–17	In HS	Student	Single
Malis	F	17	5–15	In HS	Student	Single
Munny	M	15.	2–15	In JHS	Student	Single
Narith	M	25	13–18	HS grad, some university	Office	Single
Nary	F	22	8–15	HS grad	Hospitality	Single
Pich	M	19	7–16	HS grad, vocational	Student	Single
Prak	M	25	11–17	HS grad, vocational, some university	Office	Single
Rathana	M	28	14–19	University grad	Owns small business	Married at age 23
Rotha	F	18	11–16	In HS	Student	Single
Samnang	M	14	6–14	In JHS	Student	Single
Sothy	F	17	11–17	In HS	Student	Single
Tevy	F	22	8–15	JHS grad	Musician	Single

born to adolescent girls are also prone to greater health risks and mortality. In addition, research by UNICEF found that over 30 percent of women married as girls in Cambodia had experienced domestic violence, which is higher than levels experienced by women who married as adults. Marriage before stable employment prospects are available is associated with a range of negative outcomes, and educational attainment, usually cut short by early marriage, can facilitate stable employment prospects.[9]

Although early marriage is almost universally regarded as a concern for girls, in Cambodia it is also a problem for boys because, in contrast to many other parts of the world where early marriage is common, Cambodian marriage partners tend to be close in age.[10] The "stresses of being a young husband" can be overwhelming, especially expectations that young couples will live with the bride's family and provide labor for her parents.[11] For all these reasons, the managing NGO has discouraged early marriage, and table 1 shows that they have been successful.

Employment Outcomes

Employment outcomes are somewhat complicated to summarize and to interpret because so many Cambodians have more than one job or work while they are also going to school. While most of the participants are still students, reflecting the association's discursive and programmatic emphasis on education, many are impressively hardworking, often with a regular job plus one or more part-time or seasonal jobs. It is especially popular to start small businesses on the side and to return to rural areas to help with the harvest, both of which are hard to tabulate in a tidy way. One former resident, employed as an office manager, also designs online language learning materials, and another who was working in an educational NGO was also preparing and selling food in the local market. His small business has been so successful that he recently quit his NGO job, but he still also has some other small business ventures on the side.

Analysis

All interviews were translated and transcribed in their entirety, including paralinguistic information such as pauses, fillers, false starts, repairs, laughing, and crying. I began the analysis by simply reading and rereading all of the transcripts, immersing myself in the participants' stories and gaining an intuitive sense of their current lives and memories of the center. An analysis that contained elements of both a conventional inductive content analysis and a directed content analysis was then used to identify and verify key themes and milestones.[12] Some themes resulted directly from the questions we asked, while other themes emerged spontaneously, appearing across multiple interviews even though we didn't ask explicitly about them. After deciding upon a theme to address, I reread all the transcripts searching for and highlighting all examples of that theme, both to verify the intuition that it was important to participants as well as to me, and to identify excerpts to quote as examples.

Some meta-level themes emerged out of patterns of what participants didn't say, as well as what they did say. For example, it was striking to me that no participant expressed an unambiguously negative opinion of the COC in particular or of orphanages in general, even when prompted explicitly to share the worst aspects of living in the COC. The balance of positive and negative memories and assessments led me to identify "nuance and ambivalence" as a theme that conveyed their attitudes more fully than simplified themes such as "positive things about the orphanage" and "negative things about the orphanage."

Out of the rich and often deeply moving interviews, five experiences and five reflective themes emerged as most important. The five experiences, to be presented in detail in chapter 6, are Coming to the Orphanage, Material Care, Relationships with Other Children, Visitors and Volunteers, and Leaving the Orphanage. The five reflective themes, to be described in chapter 7, are Nuance and Ambivalence, High Expectations, Their Lives Could Have Turned Out Very Differently, Positive Future Orientation, and Individual Agency and Gratitude.

The orphanage scene in Cambodia has been analyzed, promoted, enjoyed, criticized, expanded, and undone largely through the actions and words of foreign adults, with little input from the young people whose lives have been most affected by the ways it has taken shape in their homeland. In the next three chapters, I strive to balance the unbalanced narrative by providing first, in chapter 5, a careful description of the everyday life of children living in one Cambodian orphanage. It begins with the journey my daughter and I made every morning from our guest house in Siem Reap to the COC, in order to situate the COC in its community context and enable me to combine my observations into a composite "day in the life" of the resident children as it unfolds from early morning until dark. Chapters 6 and 7 follow up with insights from the interviews, organized into the above-described themes, revealing the perspectives of young adults embarking on the next stages of their lives.

5

The Rhythms of Daily Life
in the Orphanage

The Road to the Orphanage

The road to the Children's Opportunity Center (COC) leaves the town of Siem Reap and enters the gate to the Angkor Archaeological Park, where the tuk-tuk driver slows, waves to the guards, and reminds them of our destination so we don't have to pay the thirty-seven dollars for a one-day visitor's pass. Nonetheless, to get to our destination we pass directly in front of Angkor Wat; as commutes go, this one is beyond exceptional. We veer to the right under the towering faces of the Bayon temple, and as we exit the park, our turnoff from the paved road is marked by signs announcing the innumerable NGO projects that have been undertaken in this district. Cambodia has the second highest number of NGOs per capita among all countries of the world, and their presence is heavily felt here, the second poorest province of Cambodia.[1] The pitted and crumbling blacktop becomes rutted red dirt, so dusty in the dry season that motorcyclists wear face masks and so deep in gelatinous mud in the rainy season that it is frequently impassable. The orphanage is about thirty kilometers from the touristic hubbub of Siem Reap, but the trip takes over one hour for us, somewhat faster for the many villagers on their motorcycles who seek employment in the hospitality and construction industries of Siem Reap. We pass woven bamboo houses on stilts and gated villas in bright pastel colors. We pass rice fields, fishers and farmers, charcoal burners and piles of wood, a tree with cuts of meat for sale swinging in the dust, and often during the dry season, the rented canopy and folding chairs of a village wedding, which will stay for perhaps three days, blaring blessings and music on the portable speaker system over the entire journey. Along the road we see the lives of village children unfold in plain view—small children with smaller children on their hips, children in school uniforms biking and walking along the road, children squatting in the dust watching traffic and waving to us, tending oxen and buffalo, fishing, and chopping wood. Cambodia is a young country; over 42 percent of the population is under fourteen, and children seem to be everywhere.[2]

The first sight of the children who live in the orphanage might come before the orphanage is even reached. As we pass the village, which is about a kilometer before the entrance, we might see them lining up or thronging about in the primary schoolyard, although it would be hard to pick them out among the restless tide of blue and white uniforms that fills the schoolyard. Or we might see them sitting on rough wooden benches under the trees in makeshift classrooms that have been set up outside to accommodate the overflow of children that the school simply has no space for. If it's later in the day, they may already be walking back from school, waving enthusiastically and piling in on top of one another to fill the tuk-tuk if we stop for them.

The first glimpse of the orphanage itself is the row of trees and shrubs marking the edges of the compound, and the open blue and white gate with the empty guard station beside it. Although the orphanage employs a full-time guard, he is usually out driving staff and residents to various destinations or inside the compound doing handyman tasks. Foreign visitors are often surprised that security is not a big concern. Children come and go while strangers and community members enter the compound freely, although their presence is immediately noticed and monitored, and if they are unfamiliar or potentially threatening, they are escorted and never left alone on the premises. We pull into the entrance without stopping, and the tuk-tuk parks under a tree in front of the children's houses.

In appearance and atmosphere, the orphanage resembles a small village, marked by traditional architecture and patterns of living space, more than it does a large institution. The environment provides many opportunities for exploration and vigorous physical activity as well as space for children to seek alone time should they wish. It occupies a large compound, with trees, scrub, open space, and gardens. The front is bounded by the rutted road, but set back far enough that the buildings and landscaping are not covered with the fine red dust. On one side is another NGO, serving widows and children, and on the other side is the neighbors' family compound. Groups of five to nine children live in six separate houses, which surround a central playground and paved area for basketball. There is an organic vegetable garden in the back, fruit and kapok trees scattered throughout, and a cassava patch along one side. Between the main driveway and the fence to the next-door neighbors' compound is a tiled pavilion, open on three sides and holding a Buddha statue. Next to that is a two-story education building, with a meeting/supply room on the top floor and a classroom, a Western-style toilet for visitors, and a sleeping room for the director on the ground floor. Away from the buildings, among the fruit trees, is a fire pit for burning trash, and on the other side are laundry lines. Behind the houses is an open field where the children play soccer and volleyball. The kitchen and dining room are separate structures, covered but open on the sides, and there are two separate blocks of bathrooms. The pump that draws fresh water from the well is located between the kitchen and the bathrooms, and well water is piped to both.

Five of the children's houses are made of wood and raised on stilts in traditional Khmer style, with an open upstairs verandah at the front and sleeping areas inside the doorway. Underneath are raised wooden platforms and hammocks, and it is in this under-the-house space, shaded and sheltered from the rain but open to breezes and passersby, that most daily living and socializing take place. The sixth house is concrete and placed directly on the ground.[3] While children enter their own house freely, they rarely spend time inside except at night, and adults other than the housemothers rarely mount the stairs or enter the houses. Inside the houses, the children sleep next to each other on kapok-filled mats that are rolled up and pushed to the corner out of the way after the children rise in the morning.

Morning

Like most children throughout Cambodia, children at the orphanage wake up early, and it is still dark at five when they rise and gather for thirty minutes of group exercise and a run of twenty laps around the compound, followed by thirty minutes of morning chores.[4] Splashing, voices, and laughter emerge from the darkness as the children start their chores, and as it grows lighter, they can be seen sweeping the yard, piling up debris and putting it in containers, watering plants, picking up trash, and whisking dust out from inside the houses and down the stairs. They scamper around purposefully, singing, calling out, chattering, all with a high level of energy and a great deal of laughter.

Boys and girls whose turn it is to help with breakfast according to the rotating chore schedule are already in the kitchen by five thirty, helping the cook chop vegetables and fish and boil the rice. School begins at seven, and the children who have morning school bathe and put on their uniforms. There are too few schools for all of Cambodia's children, so half the elementary school-children attend school from seven to eleven in the morning and half attend from one to five in the afternoon. By the time the sun rises at six thirty, most of the morning session schoolchildren have finished their baths and are fresh and ready for breakfast in their immaculate school uniforms.

Breakfast is at six thirty. Many days it is sour fish and vegetable soup with rice; other days it might be beef braised in soy sauce with rice, or omelets, vegetables, and rice. Children eat as many servings of rice and other dishes as they wish, and at every meal there is a protein, most often freshwater fish, and a vegetable, most often morning glory.[5] Vegetables are often from the organic garden tended by the children; while fruit is eaten more rarely, some of it comes from the trees that shade the compound. Snacks and desserts are rare, although foreign visitors often feel sorry for the children because of this and so bring candy when they visit. The daily fare is simple, plain, but nutritious, and the children eat with gusto, sometimes in silence, sometimes talking animatedly. They leave individually when they finish their meal, without announcement or permission, and rinse their dishes and brush their teeth at the well pump. The adults eat separately, usually in the kitchen.

It's only one-half kilometer to the junior high school, and the teens and young adults who attend set off walking alone or in small groups. While in theory junior high school in Cambodia is for children twelve to fourteen years old, at the time a pair of twenty-year-old girls and several other youth older than fourteen were among the fifteen of the forty orphanage residents who attended the junior high school. The primary school is in the village center one kilometer away, and the children who have morning school climb onto the open flatbed moto-trailer that will take them there.[6] The rocks and ruts and lack of shock absorbers make the ride thrillingly bumpy, and frequently children who aren't attending school will ride along for the fun, even standing up in the open bed to maximize the jolt. Adults almost never have to remind children to get ready for school; the children are eager to go, and most have been waiting in the moto-trailer for several minutes before the driver revs the motorcycle engine and they bounce their way to school.

After those attending morning primary school and junior high have left, the remaining children converge into smaller groups. The groups are fluid and overlapping, although the older boys tend most often to stay in one group and the older girls tend to stay in another, while the younger children sometimes stay in their own mixed-gender group, or sometimes also split by gender. On a morning in January, toward the end of the dry season, Atith, age twelve, and Kiry, Kosal, and Leap, all age eleven, might be seen gathered on the cement area of the playground in the center of the compound, playing a version of pétanque using rubber flip-flops instead of balls, and whatever is handy to serve as the target—this day, it was a bundle of yellow cord, other days it might be a bottle cap.[7] There are always several stray shoes there, in addition to the players' own shoes. Two girls, Chanlina and Bopha, both eight, along with two boys Pran, age six, and Munny, seven, watch them silently and intently. Meanwhile, Aruni and Jorani, nine-year-old girls, have tied a chain of rubber bands together and take turns jumping it. Chanlina leaves the shoe pétanque game to join them.

Pran and Munny, the two youngest children at the time, along with eight-year-old Botum, are kneeling on the ground in front of the houses playing with the fine sand that covers the inner compound. At first they take turns drawing pictures with a stick, sometimes giggling at the silliness of the picture they have drawn and sometimes just piling up the dust and letting it run through their fingers, enjoying the texture. After about ten minutes, their focus shifts and they are carefully scraping dirt into a pile about seven inches tall in the center of the group of children. Then in turns they probe a long thin stick into the pile, and withdraw it carefully to carry as much sand as possible out on the length of the stick without it falling off. This isn't a game with winning, losing, or a score, but just awe when a child is successful and disappointment when they are not. After fifteen minutes of intense concentration Munny's eight-year-old sister Bopha joins them, then Pran leaves, Aruni joins them, Munny leaves, and after about thirty-five minutes they have all drifted off.

Later in the morning, a snapshot of the children's activity might look like this:

A group of four boys, eleven and twelve years old, are playing shoe pétanque on the paved playground area, closely watched by two younger boys, Davuth and Oudom, both ten. The players play absorbedly for long stretches of time without losing concentration, talking and laughing only in response to a play.

Two children, Pich, a boy, age twelve, and Chouma, a girl, age thirteen, are in the pavilion playing a tossing game with rubber bands. Chouma holds a large bundle of rubber bands, and Pich tosses a clump of two or three into one of the squares of the tile floor. If he gets it inside the square, she gives him another rubber band. If it lands on the crack or the wrong tile, she takes the rubber band back.

In addition to these group games, several children are engaged in solitary activities. One girl, fifteen-year-old Mliss, bathes and, with a towel wrapped around her wet hair, carries her toiletries back to the house. Ten-year-old Davuth, a boy, carries food out from the kitchen to the eating area for a snack. Pran, at six the youngest of the children, is pedaling an adult-sized bike that is standing upright with its kickstand but motionless under a tree. His legs are too short to reach the pedals from the seat, so he is sitting on the back rack, and I assume he is idly pedaling in place because he doesn't know how to ride such a large bike. But after several minutes of stationary pedaling, he suddenly pushes off from the kickstand and bikes expertly around the driveway, still seated on the back rack because he can't reach the pedals. Accomplishments like learning to ride a bike or to pump on a swing tend to pass unremarked by either children or adults. Children are not tutored or given child-scaled versions of adult tools or special aids such as training wheels; they learn to ride full-sized bikes, they clean and garden with adult-scaled tools and cleaning instruments, and they do their kitchen chores with heavy, huge, and very sharp cleavers.

As the morning warms up, Mliss and Phala, also fifteen, are dozing in hammocks under one of the houses, and the two girls Tevy and Chouma talk quietly in the shade under another house. By midmorning the groups have coalesced, splintered, and reconfigured several times. At times, groups were separated by age and gender, then they would come together for a large, inclusive game, then break off again. Because the boys' play was very physical and usually rougher, most of these large-group games provided an opportunity to see how the children responded when they got hurt. In one such instance, others of the nine- to twelve-year-old children, both boys and girls, wandered into the pavilion to join the children playing there with rubber bands. By the time eleven of them had gathered, the game switched to one involving tagging, getting "frozen," and being rescued, all played while hopping on one foot.[8] The game was rough, and the tagging turned frequently into shoving and falling, and even punching, pinching, and wrestling, but no tears. When the children got hurt, they got quiet, took deep breaths, and looked strained, and often sat out for a few minutes, but nobody acknowledged that anything hurt, by complaining, retaliating, or apologizing. Even at the game's wildest moments, the boys were careful with the girls. Although the boys frequently wrestled on the floor with each other, and the girls much less frequently wrestled with each other, there weren't any cases of boys wrestling with girls, and they poked and pulled at girls much less than at each other. Although girls sometimes distanced themselves and seemed put off by the roughness, they always joined back in enthusiastically. This was a game only for the older children, and while it was going on, the little ones sat in front of the bathhouse in their undies and splashed and laughed together playing in the water.

Children's play at the COC is active, varied, self-initiated, and self-directed. It is also physical, exuberant, and often rough. Manufactured toys were noticeably absent, but this reflects a deliberate policy decision. The COC receives many toys from well-intentioned visitors because Westerners tend to consider an abundance of toys to be an indicator of quality of life. However, toys are viewed by the staff as something of a nuisance and are kept in a room that is usually locked. The children were only occasionally allowed to play with them because, as I observed and as staff corroborated, they fought more and cooperated less when they played with the commercial toys, which tended to break quickly and then pose a disposal problem and injury hazard, since they were usually plastic and couldn't be burned in the trash fires. Although the children were always excited and delighted at the opportunity to play with the toys, the lack of toys did not affect their daily lives. I was constantly struck by the ingenuity with which they created their own games and toys out of available materials such as sticks, leaves, and stones, as well as their pets and each other.

Even on school days, school-age children have considerable free time for play; they are on their own for most of the four and a half hours or so that the other half of the group is away in school, except for when there are supplementary lessons available, which may last for one or two hours. Although the posted schedule of daily routines set aside regular time for tutoring in math, Khmer, and English, at the time I was there the lessons were sporadic and infrequent, and most of the time when they weren't in school the school-age children were playing. When not playing, children of all ages spend much of their time in silent but avid observation of adult routines and skills, or in passive participation, riding as passengers behind older children on bikes and behind adults on the orphanage motorcycle. Everyone is comfortable with clusters of children standing around and staring at any event or activity that transpires, and the importance of observational learning makes my role as an observer less strange to the children. By and large they ignore me, continuing their activities unselfconsciously as I watch.

During my observations of the children, the adults were occupied with their own work. The cook cleaned up the breakfast things and spearheaded the preparations for lunch, with the help of the housemothers, who when they were not helping in the kitchen or tutoring children, occupied themselves in the compound, pulling weeds, planting flowers, grooming garden beds, or doing laundry, leaving them little time for tutoring. They appeared to pay little attention to the children throughout most of the day.

The Adults

There were seven regular staff members for the forty children of the COC at the time I began this study—the cook Sophea, two housemothers Anchali and Putrea, Sambath the team leader, a guard, an agriculture teacher, and the director, Mr. Sann.[9] In addition to the regular staff, a dance teacher and a music teacher each came two days per week. The administrative staff of the umbrella NGO, including monks and laypeople, are also regularly on site and involved with the children, in addition to providing oversight and planning. Total staff put the COC within the ratio set by MoSVY of one caregiver for every ten to fifteen children, although most of the staff are not designated caregivers and the team leader and the director were often busy with administrative tasks. In 2011 only three of the six houses had housemothers. Instead, two older girls served as housemothers for a group of younger girls, and the older girls' house and older boys' house did not have a designated housemother. Counting just the staff formally designated as housemothers would put the ratio at twenty to one, but the MoSVY guidelines are ambiguous regarding whether only staff designated as caretakers may be counted in the ratio.

Because of the ethical values of the pagoda-based Buddhist management, staff are employed under relatively good conditions: monthly salaries are a little lower than the already low salaries that public schoolteachers make, but full room and board and use of facilities (such as tools, motorcycle, and library) are included. In principle, staff get two days off per week, although since the housemothers and cook lived on site, there was not a clear distinction between days on and days off. They continued to interact with the children on their days off, and usually left only for specific events such as festivals and weddings or for infrequent trips away to visit family in other villages. The primary criterion for selecting housemothers, as explained to me by a program director, is that they have demonstrated experience interacting in a warm and responsible way with children, with either younger siblings or their own grown children.[10] None have formal training in child care or child development. Turnover was high among staff, and only one who was present at my first visit in 2008 was still employed in 2019.

Whenever I observed the staff, all behaved consistently with kindness toward the children, although scolding and direct orders were common. While overt signals of affection that Western visitors look for, such as hugs, were missing, personal space was close and physical contact frequent. Staff interactions with residents were often playful and involved teasing and a physical closeness that felt comfortable and not forced as they performed intimate tasks such as bathing and grooming. However, during the day staff rarely took the initiative to interact with children except in structured ways like academic tutoring, bathing the younger ones, or serving the rice at meals. Like mothers in most Cambodian families, the housemothers are kept very busy with day-to-day household tasks and do not spend much time playing with or supervising the children. Most adult-child interaction centers around shared work, particularly in the kitchen and in the garden. Most of the staff speech directed to children was in the form of directives, most commonly calling one by name to do something or carry something, and during the times I was present to observe, children reliably complied with adult directives immediately and without complaint. The only situation where I observed staff time dedicated to intensive, one-on-one interaction with a child involved the treatment of four-year-old Sovay, when he first came to live at the orphanage. His housemother, Anchali, made a point of bringing him over to introduce me and give me a polite greeting on his first day, and she intervened several times when he was upset with the other children. She also napped with him in the hammock when he was fussy and wouldn't sleep. However, this extra attention is only relative to the amount of time she spent with the other children. Even during his earliest days at the orphanage, when he was distraught, she more often directed other children to comfort him, which they usually did anyway without her prompting.

The fact that staff spend so little time exclusively focused on individual children, and especially that they don't play with them, is consistent with traditional village Cambodian expectations about parenting roles. Cambodian adults are not expected to play with children, and the tendency of Western visitors to play with the children was a source of commentary and amusement, and sometimes annoyance, as when I was involved in a game with the children and my driver was bored and wanted to leave. "Oh, *barangs* always want to play with the children," Anchali explained to him authoritatively, and they continued to discuss this strange behavior. Cambodian adults work very hard, and while up through the age of three or four years children are in almost continual presence of their mothers, after that they are expected to become less dependent because adults must tend to household tasks.[11] In the family compounds surrounding the orphanage I saw small children in the arms of older children more often than with adults. A lack of exclusive interaction with adults is a reality both for children at the orphanage and for children growing up with families in Cambodia, and it would be mistaken to assume a priori that this lack of exclusive adult attention signals a difference between family and orphanage life. However, it makes it even more important to examine the quality of the interactions that are most prevalent in the children's lives, namely their interactions with each other.

Noon

After eleven o'clock, the students who have morning school begin to reappear, and they rush to each adult to give them a greeting of respect, palms pressed together in what is called *sompiah*. They run upstairs to change out of their school uniforms, and at eleven thirty a child is chosen by the cook or a housemother to strike the large, loud bell to call the children to lunch. Usually the preadolescent boys jostle for this privilege and compete to make the loudest noise; rarely does a girl or younger child show interest. Children drift over to the dining hall without hurry and wait patiently until everyone is gathered; then an older child leads them in a Buddhist prayer of gratitude before they receive their food. One day lunch might be sour fish soup with chopped banana flower and a green vegetable, another day it could be salty soup with peeled cucumber and small pieces of pork. A housemother or an older girl presides over the meal, standing at the rice pot and solemnly dishing out rice to every child. After this ritual beginning, the meal is relaxed; children help themselves to seconds or thirds, and leave whenever they are done.

After lunch, just as after breakfast, the children rinse their own dishes and brush their teeth with water from the well. Two children's names are up on the rotating chore list for cleanup and wipe the tables and sweep the food scraps out the doorway to the waiting dogs. After lunch, the afternoon school students emerge, showing a dramatic transformation—children who were scrabbling in the dirt and throwing flip-flops around the playground are now in spotless white shirts and navy pants or skirts, looking very studious. They depart, and the remaining younger children nap for an hour or so, sometimes inside their houses but more often snuggled together on the woven mat covering the wooden platform under their houses or in one of the hammocks positioned to catch the afternoon breeze. Sometimes the older children nap, sometimes they play straight through the naptime, sometimes they read quietly in the shade. The day is getting hot, and their movements are measured in contrast to the morning.

School

After lunch, the afternoon schoolchildren and the junior high students walk or bike separately, in pairs or in a loose group strung out along the road. Sometimes they have a particular friend in the neighborhood, as did Tevy, whom I sometimes saw walking to the gate and waiting until another girl her own age biked up, stopped, and gave her a ride, sidesaddle on the back. The clumps thin and separate into smaller groups as the older youth turn right into an opening in the hedgerow for the shortcut to the junior high school; the younger ones continue on another half kilometer farther into town and turn left into the primary schoolyard. As they arrive they greet and are greeted by same-age, same-gender friends, and blend into groups so that if I didn't know them, it would be impossible to pick them out. Among so many other children, it is easy to see how their condition compares with their village peers. I watch carefully, but see no signs, either physical or behavioral, that would differentiate them from children living in local families. They are neither better nor more poorly dressed, neither the tallest nor the smallest, neither the thinnest nor the heaviest, and neither the best groomed nor the shabbiest. Nor do I see them aloof or excluded, bullied or bullying, or in any obvious visible way discernible from their village peers. A distinguishing feature I cannot see emerges from one of their teachers though; he worries to me that on any given day at least one-third of his students will not have done their homework. The COC children are never within that one-third, he tells me.

Education, both secular and religious, is a priority for the orphanage and for all other programs of the umbrella NGO that manages it. "We believe that at the root of all suffering is ignorance, and that loving care and a good education can provide a way out of poverty," proclaims their mission statement, reflecting the Buddhist foundations of the organization. The program philosophy of the orphanage, one of the NGO's five poverty reduction-focused programs, is to "aim to empower these children through education so as to enable them to break the cycle of poverty and strive for a brighter future." This philosophical commitment is implemented in a number of ways. Resident children all attend local public schools, except for the one child who is under six and therefore too young to start. The orphanage also offers on-site enrichment classes in Khmer, English, and math, eliminating the need for the "extra lessons" with which public school teachers supplement their low salaries, and without which it is nearly impossible for children to advance to their next grade level.[12] As one of the more studious junior-high-school-age boys told me, children attend school in large part only for the attendance marks. To actually learn anything, especially to pass the annual exams, students must pay for private tutoring from teachers. Teacher salaries are very low, so they put their efforts into private tutoring, and I was continually surprised by how many times I unexpectedly found the children home rather than in school because the teachers were absent or the classrooms were being used for other purposes.

A designated study time is part of the regular schedule for all residents and children receive homework help from housemothers and from older children. Homework is monitored so that the children turn it in on time, and everyone takes an interest in the children's studies. One afternoon when I was there, my tuk-tuk driver came sheepishly over to me asking, "Can you help me?" because one of the seventh grade girls had failed her math test, and she was trying to figure out the correct answers on problems she had missed. He didn't know the correct answer, and I didn't either, and soon the entire staff was involved in the problem. The program has set a performance goal of 85 percent or above for every child, and report that all but one is currently meeting this goal.

All of this support and supplementation helps the children succeed in the local schools, and, importantly, to overcome the limitations of the public school system, because most classes consist of mass recitation and copying whatever is written on the board. As I enter one classroom at their school, the children are sitting idly while the teacher spends the first ten minutes of class writing a list of Khmer words on the board. Then he leads the students through repetition and then recitation of the words, first as a group and then individually. The lesson seems dry to me, but the children are engaged, and shout out the words with great energy. It is clear though that by the time he goes around the room one by one to check their skill, they are memorizing the list rather than reading the words. However, this fits their expectation of how school should be, and they are enthusiastic throughout the lesson. Indeed all the children were consistently eager to go to school, and did not need to be nagged, or even reminded, to get ready. In the entire time I observed the orphanage, I saw only one incident of school refusal, and that was a student who claimed he wasn't feeling well, although the cook, who had the responsibility that day of ferrying a group of children to school, wasn't buying it. As she loaded four children onto the motorcycle for the trip to school, he refused to come out of his house and join them. Finally she left without him, and after about five minutes, he emerged, rang the bell long and loudly as a statement of protest, and walked out to the road to school. This was the only incident I observed of anything other than eager anticipation for school, an eagerness that carried over to Sundays when there is no school but sometimes are supplementary lessons in English, particularly if a foreign visitor is willing to give a guest lesson. One Sunday, I even saw Kosal, an eager student of English, dressed in his school uniform and sitting under the house with his notebook, waiting for the English class to start, and even turning down a round of shoe pétanque with the other boys so that he wouldn't be late.[13]

The nearest secondary school is too far away for the orphanage children to attend, so when they finish junior high school, youth must move into a town if they wish to continue their studies. The NGO that manages the orphanage has made an explicit commitment to support the residents in their educational endeavors, to the extent feasible, for however long they may be willing and able to study, and when I visited in 2011, Rathana and Prak, the two oldest boys in the orphanage, had just moved into the pagoda after six years of living at the orphanage. As temple boys, they receive room and board in exchange for doing chores for the monks, but they explained that the training in Khmer classical dance they had received at the orphanage has also been instrumental in making it possible for them to continue their studies. Both performed in evening restaurant dance shows in order to cover the costs of the "extra lessons" their teachers required in order to pass their courses.[14] The option of serving as temple boys is not open to girls, but the NGO has set up a residential program in Siem Reap to advance high-school-age girls' education. Students of any gender who show an aptitude for university work are partially supported until they finish, although they must also work. Narith, for example, by 2016 had left the orphanage and was working part-time in a hotel; again, it was skills he had obtained at the orphanage, namely his excellent English, that afforded him the opportunity to continue his schooling. Students who are more inclined toward vocational training receive support for that. One youth who had recently graduated from the orphanage received training in bicycle repair so he could open his own repair shop, and several girls received training at the sewing school, which is another of the projects managed by the NGO.

Afternoon

After the schoolchildren have left, quiet and heat settle in. A snapshot of the afternoon might look like this: Under House 1, there are two children stretched out on mats, and one in the hammock, talking more and more quietly until they are asleep. Under House 2, two children are also lying on mats and playing with the hammock, rocking it back and forth until one gets into it and then they both fall asleep. Under House 3, one child is swinging quietly in the hammock. One girl is sitting on a shaded bench in the playground reading her Khmer schoolbook, and two boys are nearby playing shoe pétanque, soon joined by two more. Inside House 4 one child is reading while another is underneath lying in a hammock. Voices reciting a prayer come from one of the houses, but I can't tell which one before they too fall quiet. One boy is in the kitchen helping the cook, and another is in the dining hall listening to a portable radio. As in the morning, the locations and activities are fluid and changing, although quieter and less kinetic because of the nappers. Even those who aren't sleeping seem inclined to take quiet time.

By one o'clock though the younger boys are unsettled, too tired to sleep as young children sometimes get, and they are out of the under-house spaces and racing around the playground, over to the slide, cutting each other off and climbing up it the wrong way. The children don't have to sleep, but they do need to be quiet, and Anchali comes over and yells at them to be quiet, then walks them over to House 3. They lie down together on a mat to nap, but she tells them firmly to separate. When they do everything is quiet again, although four boys continue to play shoe pétanque.

By one thirty, Sophea the cook is momentarily done with her chores, and she lies down in the hammock under House 3 for a rare rest, but the children are starting to wake up. The children under House 2 play with each other's hair, wrapping it and winding it around their hands, then move on to wrapping and winding the strands of the empty hammock in a cat's cradle kind of game. As other children wake up, they amble yawning to the bathroom, or drift over to Sophea in her hammock where one older girl begins to groom her hair. Within fifteen minutes, a group of twelve others are gathered around watching. Anchali comes over and a child grooms her hair as well. Everyone's attention is drawn. Three younger boys are watching from the porch swing, and one boy is on the bench watching them. One girl brings a red plastic chair from the kitchen over to House 3 so she can sit while she watches. It is an intimate, peaceful moment, unusual because Sophea is almost always working in the kitchen.

While most of the girls remain clustered around the hair grooming for another twenty minutes, the boys grow restless and a group of five of them takes over the swings on the playground, standing up in them and "rocket swinging" sideways at each other, until they hear one of the older boys call out to them that they are driving the flatbed truck into town. The boys bail out of their swings and run to jump on. One struggles to catch up, and when they pull out of the exit without him, he keeps running until they slow down and he jumps on while it is still moving. At this moment, the group enthralled by Sophea's hair breaks up, and one of the girls rings the bell. They all rush to the dining area for a special snack of coconut milk, rice, sugar, and beans brought by a visitor. By two thirty, snack is over and the rhythm of activities has reclaimed its customary busyness. The three youngest boys are bulldozing the sand with pieces of scrap lumber, while the girls are gardening—one has a digging tool and is clearing growth from the front by the driveway, and the other is clipping the hedge. One smaller girl takes the scraps over to compost by a tree.

On a different day, a snapshot of the compound after lunch looks like this: Four boys are playing shoe pétanque, while a younger boy and girl stand silently watching. Three children are on mats and one is in the hammock under House 2, and four children are spread out on mats under House 1. Two boys are biking slowly and deliberatively around the compound savoring lollipops in their mouths, one of the younger boys is walking around aimlessly with a plastic wash tub on his head, knocking on it from the inside, and one midaged boy is sitting alone contentedly making a long chain out of rubber bands tied together. At one o'clock, earlier than usual, Leap asks the cook for permission to ring the bell, and all the nappers get up. By two o'clock, the groups have reconfigured; two boys are playing shoe pétanque with three smaller ones watching, one boy is sitting on a bench by himself in front of the classroom, happily stacking and restacking empty pencil boxes. Three separate groups are in the pavilion—one playing "rock, paper, scissors," one playing rubber band pétanque, and one running around shooting rubber bands at each other. Mliss is sitting on the stairs of House 5, staring into space contemplatively. At age fifteen, she is the oldest child left in the compound on this afternoon, and she seems to be at loose ends. After about fifteen minutes she comes to the playground, wanders around, stands on the swing, now sits swinging on it, and finally settles into the hammock under House 2.

Later in the afternoon, as the pace picks up again, the children become especially boisterous, running and chasing each other around the yard and up and down the playground equipment, shrieking and hitting each other. One of the smallest girls, eight-year-old Botum, who is generally somewhat timid, seems overwhelmed by all this and seeks the company of adults until Bopha, another eight-year-old girl, calls her over to the bench to play the rubber band pickup game, so together they can quietly avoid the pandemonium. Malis, age nine, is right in the thick of all this increasing wildness, which goes on for some twenty minutes, until suddenly Anchali calls Malis and Botum over to her at the well. She hands them a bundle of sticks to carry to the kitchen, and the two are immediately companionably occupied in carrying things back and forth until things calm down again. Again, I am struck. Anchali was occupied with building up the woven bamboo screen surrounding the well area so it could be used for bathing—she wasn't even paying attention, I thought. Did she know it was time to intervene, and did she know that targeting these two particular girls for her intervention was the best way to restore calm and confidence? While the adults responsible for the children do not spend their time performing the exclusive activity of watching them, they are aware of children's activities in a way that is not legible to me.

The junior high school students have full-day school but come home at different times, depending on the schedule of classes and whether they have extracurricular activities, school chores or meetings, or just want to stay and hang out with friends. On this afternoon, they begin to trickle in a little after three o'clock. They enter in high spirits, singing and laughing, greeting the adults with respect but teasing and joking after the *sompiah*. Most of them are considerably older than the twelve- to fourteen-year-old age group that should be attending junior high school, and their relationships with staff are friendly, casually jokey, and physical. Eighteen-year-old Rainsey laughs and jokes loudly with Sak, then grabs her wrist, and she slaps at him, both still laughing, as he goes to rest in the hammock under House 1, where Botum and Bopha are playing in the dirt.

Meanwhile, Munny, age seven, and Pran, age six, have been wrestling on the ground, throwing dirt and giggling in the driveway. They go to House I and gather Botum and Bopha, then they find Malis and the guard's son and go off into the scrub. When they disappear in the bushes, Mliss looks alarmed and follows them, talks earnestly with them, and they drift back and go play on the swings. After that burst of activity the children seem tired and hungry, and their behavior becomes increasingly disorganized until Sovay, Pran, and Munny appear with a stash of soursop fruits that they have gathered from the ground under the trees. Sovay has so many in his pockets that it looks like the weight will pull his pants down. They wander discreetly to the pavilion, where Bopha joins them. I find them there sitting cross legged facing each other, eating the fruits in companionable silence and secrecy. Pran and Munny walk back from the pavilion holding hands, the others following separately, calm restored.

Throughout this cycling between quiet play, increasing disorganization, private snacking, and restored calm and focus, the housemothers have left the children almost completely on their own. They don't seem engaged with the children's activities all afternoon until bath time, which in Cambodian families is another time for intimacy and responsibility, when parents give focused attention to their young children. "Come, come, come" calls Anchali and the children emerge from their houses in their bath gear—wrapped in towels or sarongs, hair in shower caps or loose, carrying soap, brushes, shower scrubs. Bath time refreshes the children and becomes its own playtime. On this particular afternoon, Botum and Bopha drag their bath gear in a huge plant leaf. At the bathroom the children prance and pose as the housemother pours cold water over them, soaps them up, shampoos their hair, then pours water over them again and sends them to the clothesline to get clean underwear. Botum drags her bath gear back to her house in the giant leaf, while Pran runs around naked. The housemother ignores him and supervises Munny as he hangs his wet bath gear up on the clothes line.

Discipline and Conflict

Although to my eye it often looked as though the adults were oblivious to the children even at times when their behavior seemed risky, there were regular events, such as bath time and serving the rice at mealtime, that signaled the adults' caretaker status and provided appropriate indicators of responsibility and intimacy.[15] It is part of a caretaker's role to bathe children and give them rice; it is not part of their role to tell them how to play. The children also appear to recognize this, and there was no tattling and very little running to adults to ask them to intervene.

On Sundays when there is no school, behavior gets wilder more quickly, perhaps because of the greater amount of free time and the larger number of children that were present all at once, and perhaps also because the children were given a small amount of spending money each school day to spend on snacks. They didn't snack at the orphanage unless they could forage fruit or green kapoks from the garden, or were able to talk the cook out of the brown crusty rice at the bottom of the pot. Because adults intervened so rarely, Sundays were therefore my best opportunity to observe how the children expressed and responded to conflict, and how adults disciplined the children.

Quarrels were most likely to break out just before meals, when the children's play seemed to become disorganized and they became more irritable and less purposeful in their behavior. However, even on Sundays when all the children were present, I actually saw very few instances of acting out while I was there, and fewer still of adults disciplining children. Although the children's interactions were physical and often rough, and the boys especially enjoyed play fighting, true fights were rare and usually mediated effectively by the children themselves, either by older children intervening or by the participants themselves taking distance to regain self-control. The children got hurt and showed visible pain quite regularly, but they neither sought nor received sympathy from adults when pain resulted from ordinary roughhousing, such as when play fighting got out of control, or when their eagerness to push their limits in climbing or jumping resulted in a fall. Typically the housemothers seemed rather skilled at discerning true conflict from rough and tumble play, and although they were occupied with their work and to me didn't seem like they were even paying attention, they intervened with fights but not with rough play.

There was no response from the adults as Pran and Munny chased each other around the compound, even through the kitchen, throwing sand and rocks at each other, giggling and hitting each other, with Munny finally swinging a toy truck at Pran. Rough as this was, the adults gave hardly a second glance. Nor did they intervene when the children appeared to be testing each other in the stick fights and pushing matches that the older boys regularly launch; the pushing gets hard enough for them to knock each other off balance, but each boy gives as good as he gets. If only two children were fighting and they were of the same age, they were almost invariably left by the adults to resolve it themselves, although sometimes other children would distract or remove one child from the scene. Children are expected to learn to manage their own emotions, and rather than complaining or accusing, they usually become noticeably quiet while regaining their composure. This is a necessary skill because adults as well as children, girls as well as boys, are physical in their teasing and affection, and although sometimes it really hurts, flinching or lashing out is not appropriate. After I have been visiting regularly for several weeks, the girls include me in their roughness as well, often greeting me by pinching my cheeks or waist, much harder than I am used to.

Some children were clearly rougher than others, but there didn't seem to be any regular targets. Conversations with staff there, as well as at other orphanages in Siem Reap, confirm that children come to orphanage care with health and behavior issues indicative of extremely difficult backgrounds, especially aggression, anxiety, blunted affect, hyperactivity, and hoarding or stealing, but that these markedly improve the longer children are receiving care. Recognizing the challenges that the children face as well as the issues such as domestic violence that many of them have already experienced, policy guidelines stress patience and loving kindness rather than punitive approaches to misbehavior.

The orphanage has an explicit policy against corporal punishment, although management was not always successful in ensuring that care staff adhered to the policy. Corporal punishment is legally permitted in alternative care centers, and surveys show that its incidence in families and schools is high and generally approved by most Cambodians.[16] Domestic violence is also widespread, and perhaps 50 percent of Cambodian children have experienced severe beating.[17] This is one reason for the COC policy against corporal punishment, but also a reason why it's hard to prevent completely, although I never observed it myself. Instead, the methods of choice were scolding and distraction, usually assigning chores. One afternoon Bopha and Botum were squabbling over the rules of the rubber band game on the bench by the swing. After Bopha had stalked off several times because Botum had accused her of cheating, only to return and squabble some more, their housemother, who was working in the kitchen, called them both over and handed them a big bucket of water to deliver to the next-door neighbors. They set off together with the bucket between them, splashing their clothes and laughing, quarrel forgotten.

When housemothers scolded children who were arguing, or took one or both by the hand and removed them from the situation, the emphasis was never on who was "right" in the dispute, on uncovering the causes of the conflict, or on children sharing their feelings and working on collaborative solutions.[18] Either both children were scolded or the oldest one was scolded and told to yield to, comfort, or distract the younger one. Children I observed complied immediately and without complaint, although there had been teenagers who left because they did not follow the rules. The same techniques modeled by adults were used spontaneously by children when they resolved disputes among themselves, and mostly the children curbed each other's excesses, leaving the adults free to tend to the daily business of running the orphanage.

Correction of children's behavior is also deferred and depersonalized when staff save their critiques for bedtime talks in individual houses, or gatherings when everyone is present, such as morning exercise and mealtimes, or the monthly Children's Council meetings. In this way, problem behaviors are targeted in a nonconfrontational and depersonalized way in which children can be enlisted to suggest solutions. When staff become more than routinely concerned about a behavior issue, the NGO director can be enlisted to phone children or visit in person, signaling the seriousness of the situation and letting children know that the adults around them are paying attention and concerned. Another way of depersonalizing sanctions was to refer to me, the *barang* ("foreigner"), as a reason to watch one's behavior, although more often than not this was a warning that had no apparent effect. One afternoon I was chatting with team leader Sambath and Pran came up picking his nose. "Don't do that, especially in front of the foreigner," Sambath admonished, and Pran laughed and wiped it on Sambath's pants. Sambath grimaced and we all laughed. This was a rare case where I observed explicit disobedience. Although adults rarely intervened in children's behavior, children rarely defied them when they did.

Evening

Afternoon school finishes at five o'clock, and after the children arrive and greet the adults, they dash upstairs for their bathing supplies. School uniforms are shed quickly and cared for carefully, and a single uniform may be worn and outgrown by two or three children. Afternoon bathing is a relaxing social time, and children emerge smiling, and often singing, from their baths. Dinner is announced by the bell around five thirty or a little later. The children rush to eat because the sun sets around six, and they are eager to enjoy the last light. As dusk falls, the boys erupt into a spirited barefoot soccer game in the back field, playing until it is too dark to see the ball, while the girls sit in the playground swings, singing and talking quietly while grooming each other's hair. While I was observing, the COC had limited electricity because it had lost the financial support of a major longtime donor, and there were lights at night for only one hour. This was the designated study hall, when children did homework or reviewed their lessons, and the older children tutored the younger ones. If children had more than one hour of schoolwork, study hall continued by candlelight. By nine o'clock most of the younger children are stretched out on their kapok mats. By ten the older ones are expected to be in bed as well. Their days are busy, active, and stimulating, and they fall asleep quickly.

The Children

Who are these children, and why have they come to live in an orphanage? According to their files, most of the children were placed when a relative, neighbor, or village headman had contacted the NGO and requested that the child be picked up. The following excerpts from the children's files evoke the extreme difficulty, even trauma and danger, of the children's backgrounds.

She can't possible to send her to school.

. . . when her husband drunk to fighting her every time.

Finally she married new husband and left 4 children living with landlord.

She gave her youngest daughter to other to carry for begging at market.

Now his parent stays in the province hospital for get the tablet HIV every day.

Now her mother got the step husband but her father got the step wife too.

She is orphan, she don't know about information her parent.

He has the mother but his mother stay in the prison and his father died 3, 5 year ago because [his mother] killed to his father.

As the children's records make clear, not all of them are living in an orphanage because both of their parents are deceased. But neither are they there "just" because of poverty.[19] Extreme poverty undercuts all of the children's family backgrounds, but all of them face other challenges, and the NGO is committed to the principle that no parent should ever have to give up their child simply because they are poor. According to their files, thirteen of the children (about one-third) had lost both their parents at the time of placement and fourteen had lost one parent. The parents of eight of the children (one-fifth of the total) were separated or divorced at the time of placement, and an additional eight were reportedly living with both parents at the time of placement; of these, seven were homeless and one child was working to support the family. Other factors explicitly mentioned include prison, unspecified chronic illness, migration to Thailand, alcohol abuse, and "so many children." Conversations with staff revealed that another prominent reason was hostility and even abuse by a stepparent. In addition, twenty-one of the children's files explicitly mentioned the inability to attend school as a motivation.

Several of the children had been abandoned at a pagoda that at the time was serving HIV/AIDS-affected adults and families. In addition to the eleven children who lost parents to HIV/AIDS, it is likely that HIV/AIDS was involved in the deaths of several of the parents who died of unspecified causes. The parents of four children were living with HIV/AIDS at the time of placement and probably passed away soon after, as ARV treatments were still not universally available at that time.

The forty residents of the orphanage in 2011 when I conducted most of this fieldwork ranged in age from four to twenty years. One arrived as an infant of three months, one at the age of two, and the rest between the ages of three and fourteen, with an average age of seven years and eleven months.[20] The relatively high average age of children at the orphanage and the few infants and toddlers is consistent with the broader patterns found in Cambodian orphanages. Infants and toddlers tend not to be found in residential care in Cambodia, and if they are in care, they are usually accompanied by older siblings. For example, ten of the twelve children who arrived at the age of five or younger came with older siblings.[21]

The average age of residents is also high because, like many Cambodian orphanages, the COC allows youth to reside past the age of eighteen. While this practice has been subject to criticism, these concerns are fueled by foreign norms of individualism and adulthood.[22] Cambodians are more receptive to children living with their families until they marry, and even after marriage. Allowing youth to stay on after age eighteen in order to finish school was also consistent with the COC's commitment to education. Fifteen of the COC children who arrived when they were already school age had not even started school, and often late school starters cannot complete junior high or high school until age twenty or even older, especially because Cambodia also has high rates of grade failure and repetition. Of the twelve who had some schooling prior to arriving at the COC, ten were already below grade level by at least three years; the two who weren't below grade level had only just started first grade. All six children of junior high school age were still in primary school at time of arrival. Since coming to the orphanage, all of the children have advanced at least one grade level every year they have attended school, which puts them well above the average of grade advancement in Cambodia, where first grade repetition, for example, is around 20 percent.[23]

After I had been visiting COC consistently for several weeks, and as the children grew more interested in me, they struggled with what to call me. Initially, they avoided calling me anything. Then, they briefly called me Barang. They learned my name, but Cambodian children are not comfortable calling adults by their names alone. Some called me Look Khruu ("Teacher"), but that didn't really match my role either since I did little formal teaching. Finally, many independently settled on Yiey ("Grandma"), which was a comfortable fit for the relationship that I had with them. Fascinated with my daughter, and how an "old" mother such as myself could have a child their age, they delighted in teaching us other kinship terms and pointing out other family relations at the center. As they continued to list kin groups, I was astonished to learn that fully thirty-four of the forty children at the COC had either siblings or half-siblings also living there and that an additional two were cousins; the largest sibling group consists of five children who came together. All three of the children who had left the center before I arrived had siblings still living there.

The children at the COC are proud of their kinship status and readily volunteer this information even when not asked explicitly. However, on a day-to-day basis, they tend to interact more with same-age, same-gender peers. While siblings are often nurturing and supportive of each other, this was true of most of the older children toward most of the younger children. This large number of sibling groups is also typical of residential care in Cambodia. It is easier to keep sibling groups together in an orphanage than in foster care, and sibling relationships have traditionally been very important in Cambodia. Siblings care for one another during childhood and throughout adulthood, with bonds that are among the most important, as well as of the longest duration, of any they have throughout their lives.

Gender is approximately balanced at the orphanage, with twenty-one boys and nineteen girls, working out to 52 percent boys and 48 percent girls, which is somewhat more balanced than the overall pattern in Siem Reap; according to MoSVY, 57 percent of children in registered centers are boys and 43 percent are girls. However, gender ratios have been considerably more unbalanced in the past at most Cambodian orphanages. Concerns about gender ratios in Cambodian orphanages peaked in the late 1990s and early 2000s, when a discrepancy between the gender of children adopted internationally from Cambodia (majority girls) and the gender of children found in orphanages in Cambodia (majority boys) was one of the indicators leading to suspicion and documentation of widespread corruption in the adoption process because it revealed that adoption trends reflected demands of prospective parents rather than the needs of children. In 2005, there were consistently twice as many boys as girls in Cambodian orphanages; this was also true in 2009 at all of the orphanages I visited except for the COC.

The fact that the gender ratio at the COC has always been more balanced reflects the organizational priorities of the managing NGO, which has targeted education and opportunities for girls explicitly since its founding. The general pattern of larger numbers of boys in residential care stems from a Cambodian tendency to prioritize sons' education over daughters' and a preference to keep daughters closer to home, both for protection and to help with household work. As Ledgerwood writes, "Many more boys than girls attend school. Parents would like to educate both, but if forced to choose, they choose to educate boys."[24] The recent rapid growth of orphanages in Cambodia has raised the hopes of rural parents that they will be able to educate both boys and girls, and the changing gender ratios, as well as the increasing numbers of children in orphanage care, reflect this.

Health and Safety

One morning in early January, I arrived to the unexpected sound of *pinpeat* music and drums.[25] The dance classes had resumed after nearly a one-year hiatus due to lack of funding. I expected to see a boisterous, maybe even chaotic jumble of activity on the dance floor because I knew that the children had missed the dance classes and had been eager for them to resume. Instead all thirteen dancers were motionless with one foot flat on the ground and the other knee crossed awkwardly in front of them. They held the pose while the teacher strolled among them, talking on his cell phone and tapping them with a thin stick when they wiggled or relaxed out of the correct pose. After holding this seemingly uncomfortable pose for over five minutes, the effect was broken with a cough, but still no movement. Startled, I realized what an uncommon sound that was; I hadn't heard any children coughing or sniffling or sneezing the whole month I'd been coming. In fact, I hadn't seen any ailments at all of the kind one usually expects when so many children are spending all their time in close proximity to one another. I realized that I had taken for granted the surprising fact that the COC children are very healthy.[26]

The children's good health is evident in their observable fitness, coordination, and high activity levels. There were no visible signs of chronic nutritional deficiencies or untreated sores or rashes. One newly admitted child was extremely small for his age, appeared younger, and was emaciated, but he started a growth spurt soon after arriving, and his appearance quickly became more typical of Cambodian children his age; with this exception, the children were not exceptionally small or thin, although several were shorter than average.[27] At school, surrounded by their same-age peers, it was clear that their heights were within the range for same-age children in the surrounding area, and they were less thin than many of the children in the surrounding community, although none were overweight. I saw only a handful of minor health issues—one cold that circulated among about half the children, temporary eye redness, insect bites that were scratched and became inflamed, eczema in one child who was treated at the local clinic for it, and two minor injuries that required treatment at the clinic. Several of the children were receiving regular treatments for chronic medical conditions contracted previous to placement. For minor injuries and illnesses, the children are taken to a small twenty-four-hour clinic about two kilometers away, and a children's hospital in Siem Reap city provides free medical care for larger health problems. A team from the children's hospital visits on a regular basis for checkups and vaccinations. On several occasions children also showed the marks of cupping and coining, two traditional healing practices.

Although health and wellness are taken seriously and self-care is instructed and modeled—the children and staff are expected to wash their hands, brush their teeth, bathe daily, groom for lice, etc.—the attitudes toward safety and security were more relaxed. Much of the playground equipment was broken, rusty, sharp, or jagged, and the railing on the climbing structure grew increasingly wobbly. Children climbed trees, perched on the rooftops, poked at the open fire pit, and biked and rode motorcycles without helmets. Although I frequently winced and worried that somebody would fall out of a tree or choke on something while on my watch, it never happened. On the whole, the children seemed to be very well coordinated, with a good sense of their physical environment as well as their own physical abilities. The lack of concern about physical safety among the orphanage staff seemed to be consistent with what I observed in the surrounding area. Regularly I passed young children chopping wood with sharp, adult-sized axes, jumping unsupervised from trash-strewn river banks into murky water, tending charcoal fires, or playing on the side of the road and only barely glancing up when trucks rumbled by.

Similarly to the lack of preoccupation with physical safety, security is not the concern it might be in a closed, Western-style institution. The gate stays open and the guard station unoccupied throughout the day, although it is closed at night. The children freely wander the premises and are often out of sight of the staff, but for the most part they stay inside the compound except when they go to school or on errands. The orphanage has a child protection policy, and the children receive instruction in how to recognize and report abuse, but the openness can be surprising and perturbing to Western visitors. Outsiders and residents come, go, and mingle, but residents and staff are acutely aware of these comings and goings and take measures in a way that is easy to miss because it is tactful and saves the face of everyone involved. For example, one February day at the COC, a local man who was visibly intoxicated biked in off the street and hung over the pavilion rail watching the dance class, every once in a while mumbling incoherently. He stayed for about ten minutes, growing louder and more talkative. In response, adults and teenagers laughed but repeatedly suggested, kindly and respectfully, that he leave. He didn't, and finally Phala (age fourteen) picked up the man's bike and walked it to the driveway, called him, and, when he eventually came over, biked him home.

Traditional Dance and Music Classes

The highlights of the no-school days for the children are their Khmer dance and music classes (in addition to being able to sleep in on Sundays, the result of a successful proposal from the Children's Council).[28] Dance at the orphanage is considered a privilege and a luxury, and so the classes were one of the first things to be cut during the donor crisis of 2010. The children were thrilled when they resumed. Before their teacher, Samang, pulled up in the morning on his motorcycle, some students were already in the pavilion stretching, posing, and critiquing each other's form; they rushed to greet him and then assembled waiting patiently while he took his time chatting with the staff before coming over. The warmup consists of calling out a pose for the children to hold while Samang strolls among them talking on his phone and slapping a long thin stick rhythmically on his leg. Suddenly he lashes out with it to strike a student who has moved or more gently to prod and tap students into the correct position. It is evident from watching the students wince that the strikes can sting, but they thank him for the corrections. I am surprised that this doesn't violate the center's policy against corporal punishment, but it is clear from the responses of the students and the staff who gather around the class that they approve his technique.

The positions of the traditional dance are challenging, and I was impressed by how well and how willingly the children held them for many long minutes. Ranging from squatting on their toes with legs bent and hands stretched flat out in front, through extending their torso flat to the floor while maintaining legs in a half-lotus, to balancing on their knees with one leg forward and one leg pointing back, the lessons required flexibility, strength, and patience.

The music lessons were far more loose, probably because only one or two can play an instrument at the same time, and children come and go, take turns playing, watch, get up and leave, and switch instruments, joining and rejoining the ensemble seamlessly. I never saw an adult demand that they practice, but they practiced for hours nonetheless. Any time the adults got the instruments out of storage, the children were right there. Although the younger ones' banging was always very loud and often seemed random, patterns, riffs, and rhythms emerged. Both during the lessons and during informal practice sessions, the older youth tutored the younger ones by holding both hands and moving them in the correct patterns, over and over so they could be memorized. Just as with the dance classes, the children also began and continued their lessons without their teacher, even when he was away with the other adults for events such as a wedding. Their teacher, Rithy, is skilled enough to play professionally at the Royal Palace, but the salary is so low he must supplement it with lessons. He teaches at several other locations in Siem Reap but confides to me that the COC children are more "clever" than any of the others and that they are his favorites to teach.

At the COC, dance and music classes do not conflict with school or homework, and children perform for community events rather than for tourists, although earlier in the center's history they performed publicly and for donors. They are much in demand in the surrounding villages for festivals, weddings, and other special celebrations. There is not another traditional dance and music ensemble nearby, so this is viewed as a valuable service to the community and confers prestige upon the children who have these skills. In this way, the COC focus on traditional dance has served to connect the children with their community and helps the orphanage earn a reputation as a good neighbor. Neighborhood youth also view the opportunity to study classical dance as a boon, and several regularly join the classes, which gives the orphanage another way to provide service to the community as well as to foster good relationships among orphanage children and their village peers.

It is easy, though, to understand why foreigners might feel uncomfortable with the repetitive nature of the practices and the strict discipline demanded by the teacher. The dance is physically arduous, and students are required to hold challenging poses for long stretches of time. They receive negative feedback often but rarely any positive feedback, although like music teacher Rithy, dance teacher

Samang made a point of privately telling me how skilled the COC children were compared to his other students. There are indications, though, that the COC children love to dance and play music—they remain in the pavilion practicing while their teachers take long breaks, and when the teachers relax in the dining hall with the male staff, the older, more serious students voluntarily tutor the younger ones. The music teacher is a quiet man of few words, but the dance teacher has a good-natured bantering and easy joking relationship with the students, despite his use of the stick. Sometimes he simply sits them down on the cool tiles of the pavilion and talks to them of the future. One day for example he goes around the group asking each child in turn what they want to be when they grow up. Several of the girls answered "a dance teacher," and when I followed up to ask them myself, they confirmed; they weren't just saying that to curry favor with their teacher. Although the lessons are directed toward the older children, the younger ones watch intently and patiently, and on the sidelines mirror the movements. During breaks in the formal lessons, the younger children take over the instruments and the dance floor and show that this observational learning is surprisingly effective; with little formal instruction, many are already quite accomplished. The older children also enjoy teaching them, and it is clear that all the children delight in and benefit from the dance and music classes, much the same way that children in North America enjoy and benefit from practicing and performing or competing in ballet or soccer. Even after the lunch bell rings, the children keep dancing and only reluctantly give it up to make their way over to the eating area.

Interactions among Children

One morning, a boy I have never seen before is walking cautiously down the stairs of House I. This is Sovay, the four-year-old introduced at the beginning of chapter I. Six-year-old Pran is coaching him from the top stair and nine-year-old Aruni is waiting for him at the bottom. Aruni helps him off the last stair and leads him by the hand to the playground, where she seats him on the teeter-totter and gently pushes him up and down while he chants and laughs with delight. All day, I see her at his side, helping him up and down stairs, bringing things to him, wiping his nose, wiping his tears. His self-appointed big sister never leaves his side except when she goes to school, at which time another nine-year-old girl, Jorani, appears in her place. All day, he is never left alone to navigate the busy, bewildering environment that is now his home. I even see two children fighting over who gets to carry him and comfort him when he gets fussy at naptime; Pran, the victor, picks him up and Malis runs on slightly ahead of them, clearing the way.

As protective as the children are at first, as Sovay becomes more comfortable, he is treated increasingly as a member of the family rather than as a guest.

Within a few weeks the boys start to tease him the way they do each other. Munny and Botum both start to poke, trick, and provoke him, then run laughing away when he swings at them. Although at first he is unsure how to interpret this and cries, when this happens, I see Aruni fiercely scolding them; then she shoves one of them away from him. But they also call him over to play with them, and Munny invites him to go eat together. Although staff showed a special solicitousness to him when he cried during his period of adjustment, the only explicit guidance of him I saw from them was an insistence that he greet visitors with a proper *sompiah*. The other children were the principal agents of his socialization into orphanage society.

Children are not just contained by their environment; they actively contribute to their environment, and, crucially, each child is an important part of the environment of the other children. Throughout the day, the children in the COC were surrounded by a dynamic, complex, largely supportive, and always stimulating human environment consisting of relationships with older and younger residents. While the adults are occupied, the children provide each other with care, attention, interaction, and models for how to behave and engage with the world and with other people, all things that have often been found to be lacking in orphanages.

The trajectory of the children's behavior toward Sovay when he first arrived paralleled the trajectory of improvement in his own affect and behavior as well, which I was able to observe because he arrived during my 2011 observation period. Had I not known that he was new, I might have assumed that his concerning demeanor was a result of institutionalization. However, some of the behaviors he came with, combined with his extreme thinness, suggested that he may have experienced harsh circumstances prior to his arrival. This possibility was confirmed by staff, who characterized him as "like a wild animal" when encouraging the other children to be patient with him. The concerning behaviors all diminished markedly after just three weeks, and staff reported that this was typical of children after placement. Many of the children, they told me, had emotional and behavior challenges when they first arrived, but their behavior improved rather than worsened after living there for some time. By 2011, all but one child had been there for at least three years, and most of them four to six years; their affect was certainly not always positive, but they were consistently alert, animated, and appropriate. There were no indications that affect or behavior deteriorated with longer time spent in the orphanage.

Interactions among boys and girls, as well as among children of different ages, were comfortable and respectful, although children spent more time in same-gender, same-age groups than in mixed groups. Romantic or sexual relationships were explicitly forbidden by the center, both among residents as well as with nonresidents. The managing NGO has placed a particular priority on supporting disadvantaged women and girls, and their commitment to promoting opportunities for girls translates into a policy of respect and a spirit of fairness among the children. There was quite a bit of verbal teasing, pestering, and intentional annoying to provoke a response, but I never saw real, sustained fights between boys and girls, or almost no mixed-gender play fighting. On several occasions, nine-year-old Aruni struck and shoved boys who were teasing Sovay, but the boys never struck back or engaged her in any further confrontation.

There were boys' games and girls' games; girls never played shoe pétanque, for example, but preferred games involving jumping and leaping skills. Boys mainly preferred their own games, but they enjoyed showing off the skills that the girls' games called for, and they also enjoyed teasing the older girls who served as judges and coaches.

In the most popular girls' game, participants take turns running toward a line drawn in the dirt and then start leaping as they cross the line, covering as much ground as they can and counting each leap out loud while the other children count along with them. The goal is to see how far they can get with a required number of leaps, while also coming to a complete and sudden stop so that the other children can record their distance. Because it is primarily a girls' game, one of the older girls is the final judge for disputes regarding children's scores, especially if they wiggle or slide to make themselves appear to have gotten farther. There are elaborate rules for turn taking and advancement through levels of difficulty. It requires both strength and balance, and the children really fly when they leap, but most of the boys soon end up disrupting the game by flouting the rules. One morning, for example, a group of seven children, mostly girls but a few boys, are playing and a dispute breaks out about one boy's stride. The judge, fourteen-year-old Chhean, makes him go back. He yells, pouts, but complies. However, another boy teases her as she is trying to restore the game, grabs her arm, and then trails her, mocking her angry striding away from him. The group divides along gender lines, and rather than escalating, each group stalks off in a different direction to do something else. In this way, the protective camaraderie of the girls' and boys' respective groups provides an effective check on conflicts that might otherwise get out of hand, such as another incident in which one boy wrestled with a girl and pulled her shirt over her shoulder, whether inadvertently or intentionally I could not tell. She protested and pushed him away, and while he walked off smirking, she joined the crowd of girls at the leaping game.

Children provided care for each other in explicit ways as well, even the ones who had not been designated housemothers for a group of younger children. Care tasks provided included teaching and tutoring, reading to, carrying, comforting, sharing food, bathing, grooming, supervising, mediating disputes and distracting from distress, as well as running errands and fetching things for other residents.[29] Generally, the older ones (who may themselves be as young as eight or nine) perform care tasks for younger ones, and younger children fetch things or run errands for older ones. For example, I see Reksa, age eleven, bike up and hand Kannitha, age eighteen, a cup of water he has requested. I also see Munny, seven, run to retrieve the rocks that Darani, ten, shoots with his slingshot. Sometimes, this tendency to defer to older children seems unfair; for example, I see older children request that younger children trade oranges so they get the bigger one, and the little ones comply without resistance. However, often it gives younger children the chance to apprentice themselves to those with more advanced skills. For example, fetching Darani's rocks gives Munny the opportunity to stand close and avidly watch him load and shoot the slingshot, so he can learn how. Older residents also provide services that the younger ones cannot reciprocate, such as homework help.

Girls were somewhat more likely to provide care than boys were, but boys were also consistently and actively involved, particularly in teaching music. Staff at COC encouraged children to serve as tutors and caretakers for each other, and explicitly instructed children to "be a good big brother/sister," although generally the children did not need any encouragement but did so spontaneously, even to the point of fighting over who got to carry a smaller child. Children express that they enjoy taking care of younger children and of themselves and are visibly proud of their ability to display this competence.

Just as the children's interactions with each other were largely good-natured but often rough, so were their interactions with the resident animals, which during my main observation period included two adult dogs and a puppy, cats that came and went, and chickens, including a large brood of chicks that appeared one day. All had free run of the compound and were a source of entertainment, physical affection, and fascination for the children. Children picked the dogs up by clutching folds of skin on their back, draped them around their necks, stuffed them in the bike baskets, and dragged them by ropes and rubber bands. The dogs went along without resistance and followed the children wagging their tails when the children left them. They were amazingly pliant and agreeable and seemed to thrive on the attention of so many children, even when it appeared rough and intrusive to me.

The orphanage had a code of conduct for visitors that precluded some of the displays of affection that foreigners often feel orphanage children "need." Visitors were instructed not to hug the children or pick them up, and children signaled their discomfort with this when adult visitors tried. There was no lack of physical affection in their lives though, and children were very comfortable expecting to be picked up by older children. After just one day, Sovay knew to raise his arms to signal he wanted to be picked up by older children, and all the younger children were consistently more physically affectionate with my fourteen-year-old daughter than with me.

The children's interactions were often supportive and nurturing, but that doesn't mean that they were always kind to one another. They fought like siblings (as indeed many of them were), and when they got bored they teased and picked quarrels with one another for entertainment. The younger kids pestered and irritated the older ones, the older ones ignored or rebuffed the younger ones, and they regularly hurt each other's feelings. None of this though seemed very different from my own experiences growing up in a family of five siblings, or very different from the kinds of playground interactions I observed at my daughter's preschool and elementary school in a middle-class, family-oriented community in the Pacific Northwest of the United States. In fact, I was impressed by the higher level of care they showed each other, and the way that older children were more likely to interact with younger children, and more skilled in dealing with them. I was also struck by a low level of complaining and whining, and a high level of rapid compliance with adult directives, usually with enthusiasm and almost never with visible resentment. The large space and amount of free time appeared to provide valuable safety valves for children's behavior as well, especially because simply performing their daily routines required physical movement and exercise. When tensions arose with other children, they were able to take space or join another group. While these strategies for conflict management took precedence over "working it out" and "telling them how you feel" as U.S. children are taught to do, self-regulation and mastery over negative emotions are more highly valued in Cambodia than are individual self-expression and open disagreement.

Local Perceptions of the Orphanage

What goes on inside the orphanage is just one part of the story, although of course a very important one. The meaning of the orphanage experience is a separate matter from the experience itself, and here too I was caught off guard by what I discovered. Early on in my visits, when I was still reluctant to ask the children personal questions, I was surprised by a question from sixteen-year-old Narith. "How do you feel," he asked, "seeing so many children living in an orphanage?" I struggled to come up with a tactful but truthful answer expressing the dissonance between my own assumptions about orphanages and what I was seeing at the COC. While I hedged, he volunteered, "I felt very happy to come live here." I asked him why, and he answered, "Because I would be able to study." Narith's younger cousin also lives at the orphanage, and Narith reported he was happy about that for the same reason—the educational success he had attained at the orphanage would have otherwise been beyond his grasp after his father deserted his mother and him. Children's own perceptions of living in an orphanage were surprisingly positive, as were the perceptions of the surrounding community.

A very large potential challenge for children growing up in orphanages is inherent not to their experience within the orphanage itself but rather to

external judgments and orphanage interactions with the wider community, especially the potential for stigma. Stigma is especially important to consider in Cambodia because of the importance of social networks and family connections, and
the fact that many of the children in orphanages may come from families with
stigmatized behaviors or circumstances. However, the COC possessed many structural features and practices, some intentional and some inadvertent, that further
reduced stigma for the children that lived there. They included desirable facilities (e.g., playground, dance classes, transportation), academic success, good care,
desirable skills (e.g., music, English), and a sound moral education enhanced by
their connection with a well-regarded Buddhist pagoda. The COC shared many of
these assets with children from the neighborhood and took measures to be a good
neighbor by letting village people take shortcuts across their property, allowing
neighbors' chickens to forage on the premises, and sharing water with neighbors
who had a problem with their own well. My very first visit to the COC coincided
with a construction project, and I was impressed by the number of community
members who pitched in to help.

Materially, the orphanage children were neither the worst off nor the best
off of their peers in the community, and this helped them to fit in without stigma
as well. The village has a wide range of wealth levels, from desperately poor to
quite well-off, and the orphanage children are comfortably in the middle. They
each have a backpack for schoolbooks, so they don't have to carry their school
supplies in plastic bags as do the poorest of the village children. But their back-
packs are well-worn rather than shiny and new like those of the really well-off
village children. Similarly, they all have school uniforms that are clean, mended,
and matching, but many are hand-me-downs, distinguishing them from the very
poorest children who have only partial or mismatched, torn, or dirty uniforms,
and distinguishing them from the wealthiest children, whose uniforms are new
and often fashionably cut. In part, this positioning midway between an appearance of wealth and an appearance of poverty is deliberately cultivated; visitors
regularly donate new and attractive school supplies, but these are carefully hus-
banded, and articles are replaced only when they really need to be. Although
there are reports of orphanages that keep children shabby in order to trigger
sympathy and donations from foreign visitors, visitors to the COC are uniformly
struck by the children's good condition, and the attractiveness of the children
is better motivation for donations than pity would be. Donors comment "keep
up the good work" rather than expressing any concerns about neediness or
desperation.[30]

Established practices of child circulation also minimize stigma, as discussed
in chapter 2, by affording interpretations of out-of-family residence that are not
inherently negative. When orphanage staff, teachers, and neighbors do not view
the children in their charge as castoffs or as tragic products of inherently unfit
parents, they are probably more likely to treat the children as beings worthy of

respect and care, further reducing potential negative consequences. As I got to know the staff better, the details of their private lives that emerged illuminated this point. Director Sann informed me that because he and his wife both work, they sent their oldest daughter to another province to live with her grandmother. They see her once or twice a year. When I discussed this with another staff member, she shrugged and said, "It is very difficult and expensive to raise a child." To her, there was nothing worrisome or irresponsible about this, and she was clear that I should not judge him for it or assume the outcome would be negative.

It was difficult for me to learn all the children's names and faces because they seemed to keep changing. As I got better at matching the names and the faces, I realized that they really did keep changing because the COC is a surprisingly popular destination for children who are not regular residents. For example, a boy I had never seen before, whom I watched carefully for signs of adjustment assuming he was new, turned out to be the guard's son who accompanied his father and played while his father worked. Neighbor children came to play, friends and relatives of staff dropped their children off for babysitting, village youth thronged to the dance classes, and entire families took shortcuts through the compound or stopped to beg for food, which was always given. It became clear that the orphanage was regarded not necessarily with suspicion or pity, but rather as a safe and desirable place for children to be, permanently or just temporarily. Although children were not supposed to leave the premises without permission, in fact they came and went freely, with the exception that the younger ones were warned whenever they stepped onto the road because of the traffic. There was never any sense that children were being "held" there, and in fact the COC rules state that children may be expelled for misbehavior. Residence is seen as a privilege rather than a penalty, although some teenagers resisted the program's structure.

The physical openness observed in the COC contrasts with the very prominent concerns about security that are more typical of the foreign-run orphanages, many of which have gates, guards, and security systems including sign-ins and name tags for visitors, and strict rules preventing the children from exiting the premises on their own. This concern about security may inadvertently isolate children by restricting their ability to connect with the neighboring community.

Placement in the care of the COC is not an "either/or" arrangement. The COC has policies for maintaining ties among children and their families, whether living parents or extended kin, further reinforcing the perception that the COC is a place to benefit children rather than discard them. Families phoned or visited, and many children returned to their communities for holidays.[31] On Sunday mornings, it was not unusual for the cook or another adult with a phone to call a child over; they would invariably run over beaming, and talk for a good half hour or so, walking around and smiling into the phone. According to staff reports, when communication is not consistent between children and their families it is most often the families rather than the children that fail to maintain contact, something I heard from other orphanages as well. Neither staff nor residents appeared to be uncomfortable with what to Westerners is the anomaly of children living in an orphanage but being free to visit their families for holidays.

Efforts to improve the lives of orphans come with their own set of challenges, especially if the facilities are considered too desirable or attractive. Envy, rather than stigma, more often came up in conversations with Cambodians about orphanages, and some of the extremely well-resourced orphanages are discussed by locals in terms of bitter resentment, especially if they do nothing to share services or resources with the neighboring community. As at the COC, staff at some other orphanages explained that they provide services to the local community in order to avoid feelings of envy (English lessons and access to an onsite clinic are two examples), but most orphanages restrict neighborhood children from entering the premises. Privately, several told me of the distress they felt when families tried to gain admission for their children but were denied entrance by government guidelines and officials.

One of the best resourced, and most securely gated, foreign-run orphanages in Siem Reap drew particular hostility because its associated school served an elite group of children drawn from all over town, rather than the very vulnerable and underserved children from the neighborhood in which it was located. As we drove by in a tuk-tuk one day, a friend pointed and said, "You need to come back here when the cars pull up in the driveway to pick up the children. You'll see Mercedes, Explorers . . . but you won't see any children from the neighborhood that is right behind the school."[32] Anecdotally, my driver was insistent that he wanted his son, a cherished only child with two doting parents and two resident grandparents, to benefit from all the resources provided the children in the orphanage. "I want my son to go to the orphan school," he told me. The heavy foreign presence, although widely criticized, is also seen by many Cambodians as one of the most enviable aspects of orphanages, especially because of the educational resources provided.

Visitors, Volunteers, and Foreign Donations

During a two-month period, I overlapped with ten foreign volunteers and a volunteer medical team. Several other groups of donors and/or volunteers reportedly came at times when I wasn't there, but I didn't see them firsthand. As discussed in chapter 3, this steady stream of volunteers coming and going is usual rather than exceptional for the COC as well as for other orphanages in town, most of which rely heavily on foreign donations. Volunteers came to the COC for as short as a few hours, to as long as several months, sometimes for several years running, and the children had, in addition to stronger English proficiency than their peers at the local schools, an array of seemingly random but interesting and impressive skills, from origami to slacklining, all taught by volunteers.[33] While the objective value of some of these skills might be questioned, it was clear that the children derived pleasure and confidence from their mastery and enjoyed showing them off to other visitors. However, as discussed in chapter 3, the reliance of orphanages on foreign donors and volunteers comes with its own challenges and has sparked concern and criticism. The COC used a sponsorship model of donor support, both for individual residents as well as for specific houses and other buildings, but the projects that are appealing to donors are not always those prioritized by the Cambodian staff. For example, toilets, especially Western-style toilets, are always a high priority for foreigners, as are gender-segregated bathing rooms with lockable doors. The COC had two complete donor-provided bathroom buildings, with more than enough dedicated bathing rooms, but the children and staff did not enjoy bathing inside, and so the housemothers themselves built an outside bathing area, screened with palm leaves, for open-air bathing that was extremely popular even before it was finished. This was considerably less expensive than the concrete bathroom blocks provided by donors. Although donations could have been better spent elsewhere, foreign visitors view traditional bathing arrangement as "primitive" and consciously or unconsciously use it as an indicator of how "bleak" children's lives in an orphanage can be.[34]

Volunteers do not always have the skills or the desire to volunteer in ways that the orphanage staff prioritize. For example, in 2010 COC management had posted notices seeking volunteer teachers of photography, art, and singing for the children, but had not so far met with success, so most volunteers provided the children with unstructured English practice as they played or did activities together. As criticisms of orphanage volunteering gathered momentum, restrictions on volunteers at the COC were increasingly tightened, and the website stopped featuring volunteer opportunities there.

Conclusion

My observations show that daily life in the COC did not conform to the popular Western stereotype of orphanage care, and the resident children did not conform to the popular Western stereotype of institutionalized children.[35] They were well fed, well educated and well taken care of, and their material conditions surpassed those of many of the children in the surrounding rural areas. One of the reasons that this was possible is certainly because of the resources provided by foreign visitors. Another is because orphanages in Cambodia are distinctively Cambodian institutions, conceived of and structured differently from orphanages in other social settings. In the next chapter, I complement these insights gained through observation and see how well my observations lined up with the children's own memories of their lived experience, by presenting the results of follow-up interviews with former residents in fall 2019, right after the COC closed forever.

6

The Orphanage Remembered

Milestones and Experiences

On September 28, 2019, the Children's Opportunity Center (COC) closed its gates forever. On Facebook, the staff extended their "sincere thanks to all donors and friends" who helped the orphanage provide "a happy, secure, warm smiling life with good care and education through loving-kindness and compassionate care." They reassured followers that all of the children who were still living there had been either reintegrated with family or offered a place in other residential programs. For five girls, this was a residence for high-school-age girls in Siem Reap that provided them with room, board, and academic support. Two boys became temple boys in a Buddhist pagoda. Four were reintegrated with family members, receiving continued health and educational support from the NGO.

The closing was the final step in a decade-long process to reduce reliance on orphanages, as discussed in chapter 3. Since 2010, the center had received increasingly intense pressure to stop accepting new residents and to reintegrate as many as possible with relatives. The number of children living in the COC had peaked at forty-three in early 2011 and begun its decline when nine residents left and only three were admitted. Departures continued to outnumber admissions every year thereafter. By late 2016 there were only twenty-two children in residence, and in 2017 there were nineteen. By the end of September 2019, when the center finally closed forever, there were only eleven children left.

I traveled to Siem Reap in October and November 2019, with the goal of interviewing former residents and staff; my methods are described in greater detail in chapter 4. The closing of the center provided an opportunity for former residents to consider the whole of their experience there, without being put in the awkward position of criticizing the organization and staff while they still depended on them. Living in an orphanage had been a defining experience for all of them, and many were eager to explore their feelings about the center and the implications of their time there. Most thanked me for the opportunity to reflect on their experiences and give their views.

As shown in table 1 in chapter 4, all the participants are employed, in school, or both. Given the really challenging circumstances all of them faced prior to going to live in the COC, they are faring well according to these objective indicators. However, the bare listing of outcomes cannot begin to convey the richness and intricacy of the former residents' lives. They have come of age in an extraordinary period of Cambodia's history, the most decades of independence and peace since the mid-nineteenth century, spanning the utter devastation of Cambodia of the 1990s to the relative stability and opportunity of the 2010s. In the remainder of this chapter, I share what former COC residents themselves say about their lives there, organized around the five milestones and experiences, shown in table 2, that emerged as important to the participants. In chapter 7 I discuss five themes that emerged as important in participants' reflections on those experiences.

But first, I'll begin with the stories of two of the former residents, Charaya and Bopha, to show how a life trajectory takes shape when growing up in an orphanage.

Charaya's Story

A neighborhood friend talked Charaya into sniffing glue when he was eight, and he describes his early childhood as "really, really destructive. . . . Actually," he recounts, "I was growing up in a family where violation had been conducted throughout my childhood, so I experienced so much difficulty and so much stress and so much depression before I got into COC."

He remembers the day he went to live in the orphanage as the most exciting day of his life. It was just after he turned nine. "So the first day I got the opportunity to go to COC . . . I got really excited because at that time I didn't have any new clothes. So we had donors who bought us new clothes, new toothbrush. I never brushed my teeth when I was living with my family so it was exciting! I was even wondering what type of thing it is. My clothes, my toothbrush, I got my bag, I got everything that I never dreamed of getting in my childhood so I was really excited!"

Did he cry? "No, not at all actually. Actually, the relationship between me and my parents had not been very, very good ever since I was born because I didn't get the comfort, I didn't get the intimacy from them. So even though I moved away from them I didn't have any feeling of missing them at all. . . . I think the best thing was . . . that I got enough food to eat. And I got enough clothes to wear, and I got a kind of education that I supposed to get as a child."

Although he was critical of the way COC was managed during his teenage years, he remains nostalgic for his early days at COC. "Life at that time was

TABLE 2

Experiences and Milestones

Coming to the orphanage

We were so afraid to stay there by ourselves. It took us some time until we made some friends there so we could feel at home (Bopha, F, age 4 at arrival, 16 at interview)

My best memory was when I moved to live in COC. At the beginning I received a very warm welcome. (Chaya, F, age 8 at arrival, 16 at interview)

When I went to COC the first time, I was so crying. One week. I missed my home, yeah, I missed my hometown, I missed my mom, I missed my friends. (Narith, M, age 13 at arrival, 25 at interview)

Material care: Physical needs were well met

I felt so warm when living there like living at home too. At COC Mom always took care of me when I was sick and she always prepared me rice and food and stay near me either day or night. (Arunny, F, age 8 at arrival, 17 at interview)

Sometimes it was delicious and sometimes it was not. But if you ask that was it enough? For me, I think that it was always enough. (Kolab, F, age 8 at arrival, 22 at interview)

I know that some people outside of the center always feel jealous of us. They think we have a better place to stay, better food to eat, and better education. (Kosal, M, age 6 at arrival, 19 at interview)

Relationships with the other children: They matter—a lot

When we have problems, we like sharing with one another. (Tevy, F, age 8 at arrival, 22 at interview)

Back home, I never felt close with my siblings, but I felt closeness when I moved to COC. And I always missed everyone at COC when I went somewhere, like missing my young brothers or sisters, but I never missed anyone at home. (Arunny, F, age 8 at arrival, 17 at interview)

We were like real siblings. (Bopha, F, age 4 at arrival, 16 at interview)

Visitors and volunteers: Appreciated and enjoyed

I felt so warm and close to them. I love that feeling. . . . I love all visitors. When they went there, I was so happy. (Nary, F, age 8 at arrival, 22 at interview)

Without volunteers, we wouldn't be able to see the world in a different way like we have. (Charaya, M, age 8 at arrival, 22 at interview)

But some visitors showed bad examples for the children. For example: some visitors was wearing sexy clothes and some came with their partners and kissed each other in front of the children. (Achariya, F, age 11 at arrival, 17 at interview)

(continued)

Table 2. Experiences and Milestones (continued)

Leaving the orphanage

Happy. Because I leave from COC, I go to the next step. . . . It's not like regret for COC . . . but sometimes we miss the many good time we have in COC. (Rathana, M, age 14 at arrival, 28 at interview)

I felt great actually! (Charaya, M, age 8 at arrival, 22 at interview)

When I left, I missed all the good things there, those children were all my friends. We were playing together. (Nary, F, age 8 at arrival, 22 at interview)

amazing," he recounts, unable to contain a chuckle. "We went anywhere around the country. You know we went to perform the music . . . went to Sihanoukville, we went everywhere around the country, and [a donor] pay for everything. It's not about him paying for us to go to other places, but the comfort, the kind heart, the kind mind, that he given us that show us the, the feeling, that . . . comfort."

I remember Charaya as a poised and friendly fourteen-year-old who was clearly supersmart and who confidently engaged me and other visitors in conversations about the wider world while sharing insightfully about Cambodia. I have a photo of him then, lying in a hammock underneath one of the houses, reading the newspaper out loud to the younger children, who are crowded around him, eager to hear news of conflict that had erupted with Thailand that week. His English was already quite good, and even more striking was his dedication to self-improvement. He daringly tried out new vocabulary on us and unhesitatingly asked for clarification when he didn't understand something. After he finished ninth grade, he started high school in a rural community, but concluded, "I saw no opportunity being there and especially there is no qualified teachers that I feel I can rely on," so he moved to Siem Reap city, where he tried a number of living arrangements, including his mother's house until she abruptly moved to another province, and eventually he graduated from high school while living in a pagoda. He found a variety of jobs, including security guard and teacher; by then, his English skills were so refined that the COC hired him back as an English teacher for the remaining children.

He enrolled at one of the best private universities in Siem Reap, but the combination of working to make ends meet and being torn between too many different future career possibilities, led him to suspend his studies and work full-time. "At that time I had many, many plans, . . . too many plans," he explains. "At that time I wanted to be, about 30 percent of my mind wanting to be in politics. . . . And about 30 percent of me wanted to be successful in academic studies and about the other 30 percent I wanna be a businessman. So things just kinda get messed up so, I ended up suspending my university studies for a while."

Charaya is currently working as a professional interpreter and as an office manager for a small business. He continues to study in the evenings, adding Thai, Chinese, and video editing skills to his already highly proficient English. And, like many Cambodians, he has other ventures on the side. He and his partner are developing an online learning platform featuring engaging, interactive Chinese lessons for Khmer speakers. Charaya sees his work not just as a key to a successful livelihood and fulfilling family life but also as a way to provide other Cambodians with more opportunity and to become a change maker himself through the avenues for social engagement that being an interpreter opens up. "Not a politician," he hastens to add, "but just somebody who can be involved in helping processing the politics of Cambodia," somebody who can translate Cambodian politics into English for speakers of other languages to better understand the situation. "So that is my long-term goal," he says proudly, but he has other big plans—he and his partner plan to be married in two or three years, after she has finished her master's degree.

Charaya is very matter-of-fact about where he would be right now if it weren't for COC. "I would be in prison by now," he says without hesitation. That is where the friend who introduced him to glue sniffing a dozen years ago has ended up. However, Charaya is also one of COC's most vocal critics. He identifies management practices that he believes caused a decline in effectiveness of the programming, especially for teenagers, who he says lacked the mentoring and guidance that could have prevented misbehavior and, especially, kept them in school. "Children just kind of ignore the regulations in the COC. . . . Things just get worse from year to year." He doesn't excuse himself, although looking back he wishes that the center had been more effective at motivating him, saying, "At that time I had very, very, very little knowledge of things and also at that time I was just kind of lazy. And sometime when there is no regulation you get used to the situation. So people just kind of get lazier, and you decide to follow them and get lazier too."

He describes various teenaged residents' escapades involving truancy, fighting, and forbidden relationships and condemns the way staff allowed some teenaged residents to foreclose their futures through lack of attention to their studies, which became more challenging even as other things became more distracting. He is especially reproachful for how several children were returned to their home communities during the first big push toward family reunification around 2011–12, rather than being counseled about other options, including the long-term benefits of further schooling, although he admits that at that time he himself also advised residents to leave and return to their families. Speaking of one he explains, "So if she had been given the opportunity to have some consultancy, or you know some things she would end up to be in [another program] and get the good education. At that time she was having a little bit of misbehavior among her friends, and [the staff] kind of saw that . . . negativity, so rather than finding ways, the best way to help her, so sending her to her parents . . . would be the . . . ways . . . so I think she regretted after that when she ended up to be a worker."

Charaya struggles with his own high expectations and how he would define success. He attributes great potential to the COC to not just care for residents and help them overcome previous abuse and neglect, but help them enter Cambodia's growing middle class. "Kids that come to COC, they all, you know they're all negatively affected kids. If you're talking about the good thing about COC, it's that it's very good to help the kids to become better. . . . But I just, I just didn't get satisfied. I didn't get complacent. . . . I want them just to be the best as they can." And for him, that means not just providing good-quality daily care and the possibility of attending school, but effective motivation and mentoring so that the residents would *want* to stay in school and would even exceed in school. "So COC, COC has been focusing on providing kids support, not to be following on the bad path, rather than seeing the bright future that they should." He reflects, then wonders out loud, "Probably I have too high expectation of COC."

Bopha's Story

Bopha was four years old when she went to live in COC. Although she begins our interview by saying "I don't remember. I stayed there since I was a child so I cannot remember," as she gets warmed up she starts to describe how her mother fled an abusive husband with her two young children and lived on the street with them, before finding a temporary shelter with an organization helping single mothers, widows, and survivors of domestic violence. Through that organization her mother met COC staff and left Bopha and her younger brother there for what she said would be three months so she could go to the city and find work. Instead, Bopha lived in the orphanage until age fifteen, when she transferred to a boarding school program in Siem Reap city, where she is currently starting her senior year of high school.

"I remember my first day at COC. There were a lot of people waiting and they welcomed me and brought me to play and buy something to eat. There was some stuff that kids loved to do. After that, we went to study English. However, I was just a child back then so I didn't study much." That first day, "I am not quite sure if I cried or not," she recounts, because her mom told her "to wait her for only three months there." But her mother did not return and so "I cried later, after I knew that my mum left me there because she promised to let me stay only three months. . . . Later we knew she lied and we started to feel scared. My brother and I were standing and holding hands. We were so afraid to stay there by ourselves. It took us some time until we made some friends there so we could feel at home."

My first memory of Bopha is as a shy but alert and smiling eight-year-old who looked up when I arrived on my first day there but remained sitting on the ground among a small cluster of children. They were entirely focused on a game that involved sliding a twig into a pile of dirt, and carefully pulling it out to see how much dirt they could keep balanced on top of it. It was the kind of absorbing, seemingly simple but actually quite challenging game that they always seemed to be spontaneously creating for themselves, and Bopha was often one of the central players in the groups.

She describes an environment that was rich in caring relationships. "We were like real siblings," she says of the other children. "Many students loved me, especially the younger ones." She describes the many ways the children provided care for each other. "Some older kids were responsible for looking after the younger ones. . . . Since there were many people, older ones need to help our mother's [housemother's] work by looking after the younger ones including putting them to sleep, bathing them, and brushing their teeth." She is aware of the amount of work that went into caring for so many residents. "Some mothers looked after children but some worked in the kitchen. Since we had more children and fewer staff, our older students needed to look after the younger ones." Mealtimes were singled out as memorable times that cemented the family feeling. "When the meal was ready, we went to have it all together. . . . Foods were delicious. Our mother knew how to prepare food that we all loved."

Bopha's recollections of routines and relationships are highly granular, illustrated by the kinds of details that stand out most vividly to young children, complemented with commentary from her current perspective as a mature sixteen-year-old. She recounts serving portions ("Foods were often distributed fairly and equally. . . . Normally each person got two bananas"), study time ("After school, we needed to study. . . . I was the top one in my class and I was also a class master"), excursions to the pagoda for dharma class ("We sat together and learned how to recite and chant dharma, the young ones siting in the front with the older ones at the back. We learned how to recite Buddhist scripts from the very basic ones. When I was young, I didn't remember much"), morning exercise ("We also needed to get up early in the morning around 4:30 A.M. to do exercise. Our mother took us for a run. We were together in group. We did that every morning until now except for the rainy days when we are not allowed to do that. For the older ones, they could play in the rain but our mother was stricter with the younger ones so she wouldn't let us play in the rain because of catching cold. Older ones knew how to look after themselves"), and a special day when her housemother made chocolate milk and let them watch a love story on TV ("Normally we weren't allowed to watch the love story").

Bopha takes stock of her life thoughtfully and chooses her words carefully. "To me, I lived there for a long time. I think I feel that my life there was like my real home. . . . Without COC, my life would be a lonely one. I didn't have anyone to rely on. I might go astray along the street. If we didn't go to school, we might end up doing something. We wouldn't be able to read and write. We were so young back then, the three of us might pick up trash on the street or face some dangers because we couldn't help ourselves."

Bopha is a good student, and everyone expects her to pass the graduation exam. She hopes to become a police officer; after she and my research assistant have an earnest conversation about good and bad police officers, she agrees that she will become one of the good ones and "bring justice for everyone."

As one of the very first children to join the COC, and as one who spent her entire childhood there, Bopha's life story is integrally wound up with the COC's history, and its closure hits home deeply. "I feel sad to hear that. . . . I would like the center to continue to accommodate more children who struggle financially with school, and those whose parents are desperate or pass away. . . . I really want it to be continued." She is aware that its closure leaves a gap for families who are still in distress, explaining, "There are some people trying to apply too but they won't accept," and she recognizes the dilemma that it brings to her own family. Her mother wanted to bring her brother to live in Phnom Penh, but Bopha was concerned, explaining, "After COC was closed down, my mother wanted to take my little brother to stay with her but I convinced her to let him stay with father monk. He agreed to let him stay with the monk and I also asked him to see if he wanted to stay there in the pagoda. He agreed with me. . . . My brother stayed with me since he was a baby."

Charaya's and Bopha's stories were chosen not just because they make appealing narratives with apparently happy endings. Together they illustrate the main themes that run through all the stories, and although Charaya's and Bopha's stories introduce a range of experiences and opinions, they are not outliers. Are they typical? Perhaps the most striking theme to emerge from the interviews is that there is no single typical story, no one typical outcome, and no one typical assessment of their childhood in the orphanage. For that reason, in the remaining sections of this chapter I describe in more detail what the interviews revealed about five important events and experiences in the lives of the COC residents, illustrated with passages in the participants' own words. The events and experiences to be covered are coming to the orphanage, material care, relationships with the other children, visitors and volunteers, and leaving the orphanage.

Coming to the Orphanage

Nearly everyone cried when they first came to stay at the orphanage, although many laughed about it years later when they told me their arrival stories. Most of the participants were pleased to have an opportunity to recount their stories, and while the distress they described was wrenching to hear, all also described adapting and coming to appreciate their life in the orphanage, although not necessarily to enjoy every aspect of it. As Sothy and Mach summarize here, fear was the dominant emotion causing distress when they first came to live at the orphanage. Sothy came to COC because of her father's new wife's antagonism toward her, forcing her to quit school and live a hand-to-mouth existence with her aunt: "I was eleven. I felt afraid of everyone. I was crying when I arrived and I wanted to return home. After a few days I started to adapt with the change." Her friend Mach, who joined at age ten because of a tragedy resulting in loss of her parents, agreed that it was frightening to stay there: "For me, I was afraid when I arrived, but after the warm welcome and greeting by all COC staff and children there, I started to feel comfortable."

Sometimes children's previous knowledge or assumptions heightened the fear. Arunny, her friend Achariya, and the interviewer all had a good laugh about her apprehensions about human trafficking: "First, I was scared to stay in COC because I thought of human trafficking. Then [staff member] told me that it is nearby Angkor Wat then I agreed to come because I wanted to see Angkor Wat. When I arrived COC I asked my father [head monk] that—where is Angkor Wat? Why couldn't I see it? He replied 'Angkor is not here but we can go to visit any day.' When I first arrived here I felt very homesick and cried."

Sometimes the children's fear was on behalf of family members left behind, which compounded the feeling of homesickness. Achariya, for instance, whose father's violence and alcohol abuse had driven her mother to seek a safer place for her children to live, worried about leaving her mother to face his violence alone. She told a touching story of how her extended family pulled together to enable Achariya to stay in the orphanage to pursue her education: "I was still thinking about my mother because my two sisters already left her and only me was the oldest in the family. So that I should help my mother in case my father get drunk and provoke my mother I could help her. Then my older sister told me that no worries, our grandmother would be able to take care of our mom. So I could come to study here and my grandmother stayed with my mom."

While one of the criticisms of Cambodian orphanages is that children are often placed under fraudulent pretexts, the only cases of false expectations that came out in the interviews originated from the children's families, not from orphanage staff. Ary, seven at the time, interviewed along with her friend Botum, describes how her mother tried to protect her feelings by exaggerating how attractive the place was:

> First time, my mother lied to me that the place you were going was full of gold. [She and Botum are cracking up.] Because she told me that I would have nice clothes, so I wanted to go. I remember the first day, when I arrived I didn't think about what she told me. I just went to play with other kids. . . . My mom left after one night. I started to cry and then I felt

better and went to play again. Then, I felt normal like any other kids. I do miss my home sometimes but I never cried since then.

Similarly, Mach's grandmother told her there was a swimming pool at the COC, although there wasn't one. Interestingly, such embellishments did not seem to cause resentment for the children, as she relates here: "I was so hesitated and I told my grandmother that I didn't want to live there, but she boasted about COC that there was a swimming pool and a lot of things that could make me happy, so I decided to live there if there were things as what she said. But when I arrived I didn't see anything! But I didn't feel angry with my grandmother because even if I stayed at home I was not able to receive education too."

Participants gave various reasons for why they were able to overcome their fear and homesickness and to adjust to life in the center. Prak, who was eleven, explains that it took him a couple of months to feel adjusted, and that it was largely an act of conscious will on his part:

PRAK: The first day is very, like, sad. . . . It's sad because on that time I just was a kid, so I just miss my parents, especially mom, and then was just crying. And after a few weeks it still was sad but a little bit better, and then I just felt fine.

INTERVIEWER: Do you remember what helped you feel comfortable? When you decided it was okay to be at COC, what did you like about it?

PRAK: Actually . . . because it had not changed. . . . Because you cannot change the situation, you change your feelings. And then, it's okay. And then I said "Okay, this is the best place that I can improve or develop my knowledge and myself."

Mixed feelings pervaded many of the children's arrival stories. The change wasn't only the move from family to orphanage but an entire constellation of changes in physical and human environment. Many of the children came from rural areas that were quite isolated at that time. For example, Narith was ten when he arrived, and he recalls feeling intrigued by the COC environment: "That day I was so surprised. Because actually before that day I lived in the country-side, didn't see people too much. When I went to COC, I saw a lot of children and I had a lot of friends. I feel like, so confident. . . . Yeah, it felt so confident and comfortable for a child. Because actually you know that when we are a child we like to play. When we see a lot of kids doing things, having fun, it's like, so comforting."

Despite Narith's positive first impressions, when the reality of staying there apart from his family sank in, he cried profusely: "You know when I went to COC the first time, I was so crying. One week. I missed my home, yeah, I missed my hometown, I missed my mom, I missed my friends. Yeah." His own experience of anguish helped him empathize with the other children he later observed crying: "Especially some people, when they go to COC the first time, they were so crying. They missed their family and then you have some kids, they want to go back home also. . . . Their feeling of being away from their family for the first time is so, so lonely."

Not everyone cried. Charaya, as summarized at the beginning of this chapter, did not cry but instead remembered feelings of relief and excitement. Other participants remember the efforts staff and other residents made to welcome them as outweighing the fear and homesickness so that their arrival at COC was recalled as positive, especially in combination with their later positive experiences. Chaya, who arrived at age eight, answered the question about her best memory from COC by saying, "My best memory was when I moved to live in COC. At the beginning I received a very warm welcome from Mom and Dad.[1] She taught me and Dad always called us to ask about the lessons and taught us to read A, B, C. And also I learned to pray too so I think that I am lucky."

Although most participants indicated that they understood the reasons why they were placed in the orphanage, as explained in chapter 4, we intentionally did not pursue that topic after seeing the distress it could cause. Some details emerged anyway though. We heard stories of violence, a neighborhood plagued by drug abuse, illness and deaths of parents, abandonment, and extreme hunger, and for some children, like Charaya, escaping these traumas outweighed the homesickness and fear. Similarly, Rathana recounts how arriving at COC relieved fear rather than caused it because although he had been working, he not been receiving food regularly before he went there:

INTERVIEWER: So, so a question about COC, do you remember the first day that you went to live at COC?

RATHANA: Yeah. I remember. I won't forget! For me, very excited. Because when I lived with my family I'm very scared about not having rice to eat, not having food. . . . I'm very scared because I have many experiences with my family no rice, and then no rice. . . . I went to work for the neighbor and then got food from him. So this is my problem. And then when I come in the first day into COC I'm very happy. Yeah, I cannot say how that feels because this is like, like God helped me, because you have so much food. Yeah, so much food because Mom, she says at COC 'Oh, you can eat it all.' All the food that I can eat.[2]

For some children, the move to the orphanage was wholly supported by their families, and for others it was complicated by disagreement on the part of family members or neighbors. Arunny recalls resistance from her grandmother and her aunt, who wanted her to care for her younger brother and look after the house after her parents' deaths. Although all three children were offered places in the COC, only Arunny and her brother were permitted to go because the family did not want to lose the labor of all three:

Before my grandmother wanted me to stay with her too and she said that if I went there I could also look after my younger brother. . . . Before we didn't want our younger brother to stay at the hometown because when I called my older sister, she said that if he stays there, we might ask him to discontinue studying and then back to [work in the] fields. And then I said if they asked my brother to go there for work, I wouldn't allow it. I'd better let him to stay here. . . . At first my father [head monk] also wanted my sister to stay in COC with me but later my aunt didn't allow it, because she wanted my sister to look after the house. And my grandmother didn't allow my sister to stay in COC too, because my younger brother and I already moved to COC.

Rotha's parents split up when she was a week old, and although both had remarried, neither was willing to let her live with their new families. She was living at her grandparents' home, but it was too far from any schools at that time for her to continue attending. By age eleven, "I had almost quit my school," she recounts, when she was invited to join the COC. Despite all the challenges she faced, her family was still criticized by the neighbors when her grandmother gave approval:

People always say my family should be afford to raise me since they [grandparents] have only one child. . . . So, they wonder why my family can't raise me like that and why I need to be sent to an orphanage like that. My grandmother told the villagers that she was poor and unable to raise me. Thus, placing me at COC was not welcomed by the villagers. However, after they knew how well I lived my life at COC, and how I was able to continue my education, they said sorry to me and they said they were afraid that I was cheated by COC or something like that. There were many organizations in the past cheating villagers.

Rotha's description of how comfortably she lived at the COC, in contrast to her fellow villagers' worries that she would be exploited or mistreated, was a common theme throughout the interviews. All participants agreed that their physical needs had been well met by the COC.

Material Care: Physical Needs Were Well Met

Participants all reported that they were sheltered and clothed appropriately and comfortably (although several recalled how itchy and uncomfortable it was to wear underwear for the first time when they arrived there). They agreed that they received regular health and dental care and that the physical environment was peaceful and suitable for exercise and relaxation, although somewhat boring for some of them at times. While the food may not have been always exciting—when

I asked Narith what he remembered about the food he groaned and then laughed, "I remember the morning glory soup"—meals were balanced, and much of the food was fresh since it came from the center's own garden.[3]

Despite the pivotal nature of children's physical well-being in the broader debate about orphanage care, the satisfactory material conditions at the COC barely seemed worth mentioning for most of the former residents. Even those who were most critical took for granted that their physical care had been good and were blasé about how it had been maintained even during the worst budget crisis. Rather than focusing on their physical care, they were more eager to talk about the relationships they forged and maintained there, especially with the other residents.

Relationships with the Other Children: They Matter—a Lot

In an orphanage, other children are a significant part of each other's environment, and relationships with other residents featured prominently in the interviews, even though we actually didn't ask any questions about that topic. Western paradigms of child development often emphasize the importance of the adult-child dyad at the expense of child-child relationships, but in Cambodia families expect older children to take care of younger children, and this expectation seamlessly carries over to institutional settings. In the COC, peer relationships were valued for caretaking, for fun, and for academic support as well as learning to self-regulate and manage conflict. The camaraderie of living with so many children, especially ones who came from similar backgrounds, was recalled with nostalgia by many former residents. As Daevy explained,

> I lived with many other kids. They were all my friends. At first, it was hard for me to adapt to the life there. I wanted to leave that place. However, there were people encouraging to stay because the better opportunities there so when I continued to stay, I knew that what they said was right. I had a chance to go to school, to have more clothes, and personal toiletries including toothpaste for me to use. I had what I needed as well as many friends I have known there. After we left the center, we still talk and treat each other as friends. No one looks down on others.

Children recalled giving and receiving a wide range of care—bathing and feeding, homework help, and carrying little ones around and comforting them when they were upset, for example. This ability to be integrated into a warm, reciprocal caring network of other children is one of the things that Bopha remembers most fondly:

> I loved being there. . . . Some older kids were responsible for looking after the younger ones. . . . Since there were many people, older ones need to

help our mother's work by looking after the younger ones including putting them to sleep, bathing them, and brushing their teeth, and other related hygiene and health tasks.... Some older kids taught me some basic math including arithmetic.... Back then, we were small so we didn't know how to take our own bath.... We didn't know how to wash ourselves so the older ones bathed us. After arriving from school, they brought us to take a bath and then get ready for lunch.

The care provided by other residents prevented the structural neglect that has been reported in some of the worst Eastern European orphanages. Bopha was four when she arrived, and she recalled how children younger than her were not placed in cribs and left unattended. "So you were young?" prompted the interviewer, and she responded, "Yes, very small. But Malis was even smaller. She was carried and looked after like a baby by the older ones at COC back then."

For children with challenging backgrounds, COC provided role models for age-appropriate behavior, especially with respect to successful study habits, since most of the children's families had little experience with the norms and expectations of the formal school system. When asked about what she would tell her future child about her life in the COC, Achariya focused on the value of examples set by other residents, saying, "I would advise my child to study hard and follow someone who is clever."

Slightly older peer models can be equally if not more effective as adults in teaching and modeling new skills, and at the COC older residents provided scaffolding for the younger ones' increasing proficiency, especially in the area of life skills.[4] All the residents had regularly assigned chores according to their age and ability, and older ones could help the younger ones master increasing levels of challenge:

INTERVIEWER: What about small kids, do they have to work, too?

ARY: Yes. They also do their jobs based on their age. They work under the supervision of the bigger ones.

INTERVIEWER: Did you also wash your own clothes?

BOTUM: When I was little, my older sister did that for me. Sometimes my housemother was the one who did that.

INTERVIEWER: So how old were you when you could wash your own clothes?

BOTUM: When I was around thirteen or fourteen. My older sister taught me how to do it.

INTERVIEWER: Did you feel upset because she stopped washing your clothes?

BOTUM: No. This is my own clothes so I can do it.

Participants did not express feeling shortchanged by receiving care from other residents instead of adults, nor did any express resentment at having to provide care for others. There were even some spontaneous comments about how living in the center had prepared them to parent their own children. For example, asked what she will tell her children about her childhood in an orphanage, Bopha said that she will guide them the same way she was guided by staff and residents: "If that day comes, I will tell them about my good experience at COC. . . . I will use the same advice I got from the center to teach my children."

This is not to say that participants shared only an idealized or sugarcoated version of life in the orphanage. When asked whether he ever fought or cried, Kosal for example explained patiently, as though pointing out the obvious, "Every day we fought and cried because we were so little and innocent." Children were not reluctant to share episodes that cast themselves in a negative light, and some of their fondest memories recalled times when they were naughty or disobedient. Achariya for example told us of dragging her feet going back to the center because it was more fun to explore the countryside, recalling with evident pleasure, "Sometimes, when we left school early before noon, I, my friends Mach and Arunny didn't want to go home. We all went into the forest to find something to eat, then went back home later. Sometimes, we delayed the time to arrive home because we were lazy to pray. When we arrived home late we didn't need to pray, we all could go to eat directly."

Achariya also recalls escapades between the boys and the girls at the center, which brought peals of laughter from everyone present, who nodded in recognition. "I was happy with my living there," she recounted. "For example, Mom always restricted us and she didn't allow us to go across the houses to play between boys and girls, but when she and all the COC staff were busy with meetings . . . we all switched off the lights and played happily all together upstairs in one of the houses. We were always keen to do something that was not allowed by Mom."

While the other children were the sources of the residents' greatest joy, they were also the sources of greatest frustration, even anguish, and open conflict and rivalry were also described in the interviews. When asked what the worst thing at COC was, Mach and Sothy agreed that favoritism, or the perception of favoritism, had created rivalries and hurt feelings that still stung. Teasing, gossiping, and cliquishness were particular sources of unhappiness that emerged as a frequent theme for several female, but no male, interviewees. Sothy explained,

> What I hate is when someone who lived with me always backstabbed or gossiped about me and told Mom bad things about me to make Mom hate me, even though I was not like what they said. They always insinuated about us like this, and said we were two-headed fish.[5] But Mom used to tell us that if anyone gossips or badmouths us, we don't need to reply back, so we all remained silent. They still continued to badmouth us.

Finally, they felt ashamed when we always kept silent and they then stopped saying anything bad about us anymore.

Resolving conflicts among residents was an area in which staff were increasingly active through the years. While in 2011 I observed relatively little adult intervention in children's fights, the cohort of residents who arrived after 2012 appreciated staff efforts to mediate conflict and to advise them on strategies to do so themselves. Staff recalled having to arbitrate when older residents asked younger ones for their possessions or told them to perform chores for them, and some participants reported jealousy and resentment over perceived favoritism on the part of some staff. While interactions with other children were among both the best as well as the worst things former residents remembered, the adults were available to counsel and intervene in ways that the residents appreciated, even if they didn't always make use of them:

INTERVIEWER: Do you have anything you don't like?

ARY: Sometimes I have some argument with others. It makes me sad and disappointed. Some people try to tease me.

INTERVIEWER: So what do you do then?

ARY: I go and let our mother know about this. She tries to stop them and discipline them.

INTERVIEWER: What about Botum?

BOTUM: I go and inform my mother. Sometimes I call them bastard. I use some swear words. I know it is bad so I try to change my behavior later on.

Staff were well aware of the inevitable rivalries, and sometimes harnessed competition as a way to encourage everyone to study harder, through small rewards given to residents who excelled. This kind of motivation, rather than top-down enforcement of expectations, also was more frequent in the later years of the center, and residents who experienced it report that it was effective, although it came with its own complications, as Achariya describes: "If anyone of us got perfect scores, Mom would always buy them a packet of dessert or candies as a gift. We enjoyed the way we used to live, even though we argued with each other sometimes, but whenever I remember it, it makes me laugh. Sometimes, we felt jealous when seeing Mom giving something to someone and we started thinking that we already did our best, so why couldn't we get anything from Mom like they did. Actually, Mom gave it to whoever who did the best and wanted us to follow that person. This is Mom's methodology to inspire us."

Often, though, the residents' loyalty aligned with the other children, especially when it came to harsh discipline. Although management worked hard to solve the problem of corporal punishment, it was an issue with certain staff members, and this was quite troubling for children who came from family situations where violence was real and frightening. Achariya responded to the question about dissatisfactions with the COC by saying, "For me, I disliked seeing Mom hitting the children. I felt so pitiful when I saw them crying and like she was hitting my younger brother or sister. . . . Sometimes, the children did wrong but I didn't want her to hit them like that. I want her to find other way to punish them."

Sibling rivalry and shared naughtiness are negative aspects of life in the orphanage, but they also make it more like a real family, and indeed some participants used the word "family" in describing it. Some, like Arunny below, spoke of missing COC when they returned to their relatives for holidays, saying, "Back home, I never felt close with my siblings, but I felt closeness when I moved to COC. And I always missed everyone at COC when I went somewhere, like missing my young brothers or sisters, but I never missed anyone at home. . . . When Mom at COC allowed me to visit home for five days, I always asked her, 'Why is it so short?' But when she allowed me to go for ten days, I always felt missing COC so much."

The peer relationships with the other residents helped fill gaps in the children's lives that were created by some of the emotional struggles that were ongoing in their families of origin. Below, Tevy explains how she feels closer to and shares more with her friends from the COC than her relatives, because her relatives' responses lead to tensions when she speaks honestly about things that matter to her:

> I miss my friends at COC more than my family because I feel they are so far apart. . . . If you ask me, "Do I love them?" Yes, of course. But I won't go and hug them and say "I love you." I don't feel that close. . . . If I talk to them [relatives], they might think completely opposite from us. So if we continue to discuss, it might lead to arguments. It doesn't matter what we discuss about, they definitely disagree so it is better to stay quiet. My mother works in Thailand. She sometimes comes to visit me. When we meet, it is just okay.

Several of the former residents are still close friends, and most make an effort to stay in touch, hold reunions, and keep up with each other through social media and various group chats they have set up. In addition to the relationships with the other residents, participants consistently described fond memories and nostalgia for an aspect of orphanage life that has become quite controversial, namely the visitors and volunteers who were frequently to be found at the COC.

Visitors and Volunteers: Appreciated and Enjoyed

The questions about volunteers almost always sparked a noticeable change of affect, often accompanied by smiles, chuckles, and more animated body language. The steady stream of foreign visitors was a source of enjoyment for all the participants, especially during the center's early years. The frequent arrival and departure of foreign visitors is one of the most criticized aspects of daily life in Cambodian orphanages, so it is striking that three-quarters of the participants explicitly answered that there were no drawbacks at all to the many visitors and volunteers that they remember. Among those who did have some "worst things" to share, their on-balance assessment was still that the volunteers were highly positive.

The most common complaint about foreign visitors, expressed by five participants, was inappropriate behavior, including sexy clothing, smoking, and public displays of affection. Achariya pointed out, "But some visitors showed bad examples for the children. For example: some visitors was wearing sexy clothes and some came with their partners and kissed each other in front of the children." Narith had an even more concerning example: "Some volunteers they go there and then they smoke. It's not a good sign to show the children."

The other criticism, voiced by only one participant, was of volunteers who "just taught the kids to know how to play. . . . They don't give them the good ability to upgrade themselves in future." On balance though, even he believed that the volunteers were "a great thing." All participants agreed that volunteers often played with the children, but for most of them, this was a "best thing," not a "worst thing" about the visitors.

The issue of residents becoming sad and crying when volunteers left was mentioned in two interviews, but it was not presented as a drawback. Rather, it arose in response to the question about what was good about the volunteers.[6] When asked how she felt about the foreign visitors, Arunny laughed and teasingly said, "You'd better ask Achariya. She always cried when visitors left," but then she went on to say, "We enjoyed playing with them closely so when they left, we cried too."[7] The worst thing for her was not that the visitors made them sad when they left, but "when they wore shorts and hugged each other in front of the children."

Over one-half of the participants simply had no "worst" thing to recount about the foreign visitors, even when explicitly asked for one. As Sothy explained, "I don't have anything I dislike. I have only what I like." Even though I pushed back with some of the older participants I was interviewing in English, I was unable to elicit much in the way of negative statements about the volunteers. When I asked Charaya if he thought there were too many volunteers he responded, "I enjoyed as many as possible. . . . To me, I think there's no negatives." Rotha echoed this appraisal in response to the prompt asking for something that wasn't good: "When there were no visitors, I guess. [Laughing] . . . I love playing." Indeed, for most of the participants, the most important benefit of volunteers was that they were fun. Nary reminisced, "I felt so warm and close to them. I love that feeling. . . . I love all visitors. When they went there, I was so happy."

The most important concrete asset provided by the volunteers, according to the participants, was English language learning. Despite the criticism of volunteer tourism that maintains that teachers without professional training are next to useless, the residents themselves saw real advantages to having fun, motivated volunteers to speak English with.[8] They expressed an intuitive understanding of the value of exposure to authentic language in a communicative context, practicing without fear of making mistakes, hearing accurate pronunciation models, and, in contrast to language learning in a formal classroom setting, having their attention fully engaged because interacting with volunteers in English was fun rather than boring.

The importance of simply increasing one's confidence while interacting with foreigners is easy to underestimate, but it is important for foreigners to bear in mind just how intimidating we can be. We often forget about the privilege and prestige that English proficiency automatically confers, and how just achieving a level of comfort interacting with foreigners can be an asset in Siem Reap.[9] Chaya noted this when she explained, "I felt happy because I had a chance to play with them without being afraid and dared to speak with them. Even though I knew only a little English but I dared to talk with them too." Sothy agreed with this point, saying, "I had a chance to know the visitors, because at home although I used to see many visitors before, but I didn't dare to talk or play with them, only seeing from afar." The visitors' playful approach to teaching and learning contrasted with the sometimes harsh and ineffective techniques used in schools. As Achariya explained, "What's special is we can practice speaking English with them, playing with them and they show us the way to use English language. They told us that speaking English it's not important whether you speak right or wrong because they don't mind you, but what's important is don't be shy. Sometimes I don't know how to use English language clearly so we don't need to think about grammar. Or sometimes our English pronunciation is not good, yet they don't get angry with us too.[10] They gave us a lot of good advice."

Foreign visitors also provided a window onto the wider world, which was exciting for the residents and sparked an interest in other cultures. Charaya explained how the simple idea that things were different elsewhere helped him recognize that things could be different in Cambodia, and helped inspire his interest in politics: "Without volunteers, we wouldn't be able to see the world in a different way like we have." Similarly, although Mach had reservations about visitors who "behaved improperly," she decided that exposure to different cultural behaviors was on balance positive: "I think that there's only a few things I dislike. But there are many things I like about their behaviors, which are totally different from Cambodians. For example, when they finished eating anything they always put plastic bags in the bin or if they couldn't find the bin they would keep in their pockets. So I felt that their countries are very developed and they have good order and no rubbish. I think that it is a good example for the

Cambodian children." Likewise, Prak recounted how his resistance to one volunteer, who was more assertive than most young Cambodian women, gave way to appreciation when he finally came to understand that she was not being disrespectful when she teased him: "Kaley is both good and at that time I feel like . . . I'm angry? Not angry, but just feel something, didn't really like. But after that I said, "Oh, Kaley is very funny. She's funny." Kaley has maintained a long-term relationship with the center, and Prak, along with several other participants, was excited to tell me of her return visit last year. He insightfully summed up his assessment of how experience with the foreign visitors prepared him for his current professional success: "When we stay together at least it will improve your knowledge, like culture one, and two is English language, and three understand about different culture. They are different so you need to understand that."

While some differences took getting used to for the residents, others were immediately appealing and even validating for Chaya, who valued how foreigners were positioned outside of local social class and urban/rural hierarchies: "I have only what I like about them. I like them because they have no discrimination. They spoke with everyone, without discrimination like some Khmers."

Botum appreciated how the foreigners encouraged her to go beyond local expectations about girls and sports. When asked about her best memory of the visitors, she said, "I always love football," and asked whether there was a worst aspect to the visitors, she replied, "I don't have any. I love all. As long as I play with them, I'm happy." Recall from chapter 5 that girls normally were not included in the spontaneous soccer games that arose in the evenings. Although recently the Cambodian government has encouraged more girls to participate in traditionally male sports like soccer, when Botum was younger the foreigners provided her a rare opportunity to be included in the games.

Concerns about child protection and the potential for abuse form a large part of the concern about foreign volunteers, as discussed in chapter 3, but I did not explicitly ask about abuse in the interviews.[11] Nonetheless, a few references were made. There was some discussion of an early volunteer who was very popular with the children, partly because he took them on trips throughout the country and paid for them to stay in hotels with him, although the participant who discussed this clarified "in different rooms." This volunteer's visits had abruptly stopped before I had begun visiting the COC. I had heard rumors that further visits by him had been blocked out of concern for child protection, although the participant who mentioned him assured me that nothing inappropriate had ever happened. This scenario was recalled as a potential "close call" by one member of the center management who said that it had been hard to hire professional English teachers, so that relying on volunteers was "not so good, but we have no choice." Like most orphanages after the 2000s, COC had a child protection policy, and there was some spontaneous evidence that children had taken it to heart when Rotha described how she had refused when a volunteer tried to give her money: "My housemother told us like that. She told us any foreigner who offered us any cash, we were not allowed to take it [so she] told him we didn't take any cash here. If he wanted to give me something, he could donate to the center and use it as a fund for organizing a party for the center or something like that."

Although another large concern about volunteer tourism pertains to the ways in which children may be treated as commodities for the enjoyment of foreign visitors, in the interviews an alternative perspective emerged in which the residents sometimes felt as though they were the ones commodifying the volunteers.[12] The residents held a certain amount of power vis-à-vis the visitors because of their ability to talk about them in Khmer, and they used this to their advantage when they thought visitors were behaving inappropriately. Mach explained, "Some visitors, when we saw them behave improperly, we would always backbite them." If they could understand Khmer language, she continues, they would have been shocked.

While the wealth, age, power, prestige, and mobility differentials are real and all contribute to a staggering gap in inequality between the visitors and the residents, the residents themselves often saw interactions with foreign visitors as a real exchange, and they recognized that they had knowledge and skills to share with the visitors, such as teaching traditional games. For example, Bopha said about her favorite thing with visitors, "What I liked doing with those visitors was to invite them to play Khmer games with us. They played with us and we invited to play our games too."

Although one aspect of commodification that has been reported in Cambodian orphanages is the intentional posing of children as deprived through dressing them shabbily, some of the children's spontaneous statements spoke to the dignity with which they intentionally presented themselves. For example, Bopha described how "back then, every time we knew that visitors were coming to visit our place, we tended to dress up beautifully and get ready to welcome them." When asked whether anyone told them to do that, she said, "No. . . . We wanted to have fun. We normally played with our older brothers and sisters so it was better to have fun with those visitors too. We preferred a large group of visitors."

Throughout their interactions with foreign visitors, the residents retained a measure of pride in their abilities and their circumstances. They were advised by staff to treat the visitors like guests in their home, an inversion of the advice that is given to foreigners that they should not drop in on orphanages because it is the children's home. Achariya mentioned how the housemothers had to warn the children not to take advantage of the foreigners' good nature and how the staff too enjoyed the foreigners' visits: "All COC staff also felt happy with the visitors. . . . Sometimes, Mom told us that we should play carefully with the visitors even if they always forgive us but we should only play in a proper way with them or respect them."

Leaving the Orphanage

Leaving the orphanage evoked complicated feelings, just as coming to live at the orphanage had. Some participants had felt ready to leave and were looking forward to the next stage of their lives; Narith for example said bluntly, "I felt enough with COC!" Others, like Sothy, did not want to leave and spoke of missing it terribly: "I felt missing. I missed everyone and especially all my close friends that I used to live with, like my siblings and Mom who always gave me good advice. . . . I felt that I didn't want to be far from there but I have to continue my studies. So I decided to leave. . . . It felt like our family."

Complicated feelings were common even among participants who had been ready to leave so they could continue their schooling in the city. Although Rathana was eager to move into Siem Reap because there were no high schools close to COC, he remembers life there fondly, and even events that might not seem nostalgia-inducing, such as early morning chores and scoldings by the staff, are reasons for him to grow nostalgic:

> For me, I can say that also happy. Because I leave COC, and I go to the next step. . . . The next point to catch my dream, my imagination. It's not like regret for COC. . . . But just sometimes we miss the many good times we had in COC. . . . In the nighttime, just sitting together around in a circle, we talk, reading the books. And every morning, every 5 A.M. in the morning [laughs], we have some exercise and sometimes have some work to do. And if we're lazy, the manager "Wuh wuh wuh!" [mimics scolding, laughs] And we have to run around again. The good times that we miss, we cannot get back. [laughs]

Some residents intentionally chose to leave COC early, before they had finished junior high school. Although this often meant returning to live with relatives, for most of them a longing for family life was much less important than was the longing to escape rules and structure, especially and somewhat ironically, being obliged to attend school and study hard.

Both Nary and Tevy, who chose to leave COC when they were fourteen, spoke with insight but also incomprehension about the choice they made to leave at such a young age, as well as their dismay when they realized that "freedom" meant having to work, support themselves, feed themselves, and navigate the whole complicated world of "adulting" of which they had been blissfully unaware as children. As Tevy explained, "We felt that we didn't have much freedom.

I loved to play but I was lazy to study. . . . I didn't have any problem there, but I just didn't want to go to school." Today, from the vantage point of a twenty-two-year-old who has worked hard to craft a successful career, she regrets missed opportunities but is proud of her accomplishments and sympathizes with her restless fourteen-year-old self: "I was naughty," she chuckles, then reflects, saying, "I laugh about my past. I feel that my past was so ridiculous. It sounds so strange when we try to think about that now." When asked what advice she would give to a child newly arrived at the orphanage, she urged more patience with respect to the rules: "I will tell them, especially girls, 'Sometimes you feel pressure about rules and regulations there, but if you can go through them, you will receive good result, good education and other supports.'"

Her friend Nary, who also left before she completed ninth grade, agreed: "During the first month we left, we felt regret." She would also advise younger residents to work hard and finish school. "Don't follow my example!" she laughs. She remembers that her life was fun at the COC and recognizes that while it would have been easier had she stayed, the obstacles she faced living on her own helped her to grow as well, and she too is proud of the life she has crafted for herself. "We had a golden opportunity that someone was there to help us but why were we so lazy? We should have worked much harder. However, we feel stronger when we live in the world outside. We are now grown up, we don't wait for others to support us anymore."

Daevy is another participant who left COC as a teenager because she was resistant to the program's rules. She acknowledges that she left COC because, in her later years there, "I made some mistakes. They didn't want me to be a bad example for future kids staying there." After floundering for a while ("I didn't do anything" she says), at age twenty she now recognizes that external structure will help keep her on the path she has set for herself. After finishing vocational training, she found a live-in work situation that provides the security she wants. "That shop applies stricter rules, which I like. They don't allow us to stay outside later than 8 P.M. If we want to go out or go somewhere we need to ask for permission." What is striking is how she has grown into the self-awareness to recognize what she needs as well as the motivation to seek it out. She is earning a good salary, saving money, and sending some to her relatives, and she sees possibilities for advancement in her career. Her desire for a high level of security and structure becomes more understandable when she describes an incident with a male customer whose advances made her uncomfortable; she was grateful that the shop owner was paying attention.

The complicated feelings participants expressed about leaving the COC were deepened by the knowledge that it had been closed down. When Pich, who had left COC when he started high school, biked up for his interview, he spontaneously exclaimed with great feeling before the interview even started: "You know

COC closed? I'm sad!" For those participants who were still missing the COC, its closure felt like a personal loss to them. Achariya explained, "I feel so sorry when COC is closed. I miss everything there. When I went there sometimes I missed the place where I used to live and I missed all the past memories there. I don't want it to be closed, I want it to continue. It used to be noisy with many people there, but now it is so silent and only old houses, landscape and yard remaining." Her friend Arunny agreed: "I feel so sorry when COC is closed. When there is no one there I feel so pitiful and lonely. It used to be a lot of children playing there, but when it is closed, I feel missing the children as well as the place."

Concern about the foreclosure of opportunities for children who come from difficult backgrounds similar to their own was a common theme in discussions of the COC's closure, even among those who couldn't wait to leave. Prak, who had been highly critical of COC, expressed misgivings about its closing because it would no longer be available for children whose needs were not being met. Upon being told of its closing, he said thoughtfully, "Hm, actually, it's not good news. Closing it just feels a bit sad to me, because of the kids who can't really get the things so they can take care of themselves."

Participants' expressions of regret about the COC's closure reflected an awareness of the social and personal circumstances that have led so many families to make the choice to leave a child in an orphanage. Speaking of the closure, Bopha explains, "I feel sad to hear that. I would like the center to continue to accommodate more children who struggle financially with school and those whose parents are desperate or pass away. They can be sent there. I really want it to be continued." Her expression of regret indicates a mature understanding that although she had felt frightened and abandoned when she realized her mother was leaving her there, she now understands the level of desperation that can leave parents feeling like they have no other choice.

Her friend Rotha, who was interviewed together with her, picked up on this theme, explaining, "I feel sad too. I know there are a lot of poor children out there who need that kind of support, and students whose parents are poor and can't afford their school fees. If the center is still there, children can be sent there to continue their education."

Only one respondent, Charaya, said he was untouched by the closing. "I felt great actually," he declared when asked about it. Although Charaya had earlier declared unequivocally that his life would have been "terrible" had he not gone to live at the COC, his criticisms were also quite strong. Nonetheless, he has maintained a connection and returned to teach English to younger cohorts of residents, although he was dismayed at what he saw: "Sometimes I went to visit, what they're doing is getting lunch, getting breakfast, getting dinner, doing chores—it's just like being in prison."[13] However, as he explored his misgivings, thinking out loud in the interview, he came to the conclusion that COC was on balance preferable to families of origin for some children, just as it had been for him. His dissatisfaction with COC as a teenager had led him to encourage another resident to return to their mother at the age of fourteen, when they were both unhappy with how staff were handling discipline. He says that he now regrets the advice he gave because the early return home has turned out to considerably limit employment options. "Perhaps I was not doing a good job as the older brother," he says somewhat ruefully. He points out though that the center, under external pressure to return children to families and at the same time struggling with adolescent behavior issues, did not offer the kind of counseling that might have helped to support other options. He concludes, "So we should study about the family conditions and the situations, rather than just sending them to their family if they want to."

Among those who spoke nostalgically of missing COC, it wasn't just talk. Some had gone back to visit, while others excitedly planned reunions. Several posted pictures on Facebook of themselves there as young children, decorated with hearts, laughing emojis, and tears. One of the most poignant signs of the depth of feeling evoked by encouraging former residents to reflect on their experiences was the response of one young man after I reached out to him. He took pictures of himself wandering the deserted premises alone and posted them on Facebook, of course garnering loves and likes from other former residents. Rathana also spoke of how he goes to visit sometimes, just to reminisce: "Sometimes I go to visit COC. And sometimes, just riding a motorbike across the COC and just look at this place and also imagine about the many memories that I have there. And sometimes I feel, like I said, I miss the many activities that we have done in COC. Like telling stories and at the nighttime just talking with the brothers and sisters like this."

Nary, Daevy, and Tevy, who were all restless and eager to leave during their last years at the COC, still stay in touch and, until it closed, returned to visit and join in celebrations and ceremonies. They compare the warm relationships they continued to have there, even after quitting the program, with their more complicated, less comfortable feelings for their families of origin. "We feel different when we went back to visit the center," they agreed. "We could hug and kiss my mother there. We felt so close to them over there." And the closing of COC, despite their eagerness to leave it, leaves them sorrowful. "I feel sad for those kids who haven't finished their school. I don't know who will continue to support them," worries Nary, while Tevy concludes, "I miss all the memories there. I feel very sad."

Malis eloquently sums up the complicated blend of nostalgia for the comforts of the COC, gratitude for the advantages provided, and acceptance of the need to move on that so many of them felt—saying goodbye to the COC felt like saying goodbye to her childhood: "For me, when I left I missed Mom and my same old friends who I used to play with. When I left I kneeled down in front of Mom and said good-bye with tears in my eyes. When I arrived here I felt that this place is for adults and that place is for kids." Her thoughtful reflection on the passage of this stage of her life is typical of the nuance and complexity I found in all of the participants' interviews. In the next chapter, I delve more deeply into their own assessments of their experiences to explore some of the themes that were revealed in this rich collection of memories and reflections.

7

Reflecting Back and Looking Ahead

Interpreting the COC Experience

I had structured the interviews to encourage more objective reporting of experiences first, as a way to build up to questions requiring more reflection and
interpretation after the participants had become more comfortable. However, I
found that they didn't really need any warming up in order to dive straight into
some of the more complicated aspects of their lives in the COC. The participants
had clearly thought a lot already about their experiences, and the implications
of those experiences, and they welcomed the interviews as an opportunity to
explore further and to share their own insights. Table 3 shows the five themes
that emerged as most revealing in their reflections and interpretations of their
own experiences.

Nuance and Ambivalence

Perhaps the most striking feature of this project has been the level of thought-
fulness the participants brought to the interviews. I found them humbling in
the sincerity and seriousness with which they considered the questions, and
their reflections were often marked by honest perplexity and wholly natural
ambivalence. Hesitations and fillers convinced me that they were not giving me
pre-rehearsed statements, and sometimes they contradicted themselves as they
explored and revisited their own sometimes confounding memories, pausing frequently to reflect.[1] For example, the first day I talked to Charaya, he described
how he didn't want to leave COC when the time came, partly because he didn't
want to live with either of his parents, who he said had not provided a loving
home for him, and also partly because he had no desire to move to a city, preferring what he called the "peaceful, green" and "full of trees" COC environment.
Several days later, when I talked to him again, he said it was "boring" and
"like living in the jungle." Similarly, Prak explored the costs and benefits,

TABLE 3

Reflections

Nuance and ambivalence

I felt somewhat happy and unhappy. (Malis, F, age 5 at arrival, 17 at interview)

I gonna tell them [future children] about the experience when they are old enough to understand the story, so they get to know what is the bitterness of life, and what is the sweet part of life. (Charaya, M, age 8 at arrival, 22 at interview)

When Mom at COC allowed me to visit home for five days, I always asked her, "Why is it so short?" But when she allowed me to go for ten days, I always felt missing COC so much. (Arunny, F, age 8 at arrival, 17 at interview)

High expectations

I want to run a business by my own. I don't want to work for others forever. . . . I have to run my own business in the next ten years. (Kolab, F, age 8 at arrival, 22 at interview)

For me, I want to know English. I want to travel abroad. One more thing—I want to be a manager or director so that I can have a lot of money and my mother would be highly esteemed. (Malis, F, age 5 at arrival, 17 at interview)

When I saw people wearing those graduation gowns, I always thought to myself that I don't really know if I could be like them or not, but I motivated myself to commit in doing it. No matter what I will wear that gown! (Mach, F, age 10 at arrival, 17 at interview)

Their lives could have turned out very differently

I think if I not go to COC then . . . maybe I go to Thailand border to work as labor to get money to support my family. (Rathana, M, age 14 at arrival, 28 at interview)

If I only stayed at home, I wouldn't be able to realize that this world is so wonderful but when I moved to live here, I learned and knew a lot about life. (Achariya, F, age 11 at arrival, 17 at interview)

If there is no COC, I think my life would end up to be terrible. I was growing up in a very, very negative society, growing up in a village where most people had been using drugs. (Charaya, M, age 8 at arrival, 22 at interview)

Positive future orientation

I planned many good things. I think for the next ten years it will be a good life and good achievement for me. (Rathana, M, age 14 at arrival, 28 at interview)

If we want to have a bright future, we need to work hard at school. (Rotha, F, age 11 at arrival, 18 at interview)

(continued)

Table 3. Reflections (continued)

I think we should learn new things and find more experience in life.
  I definitely treasure those memories in my heart, but I wouldn't want to
  go back. (Kosal, M, age 6 at arrival, 19 at interview)

Individual agency and gratitude

Ten years from now, I want to have my own business and invest, and then
  I can help other people back. Because I used to live from another sponsor,
  and . . . I need to help other back. (Prak, M, age 11 at arrival, 25 at
  interview)

It is good for me to save some money to support my family. (Daevy, F, age 7
  at arrival, 20 at interview)

I really appreciate what I'd learned and support we'd received during our stay
  there. We were also satisfied with our choice we made at that time to leave
  the center because our life got stronger and stronger. We know how to look
  after ourselves and we know how to live independently. (Nary, F, age 8 at
  arrival, 22 at interview)

complexities and contradictions of living away from family when he said, "Sure,
I learned a lot. I think that this is a very good experience that I've been away
from family," but later he spoke of his regrets: "Now we're not close, me and my
family, because I've been away like fifteen years or more, so the connection . . .
is not really a family." It was clear, from the pauses where he struggled to find
the right words, that he was grappling with the inevitable trade-offs when conditions make it so hard for families with children. He concludes that he now
has a better life than he would have had, but that it has come at a cost. Prak is
also the only participant who said, spontaneously and unequivocally, "I will not
send my kid to any orphanage. . . . I will not. I promise myself that. Even if I'm
not really rich or I'm not really a good citizen, but I will not send them." Nonetheless, in comparing himself with other children who left the orphanage before
completing their studies because they missed their families or were unhappy
for other reasons, he decided that on balance, for him staying was the right
decision.

All of the participants, in fact, concluded that living at the COC had improved
their lives, even if it had often been hard and sad for them. They could miss their
families and still appreciate living in the COC; they could resent rising early to
do chores and still believe the skills they practiced are serving them well; they
could express justifiable outrage at harsh punishment and still appreciate how
the center's discipline prepared them for school and work; they could rail against
the meanness of other children and still feel nostalgic for the companionship
and camaraderie. They avoided uncomplicated conclusions.

The former residents were especially skilled at reexamining vividly recalled childhood anger and hurt through the lenses of their current more seasoned outlook. Several from the earliest cohorts were very critical of the way rules were imposed with a heavy-handed emphasis on negative consequences rather than motivation. Narith recalls the rules as arbitrary and excessive, and he remains dismayed by the way the staff seemed unable or unwilling to explain and justify them effectively. He concedes now that expectations were probably reasonable but that the staff resorted too readily to scolding, extra chores, docking their allowance, or even corporal punishment, even though that was not allowed. He describes a litany of rules that as a child he and others had resented, resisted, and still complain about: "They tell them 'Oh, the rules here, you need to wake up like this . . . you should go to take a rest, go to the kitchen, eat breakfast, what time you need to go to eat lunch, what time you go to the dinner, and then what time you should wake up and what time you should clean the garden.'" Now though he sees benefits: "Kids want to have fun, to play, they don't want to do that. But when we grow up we say 'Yeah, it's a good policy that can teach the child to know how to clean, know how to grow.' Yeah, and then how to work as a team also."

Sometimes criticisms explicitly addressed the more traditional models of adult-child authority that were prevalent throughout Cambodia when they were younger, and participants' views showed how they are aware of more modern ideas about child raising, which they find preferable. Narith continued his critique of top-down rule enforcement by explaining how staff failed to take children's own motivation into account: "They should know . . . 'Oh, this child, this child doesn't like to study so what's the plan to make them love studying?' What plan to make them love education? Or this child doesn't respect the rules. They should know why. Why they don't respect the rules. . . . The kids, they learn but they don't have the feeling to learn well, because they just learn because of the rules. . . . When you're not there they will play with their friend." He illustrates his point with the example of traditional music, which even as a school-age child he had confided to me that he didn't like. His opinion of it has not changed—in the interview he stressed how he would much rather have studied modern music. But he has a greater understanding of why staff thought it was important: "This is from the kids, but for the management, I understand them also because they want the kids learning the traditional music and dancing to create a group, and have the tourists or volunteers go and visit them. They can get more donations. Like this, I understand them also."[2]

Another area of ambivalence lay in children's feelings toward their families, which could be raw and vexing. They often felt torn between their family loyalty and their desire for the opportunities and emotional respite provided by the COC. It wasn't just that they missed their relatives; they worried about them and felt responsible for their well-being. Children can be the most hesitant to leave the most dangerous families due to worries about the safety of remaining family members. Recall, for example, Achariya's coming-to-the-orphanage story in which she tells how she worried about leaving her mother alone with her alcoholic and abusive father after her two sisters had already fled, leaving her the oldest sibling at home. It wasn't until she was reassured that other family members would keep her mother safe that she was able to pursue her dream of continuing her studies by going to live in the COC.

Participants used the interviews to explore their conflicted feelings about enjoying their life at COC while still feeling strong bonds, and guilt, toward their families, whether parents, grandparents, or siblings. Although they understood that living in the orphanage removed a major stressor from their families' lives, the pressures intensified as the children grew older because parents sometimes then wanted them to leave the COC so they could contribute to the family by working. The extent to which children worry about the safety and well-being of their families is often underestimated, but it can undermine their ability to take care of themselves or to embrace educational opportunities. The participants themselves understood this. When asked what advice she would give newcomers to the orphanage, Bopha said, "I will tell them . . . no need to worry. They should believe that their families are all safe."

Former residents had clearly reflected on the complexity of the decision to place a child in an orphanage. For example, Narith reflected, "I know no one wants to live away from their family. Even if we know living in the family is not a good future, . . . we still choose it if we can. But this is for the mind from the kid. But for the mother, they want to see their child have a good future. That's why they send them."

Feelings toward the staff were complicated, too. As discussed above, some participants still harbored anger over unpleasant punishments, although most had grown philosophical about it. For example, Achariya speaks of feeling unfairly criticized by her housemother, saying, "When Mom advised me, I was always angry with her. I thought that I was always blamed," but upon reflection, she continues, "But actually Mom always wanted us to be a good person." She recognizes that she simultaneously was able to feel both love and hatred. "Sometimes, I loved her lesser than my hatred on her, and sometimes I loved her more than my hatred on her." She recognizes how staff tried to model the patience needed to manage volatile human emotions: "Sometimes, I ignored her but she still smiled at me. Then I love her."

Many of the interviewees, especially those who were most critical, struggled with the difficulty of a final summation of their orphanage experience as either good or bad, and sometimes came to the conclusion that they had even benefitted from some of the experiences they construed as negative. Prak, whose ambivalence is also discussed above, was highly critical of several things—the harsh discipline he recalled, his feelings of estrangement from his family, and what he sees as poor employment outcomes for many of the other residents, although he himself has done well. Although for the first few weeks he was "just crying," he now says he appreciates how the COC enabled residents "to grow up with educa-tion, and good opportunity" because he is relieved to not have remained a sub-sistence farmer. "Yeah," he concludes after listing all his criticisms, "I think it's quite good," or at least, "The place is okay, because we know that like everywhere, always have problem, and have conflict or good things that happen." As Rathana explains, "Some bads, some goods, but everything . . . it's the life."

High Expectations

As discussed in chapter 6, I was somewhat surprised at how unremarkable most of the participants found the good physical care they received at the COC. When I probed further, it emerged that for the former residents themselves, the qual-ity of day-to-day care was not as important as were the outcomes, especially employment outcomes, for former residents after they had left. Their expecta-tions for outcomes though were very high indeed.

My one hour and fifteen minutes of conversation with Charaya included sub-stantive criticisms of what he saw as poor management and how it had led to low educational and employment outcomes for former residents. This was sur-prising to me because, as discussed in chapter 4, objectively their outcomes were good. Charaya apologized for what he worried was "too much negativity" and concluded, "Probably I have too high expectation of COC." However, this criti-cism about outcomes was voiced by two other participants and was especially striking because the three who were the most critical were also among the most successful—all three had graduated from high school, had some university coursework, and were engaged in stable white-collar employment. Underlying their criticisms and their own successes was the common thread of very high expectations for themselves, the other residents, and the center itself. As was explained in the preceding section, many Cambodians place very high expec-tations on children who have lived in an orphanage, and the residents them-selves have internalized a very high standard for success.

All three were willing to label former residents as successful only if they had graduated from high school and attended some university and had jobs in man-agement, administration, sales, or related kinds of office work. They were dis-missive of former residents who held jobs such as factory worker, driver, food server, mechanic, and especially farmer, despite the fact that such positions rep-resent a step upward for many former residents, given the often very challeng-ing backgrounds from which most of them came. I was quite surprised when one young woman, who has a stable position as a server in one of the best restau-rants in Siem Reap, was not included on their list of successful former residents. She and her husband, who is also employed in a good restaurant, provide their son with a stable and comfortable home, and she likes her job, is proud of her life, and was eager to meet with me and tell me about it. When I complimented her on the restaurant where she works, saying, "It must be a nice place to work," she replied, "It is. Because my boss is French." I was reminded of how in France, in contrast to the United States, restaurant work can be a real career, receiving respect and a decent living wage, underscoring how subjective criteria for assessing success can be.[3]

The high expectations extended to the previously discussed criticism that staff should have been able to motivate residents to study harder when residents themselves resisted attending school or doing their homework. Narith elaborated on his critique of poor management by explaining how it resulted directly in poor educational outcomes: "Because children, they don't know anything. It's important you tell them everything. Do not [just say] 'You need to study hard.' So when the child hears like that, yeah, when they see you they will study but when you're not there they will play with their friends." He directly attributes the inability of staff to understand how to motivate children to apply themselves to their schooling to lack of leadership: "I have only one word. I feel like the management is so poor."

High expectations were not limited to the three young men who were most critical, however. Most participants held high expectations for their own hard work and employment outcomes. Continuing education in subjects such as English or technical skills was popular, and moonlighting to sell personal care products was quite common. Those in the hospitality sector sought, and found, employment at prestigious boutique hotels rather than less desirable ones. Some former residents who pursued vocational training or blue-collar jobs kept the dream of university study alive, expressing that their jobs would enable them to support future studies. For example, Pich is enrolled in cosmetology school. This would be a stable career for which he has considerable skill, but he also is a high school graduate and plans to use salon work to support his studies of business management at university, ultimately preparing him for a more ambitious career.

Eleven of the former residents I met with are still in school, receiving academic and financial support from the NGO. In a country where only 55 percent of all high school-age youth are in school and only two-thirds of those enrolled succeed in graduating, it is still a huge deal for a child from a rural area to graduate from high school.[4] The students' dreams of the doors that will be opened by high school graduation reflect the high expectations focused on career and educational attainment. Mach, for example, shared her daydreams about her graduation day, envisioning herself dressed in a cap and gown and holding a bouquet of flowers from her friends: "I used to see students wearing their graduation gown and when I saw them I thought that I have to wear it like them. . . . I would tell my children to try hard too. I will tell them that life is not meaningless and life is effort. When I saw people wearing those graduation gowns, I always thought to myself that I don't really know if I could be like them or not, but I motivated myself to commit in doing it. No matter what I will wear that gown!"

The former residents' focus on educational and employment outcomes as the measure of quality for the orphanage itself underscores the difficulty of evaluating an institution. It is fairly straightforward to determine whether food is adequate, whether kids are attending school and doing their homework, and whether they are clothed and sheltered; it's quite difficult though to decide whether a program is successful because notions of a successful life are inherently subjective and relative. As Charaya insisted in his critique of the COC, "People should not only be given help to avoid the problem, but only should be given the opportunity to seize into the bright future."

In order to better understand the focus on prestigious employment as the benchmark for quality of care, I pushed back a little when Charaya said, "I can say 90 percent of the people left COC ended up jobless, or being in a really, really, really poor, life."[5] I countered, "If you start with someone who comes from a family where there was hitting, if you can just help them become the kind of person that doesn't hit their kids, could that mean that the program was successful, even if they don't have a good job?" When I drew his attention to this other way to define success, he was thoughtful:

> Yeah, I think, talk about the change in kids from the violent families, and the kid will be a person that's not gonna use their violence in the future . . . yeah, that's the thing that I think COC has been doing a good job with. COC helps the kids to be a better person. . . . But the thing that I just kind of feel bad about is that I don't want them to think of that as the limit of helping the kids. So people get used to achieving small things and then telling people that is a success that they could achieve, that would be the best thing that they could do. But actually, if they try to improve their leadership a little bit more, then the kids can go a little bit higher.

In Cambodia, where precarity remains at high levels, the expectation that the COC should be able to ensure a high level of prestigious employment is understandable; after all, it is why many families chose to make the painful but intentional "sacrifice of love" to place their children in an orphanage.[6] Charaya, Prak, and Narith's disappointment in the management reveals the power to transform lives that they attribute to the COC.

Their Lives Could Have Turned Out Very Differently

All of the children that we asked believed that their life would be very different today had they not gone to live in the orphanage; invariably their judgment was that it would have been worse.[7] While two of them, Narith and Prak, were especially torn about the emotional distancing from their families they had traded for an improved level of material security, they also recognized that material security improved their ability to create a warm family life with their own future partners and children. Three mentioned that they would have inevitably been distanced anyway from their families if they had remained with them because by now they would have had to migrate to work in Thailand.

Most of the former residents stressed how the COC had enabled them to stay in school longer than they could have otherwise. Mach, whose parents had both passed away, felt that since she could not live with her parents anyway, COC provided the best alternative for her. She explained how her transition to secondary school would have been jeopardized: "If I didn't move to live in COC, I still would have had to live with others. Those others would provide money for my studies, but I might be forced to stop studying when I grew up bigger because they don't have money for me to continue my studies either."

Similarly, Narith believes that he would have become a subsistence farmer like the rest of his family had he stayed with his mother. While he missed her terribly when he arrived, he still believes that on balance he prefers the outcomes he has experienced because the COC gave him "more education," so that he could find a job in the city, which he preferred over "work using the energy," that is, physical labor.[8]

While the likelihood of dropping out of school due to financial constraints loomed large in the participants' alternative scenarios, emotional stability was as important as financial support for some of them. For example, Sothy recounted how COC helped her to escape her father's new wife's resentment toward her: "I think that it is good to live here and if I were at home, I wouldn't be able to study higher because my family always had conflicts between stepmother and previous daughter."[9]

Daevy also emphasized that it wasn't just financial constraints that prevented poor children from continuing their studies successfully. She found it hard to concentrate on studying while living with six other children and her aunt, whose own living situation was already precarious. The simple logistics of monitoring the attendance and homework of so many children were daunting, and Daevy thought it was "great to stay at the center," explaining, "It is stricter. The center has rules and regulations. We need to follow them, for example, going to school instead of playing. If we stay at home, no one will check up on me to see if I go to school or not. . . . I think it is hard if we stay at home because we might have friends who invite us to go out and play more often. Having this kind of friends, we might not be able to concentrate on school. . . . For me, I think the center is better."

The social capital provided by the organization, in terms of meeting people whose paths they otherwise would never have crossed, impressed Achariya, who reminisced, "Every time I remember it again I feel that for myself it's wonderful because I have known a lot of friends. We always had unity and I learned a lot from everyone around me. If I only stayed at home I wouldn't be able to realize that this world is so wonderful. . . . I know a lot of people that I've never known before, sometimes wonderful and successful people too."

Kolab, who is currently working while attending university, understands that because the support she received from the COC benefitted her as an individual, it also is potentially beneficial for Cambodian society, especially given her chaotic and traumatic first eight years and the outcomes that could have been likely for her:

> If I was not living in COC I would probably be nomadic. I might have early marriage and not be able to study higher. And my character would be belligerent and too impulsive. . . . I might be addicted to drugs because of having bad friends or I might become a thief or do something that society despises. So I would not only not help the society but also make society hate me. [After the COC] everything was changed. I was changed from a child who used to be so irritable and nasty to be a better person. From a child who was lazy to study to be a hardworking child who wants to study till I finish all levels. I became a child who could help society.

Prak, who also is studying at university while working full-time, recognized not just the value of formal educational opportunities but also how some of the supplementary skills the residents were taught had opened doors to a different way of life for him. His dance and music skills enabled him to pay for his extra lessons and have a little leftover spending money with which to nurture friendships and networks while he was finishing high school and living as a temple boy in a pagoda: "You need to have money. Like when you go outside, you *die*, you know that feeling. You cannot just go out when you feel like it. But you [want to be] with friends, so I did a part-time job, in the evening, between around seven to nine I was dancing, and I played traditional music." Prak is the participant who expressed the most negativity about his COC experience, and he stresses that while COC opened some doors for him, his success is still largely due to his own hard work. His drive is evident in the long hours he put in, rising early for chores at the pagoda, studying, and then performing at night. He believes he would have remained a subsistence farmer if he had not gone to the COC, and he is glad to have avoided that outcome, but he also understands that leaving home meant that he does not feel as close with his mother as he would if he had stayed in his village with her, and he regrets that enormously.

Some girls felt fortunate that going to COC had enabled them to avoid an early marriage. Arunny expresses sympathy for her older sister, who had not been allowed to join the two younger siblings at the COC: "If I were at home, I would not have a good future, like my older sister. She had to stop studying and married a husband. She had to work to earn money because she didn't have enough money to continue her studies so she dropped out of school when she was in grade 8. . . . When I moved to live in COC, I had the opportunity to study and Sister told me to study hard because she didn't want me to be like her." Arunny appreciates the sacrifice her sister made and later told us how she looks forward to getting a good job so she can in turn help support her family.

Participants also understood how the realities of adult addiction affected their ability to go to school and how the COC provided guidance in helping them to avoid such destructive behaviors. Achariya explains, "I think that if I still lived with my family at my home, maybe now my father would not realize to stop drinking alcohol. . . . And also I could release the responsibility of the family too, meaning that my parents can take the amount of money [they were] supposed to spend, about 10 percent, on me to spend for my siblings or daily expenses instead. In COC we learned what is good or bad and we know clearly about grati-tude and how to respect older people and a lot more." For her family, moving to COC relieved financial and emotional stressors and provided her with a differ-ent set of expectations that made alternative futures more possible.

Even some residents who resisted the COC's heavy emphasis on schoolwork recognized that it strengthened habits of mind that later served them well. Nary, who quit COC before she finished ninth grade, was still able to successfully graduate from high school on her own. She explained that if she hadn't lived for seven years in COC, "I don't think I could get this much education," and suggests that the value of schooling extends beyond just grades completed: "My life before COC, I was so little I didn't know how to think or I never thought of anything. When we were at COC, we started learning and after that when we stay on our own, we know how to think more properly." Her friend Tevy, who also left early, agreed:

> If we didn't stay at COC, we wouldn't be able to think more critically like right now. We might just be half of what we are right now. We wouldn't be able to know how to lead our life in the society. We would just listen to our parents. If they wanted us to get married, we just did it without questioning them. That's why I'm so proud of my stay there. Girls in the countryside get married, have babies, fight with their husband, and get divorced. When they have a lot of kids, they don't know how to look after them.

Several interviewees assumed, quite realistically, that they would have gone abroad to work had they not gone to the COC.[10] Ary declared unequivocally that by the age of fourteen, "I am sure I would already stop studying and go to work in Thailand," and seventeen-year-old Botum immediately agreed: "I would also stop and go to work somewhere. Thanks for COC for that." Likewise, Rathana recognized how likely this would have been for young Cambodians of their background: "I cannot avoid from it. It would be the same like the other kids that go to the Thailand border to work."

When imagining alternative futures for themselves that did not include the COC, most participants focused on the educational opportunities they would have missed, but some mentioned other risks that COC had averted, such as homelessness, as Bopha did in her narrative at the beginning of this chapter. Later she returned to this powerful theme that clearly remained in her thoughts: "If I hadn't been able to live at COC, my family would have gone astray along the street because my parents were separated and we didn't know what to do. We couldn't imagine how we ended up."

Life on the streets was a very real alternative for several of the participants. Kosal summed it up in a matter-of-fact way: "I might have gone astray, sleeping on the street, or doing some jobs here and there because we had no education or knowledge of what the right or wrong things were. I might end up breaking my mother's heart because I didn't know what to do."

Even participants who were most critical of the COC, like Charaya, believe that it delivered them from serious negative consequences, which he struggles to describe dispassionately despite how it clearly distresses him, saying, "I think ah, if there is no COC, actually ah, if there is no COC, I think my life would end up to be terrible. I was growing up in a very, very negative society, growing up in a village where most people had been using drugs. . . . I was drawn into this by my friend, who ended up to be in prison. . . . So yeah, my life would end up to be terrible if I hadn't gone to live in COC."

The alternative futures that might have awaited clearly weighed on participants' minds and emerged even in answer to other, seemingly unrelated questions. Chaya, for example, finished her description of her best memory of COC by talking about what she thinks would have happened if she had stayed at home: "If I were at home, I didn't really think that I could study like I did in COC. I might have stopped studying and went to work in Thailand. I am the only one who has opportunity to study higher among my siblings. . . . I feel so sorry and pity them."

Former residents' conjectures about their possible alternative life courses were overall quite realistic, and all spoke with relief rather than regret about other paths they might have taken. Several used the word "lucky" to describe their lives, as Rotha winds up here after being asked about her "most special memory" of life in COC: "For me, I had a lot of them. . . . Every year we went for a trip, a place far away, too. In the past, when I stayed with my parents in my homeland, I didn't have an opportunity for any trip outside of my home town. So I was so lucky to be able to do that at COC. As an old saying goes, 'do good receive good.' So, I ended up with good people. It is really our fate."[11]

The participants were not just looking back with relief upon unpleasant hypotheticals, though. They were firmly oriented toward the future, in terms of looking ahead, imagining alternatives, and making them happen.

Positive Future Orientation

The children who went to live in the COC were chosen not because of their capacity for resilience but rather because of their vulnerability.[12] The NGO had identified them through poverty-reduction and education projects that are aimed at supporting and strengthening families; they were invited to live at the COC expressly because these family-based programs had proven insufficient for meeting their needs. Given that these children were therefore among the most vulnerable of the vulnerable, it was striking how consistently they expressed a positive orientation toward the future, including high levels of hopefulness along with concrete plans.

Many former residents had well-articulated career plans that were often ambitious, but realistic rather than grandiose, and responsive to the actual employment situation in Cambodia. Bopha wants to be a police officer and is focused on graduating from high school to improve her chances of being admitted to the Police Training Academy. Kosal has always had a knack for electronics—he fixed the organization's electrical problems while he was still a high school student—and now that he has graduated from high school he is enrolling in a technical postsecondary institute. Daevy attended an NGO sewing school and then advanced training and is now working in a custom tailoring shop in Siem Reap. Pich is attending cosmetology school. Rotha backs up her dream of becoming a Khmer teacher with a practical alternative plan of becoming a rural development officer.

While many Western critics have called into question the whole paradigm of education as the key to the future, and certainly Cambodia struggles with underemployment among university graduates, an educational orientation can build resilience and mitigate effects of earlier adverse experiences by orienting children toward future possibilities.[13] Attending school is also prestigious and thus benefits the self-esteem of the former residents and their families, as Sothy explained: "When I went home my grandmother always told me I have to be a teacher because my family loves teachers." In Cambodia also, social and professional networks are very important, and participation in formal education can cement relationships with a peer group that will help build the kinds of relationships that are helpful for success.

Some participants described aspirations that went beyond a stable livelihood and that, while ambitious, were entirely developmentally appropriate. Achariya, still in high school, spoke of her desire for a career in which she could travel internationally: "When I was in COC, my wings were still small but moving here [an educational project] I feel that my wings are growing bigger. Before I expected to be a teacher but I think that even though the job as a teacher gets high salary, but we always remain in the same place. My aim is to see the world wider so now I wish to be a writer. I want to be a three-language writer including Thai, English, and Khmer."

Love of learning, not just prestige or the instrumental goal of getting a good job, was also a career consideration that kept some of them faced toward the future, for instance Arunny, who said, "For me, I want to become a Khmer literature teacher because I love this subject and want to teach too." Those who were most oriented toward schooling appreciated being part of a peer group and community that shared this value, and this, along with the inherently future-focused nature of formal education, helped some of the adolescents avoid potentially destructive behaviors. When asked about her friends and what they liked to do together, Arunny was pleased to be able to state, "All my friends are clever students and no one likes going out." Similarly, Ary, when asked if she, like Botum, enjoyed playing soccer with foreign visitors, explained how she preferred activities that advanced her academic success: "For me, I don't really like football. I prefer some games that help my thinking process. For example, I like playing Khmer folk games including 'Monkey snatching leaves.' I think this game helps me a lot in the process of learning."

Their dreams are not just talk. In addition to working hard in school, many of the residents are also taking concrete steps toward futures that they have clearly put much thought into. Narith has worked hard in the hospitality industry, rising to the position of general manager for a boutique hotel before switching divisions from customer relations to sales, preparing him for his next move, which is to open his own small business. He is already saving money for that dream. Charaya, as described in his narrative above, already has a good job but is taking night classes on multimedia skills to develop an interactive website for Cambodians to learn Chinese. He expects that this enterprise will be flexible enough to enable him to accompany his partner when she goes to study abroad. His ideas, like Narith's, reflect awareness of and responsiveness to the current economic context as well as his goals for his personal life. Likewise, Prak is already laying the groundwork for the business he hopes to establish after he graduates; Rathana is already selling and making plans to expand his menu; the former residents who are still in school are all successful in their studies; and even the youngest ones who were on school holiday when I visited had prepared the information they needed to register for supplementary English classes.

The former residents' focus on the future also helps to build resilience by giving them a way to recast past unpleasant experiences in terms of future value. When Ary described at such length how early the residents rose and how hard they worked, we asked her whether that made her angry with her housemother. But she reminded herself of the long-term benefits of learning time management and developing a work ethic by responding, "No, she just wanted me to create a working habit. When I grow up, I can work better. If I never worked, when I moved to live with others, I would know nothing." The positive future orientation that emerged among the former residents dovetails with the findings of Emond, who found that orphans still living in the Cambodian orphanage she studied attributed their future orientation precisely to their status as orphans and their residence in an orphanage, which freed them from other kinds of cares and responsibilities to focus on their studies.[14]

Although the participants were well aware of, and grateful for, the way that the COC had changed the courses of their lives, many were conflicted about the amount of gratitude they might owe. The COC didn't hand them anything on a silver platter; it provided them with an opportunity to work hard in ways that increased their chances for success, and they understandably wanted their own work ethic and perseverance to be recognized and appreciated.

Individual Agency and Gratitude

Many of the participants struggled with tensions between the gratitude they believed they owed and the pride they felt in their own accomplishments. Narith, who is certain he would still be a subsistence farmer had he not gone to COC, makes clear that he is glad to have avoided that outcome. Nonetheless, he did not minimize the challenges he had surmounted while living there, especially his loneliness and homesickness as a newly arrived young boy from the countryside who had already experienced abandonment before he arrived. He struggled with gratitude for the educational opportunities provided by the COC while wanting to acknowledge his own hard work and the intelligent, intentional choices he has made. Other participants and staff singled him out for his determination and the position of respect and responsibility that he now holds, and he realizes that not every resident has been able to succeed as he has. As he explains, "I'm still thankful for COC. But if talking about what I will become if I'm with the family or what I will become with COC, it's like it's not specific. It depends on ourselves too. . . . The best thing about COC is it gives more opportunity for the children who live in the rural area, they can get the good education. Not too much, but it is enough."

Narith's reasonable concern about wanting to receive credit for his own intelligence, hard work, and sacrifices extends to a reluctance to disclose the fact that he grew up in an orphanage to the people he works with. His hesitance to reveal it is due to the widespread perception among Cambodians that orphanages provide advantages, which might imply that he had not succeeded on his own merits or that he had succeeded just because other people had felt sorry for him. Charaya elaborated on this theme, although his conclusion was different, explaining that he was proud to disclose his orphanage residence: "Everybody who is close to me knows I was growing up in the orphanage," he explains, because "people look up to you when you grow up in the orphanage actually. . . .

Because they think that you had a good education. Especially Cambodian people, when I told them I was growing up in an organization they said, 'Wow, that's why your English is really good, that's why your education is really good.'"

Kosal, who had just successfully graduated from high school, echoed this feeling of pride in his background, mixed with some concern that it could make him a target of envy, explaining, "I am so proud of what I have been through and I want to share this to everyone I know." He elaborates on Charaya's assertion that an orphanage background can inspire respect among other Cambodians by explaining that it can also be a source of envy: "I know that some people outside of the center always feel jealous of us. They think we have a better place to stay, better food to eat, and better education."

In Cambodia as in most societies, expressing gratitude is complicated; it can be a sign of good character and good manners but can also imply obligation or even inferiority. These Cambodian young people were as torn as their peers anywhere would be about the extent to which they should feel grateful for opportunities they had received. While many were unambiguously grateful, others were more ambivalent. Although he had made some very reasonable suggestions for improvement of the COC, Narith later confessed to me that he probably would never pass them along to the management because an apparent lack of gratitude would reflect badly back onto him. "If I talk bad about COC how will people in COC be thinking about me? They would be shocked. 'He's from COC. COC gave you food, COC gave you clothes, gave you education. And then talk bad about COC! What kind of person are you?'"

One way to reconcile gratitude with self-acknowledgment is shown by Rotha at the end of the preceding section—recognize it as fate, related to the Buddhist idea of merit; if you have done good, you will receive good. Most participants found that helping others was a way to assert their own agency and thereby balance their feelings of gratitude with the natural desire to take credit for their own success. This approach was encouraged by the NGO, whose Buddhist ethics focused on an interpretation of compassion that entailed social responsibility. Groups from the programs performed service activities and raised funds to support flood victims, among other ways they were encouraged to engage with the community. Empowering former residents as agents of change reminded them of the advantages they had received while giving them concrete ways to use those advantages to avoid feeling dependent or helpless. The idea of helping others, especially one's family members, was a source of pride, not just obligation, for many of the participants.

Providing care and support to one another while still living in the orphanage was another very powerful way that the residents of the COC claimed and cultivated agency, as described in chapters 5 and 6. The explicit sense of agency expressed by the participants stands in marked contrast to common narratives surrounding orphans and orphanages. As Emond has written, opinions about orphanages are "underpinned by a discourse of the passivity and vulnerability (and therefore incompetence and incompleteness) of children."[15] Dominant discourses of orphanages leave little space for the residents' own empowerment, and children within the care system "are regarded as dependent, powerless objects whose active contributions largely go unacknowledged."[16] However, the children of COC demonstrated considerable agency in the way they made use of resources and opportunities, in the way they advocated for siblings to also receive opportunities, and in their own reflections on their experiences and outcomes.

Prak, whose ambivalence was described in the preceding section, was the participant who wrestled most openly between acknowledging the role played by the COC and asserting his own agency as the leading factor in his success, and he was also explicit about his desire to give back. Unlike the residents who had left the center before completing their studies, Prak spoke of an intentional decision to stay despite the difficulties, which he has made an important part of his own personal story. Asked about the difference between his ability to stick it out and others' decisions to return home, he explained, "One reason is because of themselves, that they didn't see that this is the good place. . . . And then yeah, like, no chance, they don't have a high education so they work as a farmer now." Asked whether this trade-off was worth it for him, and whether he is glad that he isn't a farmer today like the rest of his family, he responds firmly, "Yes. I feel glad that I just stepped out a bit from my comfort zone, and I created my [own] comfort zone with this." He also explained that his motivation is partly driven by a desire to help others as he had been helped. "Ten years from now, I want to . . . have my own business and invest, and then I can help other people back. Because I used to live [on help] from a sponsor, and so I need to help others back." The desire to give back enables Prak to put himself in a position of efficacy instead of remaining a passive recipient of charity.

Other participants expressed a less ambivalent, less complicated gratitude to the COC and to individual staff. In response to the question about what he planned to tell his own son about his life in an orphanage, Rathana emphasized how COC had helped him and how the experience would help him be a better father, explaining with evident feeling, "I will tell him about how COC is, like I said, COC is like the god helped me. Yes, it is like the god, and also a very good place that taught me a lot. And now I can keep having a comfortable life . . . so I can help my kid and not bring him up too hard when he is young." When asked what he would say to the staff now if he had a chance, his answer focused more on the expression of unambiguous gratitude, rather than advice for improving the center: "I will say to them . . . I'm thankful to this place and thankful to all the staff. Yeah, this place, is good . . . and I think this place, I cannot forget it in my life."

Kosal likewise was able to embrace gratitude wholeheartedly by recognizing that everyone owes a debt of gratitude to others and that therefore success always entails the need for humility and gratitude. We had been speaking of whether anyone ever teased him about growing up in an orphanage, and while he said that they had, he attributed it to their jealousy, continuing, "I just want to say a few words to younger generations that they should not feel jealous. Wherever we go, we should remember our origins. Wherever we go, we should not forget those who have helped us when we are in need, those who gave us jobs or work to do. We should remember that gratitude and try to help one another. If a person commits a mistake, try to help and save them. Do not push them into a deep abyss."

While a criticism often levied against orphanage care is that it ruptures the bonds among family members, for many of these children the opposite was true—the COC enabled them to make the contributions to their families that they wanted to be able to make. In Cambodia and much of mainland Southeast Asia, milk debt is an expression used to describe the obligation that children owe to their parents. It accrues from birth and informs a social construction of children as active subjects who have incurred a debt that they must repay, rather than as passive vessels to be unendingly filled with parental concern. It is often a source of great perplexity to Westerners, who don't understand why children feel such strong responsibility to help parents who don't seem to have behaved responsibly toward them. But honoring the milk debt can confer young people with confidence and empower them with the knowledge that they are able to effectively fulfill their obligations.

Sothy and Achariya take for granted the fact that an outcome of studying further will include the ability to help their families and others less fortunate. They know they must balance their individual dreams with this obligation, despite the uneven care that they received from their parents, in Achariya's case a violently alcoholic father, and in Sothy's case a father who allowed his new wife to rupture their relationship. Achariya tempers her growing sense of independence by saying, "I also want to study or travel abroad, whenever I have enough money to support my family and myself." Her dream of a life of travel includes being able to "introduce our attractions and where we live to the world, in order to seek generous donors to help people who are difficult or poor. I want them to be better than me and support them." Her friend Sothy also weaves the ability to help her family into her future dreams, explaining, "After I pass the exam to be a teacher, I will return home and earn money to support my family."

Giving back and helping others is not just a way for orphans to reconcile the tension between gratitude and acknowledgment of the very real hardships and traumas that most of them had overcome. As Kosal points out above, none of us should "forget those who have helped us," and this was a value that

Kolab says she wants to pass on to her children. When asked what she would tell her own children someday about her experiences growing up in an orphanage, she said,

> If my children ask me I would answer to them that Mom faced more difficulty than you.[17] When I have children I think that my living condition will be better than now. So I would tell them that Mom faced more difficulty than you. Mom rode a bicycle to school and lived with many people, not like you because you have only me to take care of you. So I will tell them my previous experiences in order to get them to try hard and know how to help others. I will tell them that I could live because of someone's help so if you become rich, please help other people like they used to help me and like I help you too.

However, the tension between gratitude and self-acknowledgment can be uncomfortable, and among teenagers especially, gratitude was undermined by rebelliousness and the need to assert their lack of dependency on the COC. While criticisms of the center often had merit, they also were a way to demonstrate how well some of the former residents had done despite the programmatic weaknesses of the orphanage, and thus further testament to their own efficacy. For example, while Rathana above described how he would express his gratitude to the staff, Charaya's response placed him in a position to offer them management advice, which also displayed his own expertise, saying, "I think if was living in COC and I was as knowledgeable as I am now, I would talk to the NGO and the Board of Directors . . . to tell about the poor implementation of the regulations or education activities in COC."

Some practices implemented by the COC may have contributed to an internalized sense of agency among the residents. For example, there was a Children's Council of elected representatives, which tried, with varying degrees of success over the years, to involve residents in participatory decision making. It may have provided alternative ways to think about hierarchical authority structures. Charaya describes it today as something of a pro forma exercise: "At that time, we couldn't come up with a better solution, just 'Okay, agree,' 'Okay, agree,' that's all we did. So yeah we were given this opportunity to talk, but we didn't have the understanding to address it at that time." However, some positions taken by the children had real effect; for example, in 2011 the Children's Council was able to convince the staff to allow one day per week when the residents could sleep late.

Agency in the sense of proactive problem solving and intentional communication was explicitly taught at the center during its later years; this not only provided needed skills, especially for children who came from homes marked by conflict or desertion, but also enhanced children's own sense of agency in terms of their ability to navigate conflict and initiate solutions. Children affected by domestic violence often struggle with feelings of helplessness, compounded by their lack of skills in speaking up for themselves in constructive ways. As one staff member confided to me, the behavior and communication patterns of the residents could be quite challenging because of their family backgrounds. In the dialog below, Mach, who had been affected by violence at home, especially appreciated the scaffolding that her housemother provided her for learning to resolve her own disputes with others. Sothy, who also came to the COC because of intractable conflict within her family, chimes in at the end about learning how to reach out to reestablish communication after a conflict, having learned both the difficulty and the importance of proactive problem solving:

MACH: If my child asks me in the next ten years, I would answer to them that I was provided education and shelter by the organization staff and I used to live all together with many children. I will educate and advise my child like Mom used to educate me. I will teach them to always realize themselves [their feelings] and dare to accept the hurt or sadness. And then learn to think and solve the problems. Some problems I could solve by myself so I didn't need to tell Mom, but some problems I couldn't solve alone so I had to tell Mom to help me solve it.

INTERVIEWER: What was a problem that you couldn't solve by yourself?

MACH: Sometimes, when I argued with friends I couldn't solve this problem by myself. When we were angry, we wouldn't talk to each other so Mom always helped us to solve this problem. Mom always told us to talk to anyone we were angry with, so that we could get along together again.

SOTHY: Sometimes, when we talked to them first, they would think that we were the loser. But Mom always told us that it was not true and the person who talked first is the one who has value, not the loser.

To summarize then, the participants did not conform to the stereotype of institutionalized children as passive recipients of other people's charity; they actively made decisions about and negotiated the terms of their own lives and occupied positions of advocacy and support in the lives of others. Some of them were deeply interested in the respective roles of individual agency and external circumstances in their own success and struggled with how to express gratitude while saving face and acknowledging their own agency. Their responses were thoughtful and made clear that they had been thinking about this issue, even as they had no simple answers. And indeed, who does? It's one philosophers and psychologists continue to struggle with as well.

The participants' reflections share commonalities on the five themes of nuance and ambivalence, high expectations, the different turns their lives might have taken, positive orientation toward the future, and gratitude and giving back, but also reveal participants' own differences in background and temperament as well as variation in COC staffing, management, policies, and programming over time and changes in the external Cambodian context. Discipline and setting limits posed very different challenges in the eras pre—and post—cell phones, for example. Despite all this rich variation, one consistent pattern was that the interviewees' responses aligned with the overall greater receptiveness to residential care among Cambodians than among Westerners. Lacking was the polarization that accompanies discussions of orphanages in the West. As Reaskmey said philosophically, "I think whether living alone or with others, everywhere you go is always the same. So, living in the center and at home is similar. Both have some benefits and also drawbacks."

8

Discussion and Conclusions

Reprise and Response: Was the COC Good or Bad?

I did not expect, when I began this project back in 2008, that I would find many positive things to say about living in an orphanage. But I didn't have an agenda; I was simply wondering. As explained in chapter 1, I was surprised by the apparent well-being of many children in Cambodian orphanages, and so I sought to portray the details of life in one orphanage, as observed by me and as recalled by former residents, calling attention to the local and contingent nature of the different ways that children's needs can be met, and assuming a broad range of possible solutions to the same challenges. Approaching the situation with a complicated mix of curiosity, humility, and concern, I encountered an equally complicated mix of gratitude, resentment, and nostalgia. The most striking observation to emerge from the interviews was the earnestness and genuine good faith with which this group of young Cambodians engaged the same questions that I began with. What was it like growing up in an orphanage? What is the role of orphanages? What are the trade-offs involved in living there? When might an orphanage be a suitable choice? The former residents do not assume blanket, simplistic, one-size-fits-all approaches. They weigh benefits and drawbacks, sometimes in the same breath, and they balance disadvantages against the very real challenges that they faced while living with their families, challenges that many Cambodians continue to face. The depth and nuance that they brought to their reflections were inspiring and deeply touching. Yes some of the participants are adamant that they will never, under any circumstances, place their children in an orphanage, but yes too, even the most adamant recognize and are grateful for the fact that they have a better life than they would have had because someone made that wrenching choice for them.

Public discourses on orphanages, in Cambodia and elsewhere, are not always graced with a similar level of reflectiveness. In the scandal-reform cycle of child welfare policy and programs, we are always in danger of fighting the last war. It is indisputable that the Indian boarding schools will forever be a stain on the conscience of my own country, echoed today in the disgraceful forced separation and caging of children on our southern border. Australia similarly is still struggling with how to address the damage done to its own Stolen Generation. But the former residents I interviewed were not forcibly or fraudulently separated from their families. They often missed their families when they were staying at the orphanage, but they also missed the orphanage when they were staying with their families.

Nor did I begin this project planning to resolve the question of whether orphanages are good or bad. Indeed, throughout much of the project I had been hoping to sidestep that question and merely describe, as carefully as I could, the daily lives of children growing up in one Cambodian orphanage. My intention was thus to add to our understanding of one particular kind of childhood that was common during one particular period in Cambodia's rich history. My contributions to policy, if any, I believed, would lie in the descriptive, empirical approach I was taking, having already noted that much of the debate is long on ideological assumptions and short on evidence. However, events got away from me, and it became impossible to talk about an orphanage in Cambodia without addressing the larger context of the orphanage boom, the role of foreign volunteers and donors, and the question of whether all this was good or bad for Cambodia's children and Cambodian society. So are orphanages good or bad? Or phrased more carefully and appropriately, was it, on balance, more helpful or more harmful for children to have lived at the COC?

I have concluded that most of the critiques that are levied against orphanages, presented in chapter I, fail to align with the lived experience of the children residing in the COC. There *are* legitimate alternatives to the narrative of orphanages as the bleak institutions widespread in stereotype and fiction. Practices, not labels like "orphanage," are what have the most consequence for children's well-being, and practices can vary widely. Orphanages are culturally embedded and distinct to the social environments in which they are found.

A more important response though is that evaluations of care quality for children inevitably rely on implicit assumptions about values rather than objectively delineated criteria. Take for example the charge that orphanages are overly regimented. Certainly many of the residents, especially as teenagers, resisted the structure and rules imposed in the center. Does that mean it was overly regimented? These complaints reflect changing expectations that are increasingly being voiced by Cambodian teenagers growing up in families as well.[1] But more importantly, the term "overly" is completely subjective—what is the correct amount of structure? Structure and consistency can be therapeutic for children who come from turbulent backgrounds.[2] This issue of the inherent subjectivity of relative terms such as "overly" highlights the larger problem with much of the orphanage critique—as first proposed in chapter I, opinions about the ideal childhood are inherently subjective and based as much on values as they are on objective facts about human development.

The subjectivity inherent in assessing the quality of care is part of the broader issue of subjectivity about the very nature of childhood itself. As Wang has written, "Children's 'best interests' are not universal, but are instead shaped by the surrounding context and access to resources."[3] For example, overly rigid application of the bright line separating childhood from adulthood at age eighteen might result in residents being inadequately prepared to leave the orphanage and live on their own, based on the observation that residents often continue to stay on well into adulthood.[4] However, school drop-out and grade repetition rates are so high in Cambodia that it is not unheard of for youth over the age of eighteen to still be in junior high school. In 2008 and 2009, when I asked staff at four orphanages I visited, including the COC, what happened when children turned eighteen, they expressed pride in their commitment to permit youth to stay on as long as it took for them to be able to support themselves, usually after finishing school or vocational training. But as the Cambodian government worked closely with international organizations to regulate orphanages, increased pressure was put on them to implement policies banning eighteen-year-olds from residence. By 2011, most orphanage staff were reluctant to confirm with me that youth over the age of eighteen would be permitted to stay on and were instead eager to discuss their plans for a separate youth house or other arrangements for older residents. But, it would be entirely normal for an unmarried Cambodian twentysomething to still live in their family home, and as long as youth are in school, they need a supportive environment in which to live and learn. More to the point though, I was pleasantly surprised at how well the COC's former residents seemed to adapt to living outside the orphanage.

Similarly, the criticism that residential care is more expensive than family-based care is often taken as a truism, but it is a truism that conceals many hidden assumptions. First and foremost, cost should not supplant care quality as the primary policy consideration. Additionally, cost comparisons are often made in an "apples versus oranges" kind of way, and indeed it would be difficult to construct an absolute equivalence between foster care and residential care so that an accurate comparison could be made. Foster care funding even in wealthy societies is almost invariably inadequate, and so to then say that it is cheaper is hardly saying much.[5] As Cohen points out, foster care shortages exist widely across the United States, and foster care is cheaper than congregate care partly because foster care stipends are often insufficient to guarantee the kind of care that children need. Describing foster care providers she has known, she writes, "I have seen such caregivers dip into the stipend to pay their own expenses, run out of gas by the end of the month, fail to get children to appointments."[6] More importantly, absolute cost is not as important as whether or not anyone is willing to pay for it. If foreign donors are willing to contribute to orphanages, then orphanages may be cheaper for Cambodian society, regardless of absolute cost.

Rights-based critiques arose after most orphanages in the United States were closed and have largely replaced a distaste for regimentation with concern that orphanages violate children's human rights. While in principle all rights should be coequal and inalienable and none should be prioritized over any other, dominant discourses primarily focus on the ways that orphanages violate the child's right to a family and the ways that foreign visitors violate the child's right to dignity. But while it is indisputably true that many COC residents had living parents or other relatives, they were not always suitable or willing to care for the children. Many families instead prioritized the child's right to educational opportunity more than the right to live under the same roof with kin, and it makes sense that the right to education might become paramount when educational opportunities are unavailable. The two participants who spoke in their interviews quite regretfully and movingly about how they felt alienated from their families still believed that on balance their lives were better for having gone to live in the orphanage. The COC management believed that it was supporting the children's right to a family by helping them to maintain connections with relatives. Some of the residents recalled feeling hurt and disappointed by family members who didn't visit regularly, but this was on their relatives, not on the center staff. Certainly it was the case that transportation challenges made visits difficult, but some missed family visits were down to family members who just didn't show up. As discussed in chapter 7, several of the children explained that living separately from their families did not mean that their right to a family had been violated because studying further and hopefully getting a well-paying job would enable them to help their families in the long term. For families that are suffering, orphanage care can be even less distressing than non-kin foster care because the children can retain primary loyalty to their families, and it can result in greater stability and less changing of care arrangements than foster care does.[7] In unstable households, children themselves can be a major stressor, and sometimes just knowing their children are safe is all a parent needs from them.

The criticism that foreign-supported orphanages habituate children to foreign norms and alienate them from their culture is also at heart values-laden. I once discussed this issue with a member of the COC's leadership team, asking him whether he worried that they were socializing the children into an un-Cambodian lifestyle or expectations about a standard of living they could never realistically hope to achieve. He was actually quite offended, wondering why feeling comfortable interacting with people from other cultures, pursuing higher education, and dreaming of a nice house, stable lifestyle, and a good job in the city were somehow "culturally inappropriate" or "un-Cambodian," just because the children came from poverty or remote rural areas. Even former residents who in the interviews expressed regret because they felt alienated or distanced from their families admitted that they were glad they weren't going to end up as subsistence farmers.

Orphanages are accused of marginalizing vulnerable Cambodian children by removing them from their family and community networks and placing them in a presumably stigmatizing situation. However, my own research has revealed that stigma is not the problem for orphanages in Cambodia that it may be in other societies, and additionally the children who came to the COC were already quite marginalized in their previous living situations. Living there did not necessarily marginalize them further, and in many ways it helped integrate them and enhanced their standing in their communities.[8]

This research supports the position that visitors and volunteers can play a valuable role in enhancing residents' short-term and long-term well-being. The former COC residents were far more enthusiastic about foreign visitors and volunteers than one might expect from the widespread criticisms of voluntourism in the scholarly and popular press, and there was no evidence of harm caused by visitors. As discussed in chapter I, a leading concern about volunteers and visitors is their effect on children's development of healthy attachment capacities. However, attachment theory simply is not relevant to most children who reside in Cambodian orphanages because almost all the COC children began their residence past the age at which they could be considered vulnerable to disordered attachment. The few who joined the center as infants or toddlers were enthusiastically cared for by the staff and other residents, so they received an abundance of affection and attention. There are certainly good reasons to be careful when allowing visitors and volunteers to interact with children living in orphanages, but fear of disordered attachment was not a concern for the COC. Participants said they had gained as much from the volunteers as the volunteers had gained from them, and while they were usually sad to see the volunteers leave, this didn't seem to dampen their enthusiasm for new visitors or for the idea of visitors in general. Is it really possible, or even desirable, to protect children from all experiences that will make them feel sad? Certainly the children in the COC had already experienced more sadness than one would ever want a child to endure. On the other hand, the visitors also brought real joy into their lives.

Neither did the interviews reveal concerns about violation of children's dignity or commodification of them by volunteers. As I have written elsewhere, the concern about commodification of children in orphanages is not straightforward because intimacy and economics do not fall into mutually exclusive spheres. While in the abstract we may believe that intimacy is incompatible with monetary considerations, people regularly blend intimacy and economic activity. For many families, children's contributions to the household economy are "woven into the fabric of daily life."[9] As Zelizer has pointed out, family members "sustain each other's lives, not with love alone, but with concrete contributions to their joint material welfare."[10] For their part, staff complained to me about families that pressured their children to leave the orphanage so they could put them to work.

None of the residents expressed feeling violated by the intrusion of foreign visitors into their home; the physical layout of the COC may have mitigated this, since there were plenty of pleasant open-air common spaces in which to socialize and play, and visitors were not allowed inside the children's houses. Another practice that is widely criticized as a violation of children's dignity is the dance performances given for tourists, a practice that the COC had halted by the time I started visiting in 2008. However, the one resident who mentioned the public performances expressed nostalgia for them. In addition, the performance skills had some tangible benefits—two former residents were able to use their performance skills to support their studies, and two others are now working as professional musicians.

Whether or not visitors were wasting the children's time with games and songs is another subjective, values-based assessment. The children certainly enjoyed it, and additionally they reported that they found it beneficial. Language learning through song and play is pedagogically sound, and immersion works. In any case though, why shouldn't they get to play?

Charges of fraudulent placement and "paper orphaning" underlie much of the recent debate over whether orphanage tourism constitutes modern slavery.[11] The COC however did not make fraudulent claims to families about providing access to educational opportunity, and all participants agreed that their access to schooling was greater in the center than it would have been had they stayed with their families, although some stated that it should have been greater still. The center staff likewise never made fraudulent claims to foreigners about the children's life histories, and in particular never claimed that all of the children's parents were deceased.[12] There was more demand than capacity for places in the orphanage, and they didn't need to misrepresent themselves in order to attract residents.

Another common criticism is that too many orphanages in Cambodia are private or run by NGOs or other organizations rather than by the government and, further, that some of the private ones are for-profit enterprises, enrolling children simply in order to attract foreign donations. While it is true that the COC was supported almost entirely by foreign donors, it was not operated for a profit. Even though more families were drawn to it than there were spaces available, it would be absurd to hold the COC responsible for the root causes that made families think that it would be a good place for their children. It's simply magical thinking to believe that if the COC and other orphanages didn't exist, hostile stepparents would automatically welcome their stepchildren, migrating parents would immediately come back from Thailand, violent alcoholics would suddenly go on the wagon, or Cambodia's educational system would somehow become able to adequately serve all children living in remote rural areas. Furthermore, the assumption that state-run orphanages are somehow automatically better than private ones is an idea that generates contempt among people who have visited the state-run orphanage in Siem Reap. A former orphanage worker I spoke with said, "The Cambodian government has a center for children, but it's very terrible also. . . . You've seen?" Having also visited it, I had to agree. It compared so unfavorably that some staff from NGO orphanages, both Cambodians as well as foreigners, went there to volunteer and give donations.

The evidence for corruption invoked more perplexity than outrage for me. In two interviews, the former residents spoke of corruption at the COC, but in ways that were completely different from what I had expected. One participant spoke of a beloved staff member who had been accused of corruption, but believed that the kindness and competence shown by this staff member outweighed the possible diversion of resources for personal gain. Management confirmed to me that at times there had been problems with staff diverting cash to their own pockets, but their response had been to carefully monitor the care provided to the children to make sure they were not suffering as a result, for example by closely watching to ensure that the children were receiving adequate amounts of expensive foodstuffs. Although they tried to verify costs with suppliers as much as possible, they were philosophical about the impossibility of tracking the actual costs of fresh foods or other items purchased in the local market, and felt that as long as the children's care was not compromised, there was not really a lot they could do about it. The other accusation of corruption was also not what I expected because it involved favoritism regarding who was admitted to the orphanage, rather than any siphoning of funds for personal gain. Friends or relatives of staff were able to get their child a place at the orphanage, said one participant, even if other children were more needy.

"An Orphanage" or *Orphanages*?

The goal of this book has been to describe life in an orphanage, just one orphanage, situated in a particular time and place. However, I wish for this work to do more than provide yet another anthropological veto. The debate that rages is characterized by blanket statements about "all orphanages" and easily falls prey to nominalist fallacies equating very different kinds of settings simply because they are all referred to by the term "orphanage." Too often crucial qualifiers are left unsaid in statements such as "a family will always be better for a child than an orphanage."[13] Clearly, for this to be true the family needs to be non-neglectful and non-abusive. And yet when this is pointed out, the rejoinder is too often "well, of course, that goes without saying. I meant a normal family." However, many families are neglectful and abusive, and so it cannot go without saying. Allowing the anti-orphanage position to set the terms of the debate in this way makes it difficult to approach the topic with the necessary nuance, and it makes it hard for the growing body of literature describing evidence of good orphanages to gain a toehold in the public debate.

Because the debate over the consequences of orphanage residence favors blanket, un-nuanced solutions, policy responses are also rigid, echoing similarly ideologically and affectively fraught issues, such as sex work and the debate over whether abolition or legal regulation is the more appropriate response. The pressure put on small NGOs to implement all-or-nothing policy responses is especially problematic because they are often closer to the ways issues take shape in local communities. One NGO worker, a friend who worked in the area of domestic abuse prevention, confided in me that their organization had been pressured to sign a declaration that they would never rely on orphanage care, even though the staff didn't agree with it. In their efforts to provide support for struggling families, sometimes they found that family preservation was not appropriate and that children needed to live elsewhere for their own safety. "Alternative care, they say," this staff person complained, "but there isn't anywhere to go. All the neighbors already have children, grandma is old and she's sick. I would take, but I have two of my own, and I have to work. What are we supposed to do?" However, as a small organization, they could not raise these objections publicly.

Observations and Residents' Later Recollections in the Interviews Mostly Corresponded

In large part, the interviews with the former residents and my own observations corresponded and confirmed each other, supporting the conclusion that both are methodologically sound and can be used in research and program evaluation to gain real insights. In particular, my earlier conclusion that the center provided good-quality care and that residents' social, educational, health, and material needs were well met was corroborated by participants' own reports. My assessments of the children when they were young, concluding that they did not show signs of emotional blunting or apathy, that they experienced a full range of positive as well as negative emotions, that they had learned to self-regulate effectively, and that overall they were active, healthy, and developing appropriately, were also all confirmed by interviews and interactions with them as teenagers and adults.

My observations were most strikingly contradicted in two areas—the children's memories of punishments meted out by staff and the attitudes surrounding teenagers. I did not witness any corporal punishment and assumed the center's policy against corporal punishment was being effectively enforced. However, both staff and residents agreed that corporal punishment occurred, although it declined over the years as enforcement of the policy became more successful through staff education and selective hiring. With respect to teenagers, most of the serious tensions occurred after I had ceased my daily observations, as the cohorts that I knew as children hit their teens. An additional limitation was that I didn't have the opportunity to observe the older residents as much as the younger ones because they were in school all day and because I was not permitted to spend the night at the center.

Criteria for Measuring Care Quality Need to Be Clarified and Interrogated

In the interviews it became clear that there was a mismatch between my assessment of care quality, which I based on the daily care provided, and some of the residents' assessments, which were based on employment outcomes. One orphanage director in Siem Reap (not affiliated with the COC) was fond of saying in public presentations that their organization was raising "the next generation of leaders in Cambodia," through intensive educational and other support of children from poor backgrounds. While this is setting a very high bar, it is one that is shared by many Cambodians, including some orphanage residents themselves.

Simply enabling residents to attend school regularly, a primary goal of the COC founders, was not sufficient, according to several of the residents, even though it already advantaged most of them relative to their previous lives and their village peers. Most were the first members of their families to study beyond primary level, and they needed effective motivation and intensive support, not just access as they moved through their teen years and activities other than studying seemed more attractive. Some children complained about strictly enforced studying and homework, but in order to succeed in Cambodia's increasingly unequal society, such intensive efforts may be necessary, even if it comes at the expense of free time and engenders resentment among teenagers, who often do not yet understand the significance of schooling.

It is important to be explicit about the goals of any residential program—is it enough for residents to have safe and healthy childhoods, and to learn positive communication and discipline styles so that they can provide a stable, supportive home for their own children? Or do they need to be provided the intensive supports that will scaffold their entry into a middle-class lifestyle? When teenagers resist attending school and doing homework, should they be obliged to do these things anyway, or should they be permitted to disengage educationally? Again, this is a matter of values that need to be made clear.

In general, what matters to adults may not be salient or important to children. Just as material well-being, which has figured so prominently in the controversies surrounding orphanages, did not figure prominently in the interviews with former residents, so too were some of the concerns expressed by the residents not ones that have been of great concern in the literature. Several residents complained about the skimpy attire of foreign volunteers, or were most impressed by how they disposed of trash, but didn't say anything about the issue of commodification that adult narratives of volunteer tourism focus on. One of the most vivid memories of several former residents is of how they had been made to wear underpants for the first time at the orphanage and how much they hated it. Several mentioned this, but none mentioned feeling that they had been kept in the orphanage against their will.

Orphanages Can Support Families Even
as They Physically Separate Them

As was revealed in the interviews, many of the children retained a close bond and sense of responsibility to their families, even as they embraced the opportunities and relationships provided by the orphanage. They recognized that their orphanage residence reduced financial and emotional pressures on their families, and two unrelated participants reported that leaving their family had motivated their abusive alcoholic fathers to stop drinking. Several interviewees were proud that the opportunities provided by the center would enable them to earn enough as adults to provide financial support for their families of origin. Regret about feeling alienated from their families was tempered by the knowledge that their families had sought their placement out of a desire to give them a better life. The issue of family separation is a case where it is especially important not to overgeneralize; some children regretted feeling distanced from their families, but others were relieved to be living at a safe distance from relationships that had already alienated them.

Paid Staff and Residents Can Have Real Feelings for Each Other

It is common in the orphanage literature to treat paid staff like props or like part of the background, to focus on their perceived inadequacies, or to ignore them altogether, rather than to approach them as human beings with their own aspirations, issues, and insights, for both themselves as well as the children in their care. This reflects widespread suspicion about entrusting children to staff who are "only doing it for the money," and ambivalence more generally about paid performance of so-called women's work. And yet their role is vital and their perspectives critical.[14] The misgivings about paid child care in the West, especially in the United States, occlude appreciation of the fact that many of the COC staff sincerely cared about the children and took pride in their ability to improve the children's lives. Staff expressed some frustration and even hurt at the way they are often portrayed as corrupt or inherently second best, despite what they see as irresponsible or even abusive behavior taking place in children's families, and their own sense that they often must work hard to undo damage that has been done to children while in their relatives' care.

Interviews with both staff and residents revealed many examples of deep, sincere affection between the two. Profound grief was expressed over the deaths of two residents, one from leukemia and one in a motorcycle accident in his home village, and the death memorials observed for them every year thereafter have been genuine and moving. Some of the efforts made by staff to express love for the residents in tangible ways were touching. A decade later, Charaya recalled with wonder the staff member who set his alarm clock early every day so he could go to every house and awaken the children personally at the already-early hour of four thirty. Similarly, Mach recounted how her housemother smiled back when residents pouted and ignored her, winning back their affection even when they were furious with her. Much of the structure that was perceived by some children as rigid and uncaring was from the staff members' perspective the result of deep caring and worry over children who were, after all, objectively at risk for serious threats to health and well-being. "We care for them," said one, "but they are not ours. It's hard. Risky." They understood that the teenaged residents resented their policies as too strict, and cell phone usage became a constant battle, but the motorcycle accident in which one resident was killed served as a constant reminder of what can happen when adults are not protective enough. "You know, we love them," said one longtime staff person. "We don't want them to get hurt." While families who struggle to control their willful adolescents sometimes threaten to take them to live in an orphanage, orphanage staff believe they have to be more strict because they are responsible for someone else's children.

While much of the criticism of staff focuses on haphazard care, for their part staff eagerly took advantage of professional development opportunities addressing specialized care, such as for children who had survived domestic violence. "The violence ones we don't know," explained one. "Staff really have no capacity with that but just base on our good heart, compassion . . . I think everyone one of us that work there has a very big heart with the children."

Some "Orphanage Issues" Are Really "Pre-orphanage Issues"

It is important to distinguish living in an orphanage from the reasons children are placed there. When children in an orphanage are observed or interviewed at a single moment in time, it's difficult to sort out which feelings and behaviors derive from the orphanage itself and which are a result of the children's lives before the orphanage. As mentioned in chapter 4, we had originally planned to ask participants about their lives prior to placement, but this question proved to be so distressing that after the first two interviews we stopped asking it. But it was events that occurred before moving to the orphanage that sparked the participants' distress, not their lives in the orphanage itself. Since children enter care later in Cambodia, they have had more years to experience abuse and neglect while living in their families of origin.

While poverty is nominally the reason many children are sent to orphanages, to say that children are sent to orphanages just because they are poor is overly simplified. I noticed in the interviews that saying something like "my family was very poor and couldn't afford to send me to school" was often a face-saving way to avoid getting into the real details of their lives before the orphanage. Violence, addiction, desertion, disease, and death often accompanied the extreme poverty that most of them had experienced, but they were understandably reluctant to go into the details, and referring to family poverty was an appropriate way for them to deflect the question.

Because many of the issues that lead to orphanage placement remain unaddressed, it is important to look beyond quantitative measures of success such as how many children have been returned to families and communities. While the Cambodian government was applauded for setting a goal of moving one-third of orphanage residents to family-based by the end of 2018, such narrow criteria do not reveal the ensuing "scramble" to provide appropriate care for children when they are abruptly removed from orphanages, or the frustration of families who still find themselves unable to provide the educational access and support that their children were receiving in some orphanages.[15]

The challenges of returning children to family care in Cambodia are exacerbated by the same factors that led to the orphanage boom in the first place, and unfortunately, some of the tools that are used in wealthier societies to enhance the availability of family- and community-based care are not widely available in Cambodia. For example, stipends to defray the costs of a foster child are not sufficiently available in Cambodia. Similarly, supports such as home visits are difficult; in 2017 Cambodia's Ministry of Social Affairs still had only seventeen social workers on staff, for a population of around seventeen million; transportation infrastructure likewise is a barrier to home visits.[16]

An Orphanage Can Become a Home

Regardless of whether or not one believes that orphanages can ever be in children's best interests, once orphanages are established, it's important to be cautious about how they are disestablished. After children have lived in an orphanage for several years, that orphanage is their home. Since stability and permanence are considered to be inherently desirable for children, terminating orphanage care is not something to be taken lightly. This is particularly true when children are being returned to families who are unprepared to care for them or who previously rejected or abused them.

For better or for worse, the COC was home, a real home, for many of the children for many years. They developed meaningful relationships in the orphanage and the surrounding community, and important memories are woven into the site itself. Closing it and separating the children resulted in feelings of sadness for many of them and in true anguish for some.

More Effort Needs to Be Put into Taking Advantage of the Benefits Volunteers Have to Offer

Staff and residents at the COC recognized the complex trade-offs involved in relying on volunteers, and the interviews showed how addressing potential problems with volunteers, rather than restricting them altogether, can provide residents with advantages, especially in the area of language learning. Volunteers are sometimes disparaged for emphasizing a repetitive repertoire of games and songs. As Reas describes, "The 'head-shoulders-knees- and-toes brigade' or the 'if-you're-happy-and-you-know-it crowd' were ironically referenced by NGO workers and expatriates."[17] However, language learning through songs and games can be very effective, and repetition is necessary for learning. The interviews showed how volunteers can provide a host of benefits independent of formal curriculum and structure, such as confidence, motivation, attention, and accurate pronunciation models. I noticed a decline in English skills after foreign volunteers dwindled, and I witnessed firsthand the low quality of the local teaching staff that replaced them. One surprise that emerged from the interviews was that the residents actually preferred visits that consisted of a van load of enthusiastic young volunteers who came for a short visit, and whose contributions consisted mainly of playing games like soccer with the residents.[18] Several singled this out as their preferred interaction. This suggests that it might also be timely to retreat from the very strong arbitrary restrictions on length of duration of volunteer experiences that have increasingly been encouraged.

Education Is a Fraught but Still Valid Target for Success

The value of formal education is controversial with good reason. Education is not a panacea, and it is too often invoked formulaically as a solution for the entire host of challenges facing people living in poverty. In Cambodia as elsewhere in the world, broader social and macroeconomic conditions, combined with a kind of education arms race, mean that even getting children successfully through public school may not be sufficient to prepare them for university or for a well-paying job. The proliferation of private schools and tutoring services that increasingly attract Cambodian parents makes education a potential engine of inequality in Cambodia just as it can be in the United States.[19]

All that said, higher educational attainment improves one's chances of earning a comfortable livelihood in Cambodia. In addition, the interviews revealed that for these young people, education matters for lots of different reasons, not all of them economic. *They* define success in terms of formal educational attainment. All speak respectfully of those who have graduated from high school or enrolled in universities, and their own educational successes are a source of self-confidence and pride. Education is inherently tied to a positive future orientation, and educational aspirations kept them hopeful and optimistic and provided an incentive for attending to their well-being in other ways, such as resisting drug and alcohol use or early marriage. School also provides social opportunities and peer groups that helped to broaden their worldviews and social horizons.

Orphanages Can Cultivate Agency and Self-Efficacy

The characteristics of agency and self-efficacy are associated with resilience but are generally considered to be lacking among orphanage-raised youth. However, throughout the interviews with the COC former residents, I was repeatedly impressed with what an accomplished, ambitious, responsible, and self-reflective group of young people I was talking to. They made plans and acted upon them, they were respected and appreciated as colleagues and employees, they anticipated and solved problems, and they had realistic, concrete, and ambitious aspirations for the future.

Other Residents Can Mitigate Structural Neglect and Other Deficiencies

Other children have the potential to provide continuity of relationships as well as to perform care tasks and can help mitigate deficiencies in the staff. Although we did not specifically ask in the interviews about relationships with other residents, they came up spontaneously in ways that corroborated my observations of the importance of child-child interaction. Other residents provided significant levels of care, served as accessible role models, and provided companionship and stimulation. Caring for younger children may also give residents preparation for their roles as parents, and even events remembered negatively, such as quarrels, might help children develop self-regulation and interpersonal skills, like empathy and conflict management skills. Many of the former residents remain in contact, and some are close friends, providing them with a social network that can provide support and mutual benefits.

The contributions made to children's well-being by positive peer relationships may be a distinctive feature of the COC, or of Cambodian orphanages more generally. In contrast, when residential care is considered a last resort option, such as in the United States, it usually occurs only after one or more failed foster care placements, so that children with a history of behavior issues, often also having endured abuse and neglect, are concentrated in the presence of other children with similar histories.[20] This inevitably creates a very different human environment from the one children experienced at the COC.

Norms of Childhood Are Changing

I regularly heard anecdotes about even well-off parents who threaten to send their children to an orphanage as a way to control defiant behavior and enforce family rules.[21] However, the COC struggled with setting limits as well. Residents' resentment about authoritarian discipline and the management's struggles to find alternative modes of discipline while enforcing the rule against corporal punishment both mirror a broader dispute about the nature of the adult-child relationship, which is changing everywhere. As Gordon has written, "One of the most transcultural markers of what historians call modernity has been an ethical, or at least discursive, prioritizing of children's welfare. . . . There is no question that the dominant modern norm puts children in the privileged position."[22] Norms are changing, and orphanage residents, as recipients of NGO-sponsored rights workshops, in addition to media portrayals and interactions with foreign visitors, are often well versed in, and positively inclined toward, modern models of discipline and participation that are very different from the ones that have been prevalent historically in Cambodia.

This tension surrounding changing norms of childhood, especially expectations for teenagers, was the largest source of criticism of the COC among the participants, and several recalled staff who relied too often on harsh discipline rather than explanation and reasoning. Staff also expressed confusion and ambivalence about changing childhood norms, exacerbated by their own anxieties about being responsible "for other people's children." Their assumption that residents should respect and obey staff and follow center rules clashed with residents' desire to be consulted and motivated rather than dictated to. Staff described intense frustration trying to enforce even rules that they saw as clearly in the residents' best interests. For example, although orphanages in Cambodia have been criticized for not delivering on promises of increased educational opportunities, COC staff sometimes found it impossible to convince teenagers to take their studies seriously.

The criticisms voiced by participants about harsh discipline and corporal punishment by residential staff were corroborated by managerial staff I spoke with. They were sympathetic to the complaints and explained that it was something they had worked hard to improve over the years. Although the center always had an explicit "no corporal punishment" policy, it was sometimes very hard to enforce because corporal punishment has such widespread acceptance in Cambodia. The interviews with later cohorts of residents show that the center was increasingly effective in preventing care staff from resorting to physical punishment, but particularly in the early years it was a problem. Trainings and workshops on topics like positive discipline and child development were helpful, and later cohorts described their appreciation for some positive conflict resolution strategies they had been taught or that had been used with them.

Residents also complained that staff didn't differentiate enough between children and teenagers. It is telling that former residents, but not staff, used the term "adults" to refer to older youth in residence. The legal age of majority in Cambodia is sixteen, but in the NGO community of which the COC is a member, the hard boundary of eighteen years has been formalized by the UN Convention on the Rights of the Child.[23] Historically, when marriage occurred soon after puberty, there was little time for teenagerhood as a discrete life stage, and both staff and residents struggled with how to navigate this new space opened up between childhood and adulthood. This resulted in considerable confusion, hurt, and anger over how the teenaged residents should be treated, compounded by the fact that even some residents over the age of eighteen continued to live there so that they could finish school. At the time of the big push to return orphanage residents to their families of origin, youth were given considerable decision-making power, but what some later said was insufficient discussion about all the ramifications. Several said that staff should have done more to mentor them as they were making these largely irreversible decisions about their futures at what they recognized in retrospect as very young ages.

The organization's focus on traditional codes of behavior caused challenges especially for girls. Romantic or sexual relationships were strictly forbidden to the residents, but some reported feeling that this policy was enforced in a non-empathetic, heavy-handed way. From the organization's perspective, they could not afford to have a scandal involving one of their residents, and they believed, quite reasonably, that residents would have plenty of time to explore romantic relationships after they had completed their schooling. However, norms about relationships and dating are changing rapidly in Cambodia, and some residents believed, also quite reasonably, that it was normal and appropriate for teenagers to want to explore relationships. The strict no-relationship rule gave neither staff nor residents any tools for dealing with adolescent exploration and infatuation; residents felt they were forced to clandestinely break the rules, at some risk to themselves, and staff felt they were forced to expel transgressors or to make only half-hearted attempts to convince them to stay when the government was encouraging them to return to their families of origin anyway. Contrary to widespread allegations in the media of orphanages that kept youth in residence against their will, it was often with a sigh of relief that COC staff accommodated rebellious teenagers' wishes to return to live with their relatives.

The cohort of children that grew up in the COC was also the first in Cambodia to have access to technology, especially cell phones. Although many of the staff themselves were early adopters of cell phones and the internet, they were reluctant to give in to residents' desire to use these devices. This clash, familiar to anyone parenting in the twenty-first century, was made even more fraught by the fact that the residents used cell phones to stay in touch with their families and communities of origin. While staff were very accommodating in letting residents use center phones to speak with relatives, residents did not find this to be a satisfactory solution, especially when their families often bought them cell phones precisely so they could stay in touch more regularly.

The conflict over cell phones is an example of broader tensions between orphanage staff and the families of origin, which at times felt like the conflict between the weekend parent and the custodial parent in U.S. divorce cases. Staff complained about the indulgence and lack of limits on residents when they visited home, undermining the strict rules they nonetheless felt they had to enforce. On the other hand, who cannot sympathize with the families who wanted to treat the children like "kings on the shelf" (in the words of one disgruntled staff member) on the rare occasions when they returned home? Families felt that it was their right to pamper the children and the orphanage's job to discipline them. But staff spoke of their frustration with the attitudes, language, and behavior that residents challenged them with after visits home. They were especially disturbed by relatives who relied on the orphanage to care for younger children but then encouraged older children to return when they were able to contribute to the household by working.

Conclusion

To summarize, most of the criticisms levied against orphanages in Cambodia lack weight when applied to the COC, based on my own observations as well as my interviews with former residents and staff. The COC provided good care to children who needed it. More importantly, though, how we define good, bad, and success often depends on subjective values more than objective criteria. I believe, and most of the former residents and staff agreed, that the COC was the best option available to most of these children at the time they were placed; further, once they had lived there, the challenges posed by moving them, along with the fact that many of the issues that caused their placement in the first place remained unresolved, meant that staying in the orphanage was probably a better option than moving them somewhere else.

The orphanage boom in Cambodia represents a singular moment in Cambodia's rich history, when a confluence of factors all converged to create a rush toward residential care, suddenly, in a place where it had previously been uncommon. Already many of the social trends that facilitated the rise in orphanages have crested and are in decline—birth rates are going down, as is the number of women living alone with children; women's expressed desire for family planning is finally being met; the HIV/AIDS epidemic has been controlled; and the demographic hole where the COC children's grandparents should have been is being refilled as the war generation ages and early mortality declines. The instabilities of the war decades are receding into the past. Social services and public consciousness are tackling issues such as domestic violence, gambling, drug use, and alcoholism, and slowly but surely the education system and school attendance are improving, even in rural areas. Likewise, although it caught everyone by surprise, tourism to Siem Reap declined dramatically in 2019 and all but ceased with the COVID-19 pandemic in 2020. These unanticipated developments, along with the very intensive anti-orphanage-tourism campaign, have led to a noticeable decline in orphanages and in the donations and volunteering that contributed to their rise. Cambodia's orphanage boom is over.

The decline of orphanages has also been accelerated by active efforts to end them. On December 18, 2019, the UN General Assembly officially condemned orphanage care. The Resolution on the Rights of the Child, with a key focus on children without parental care, began with the familiar emphasis on the child's right to be cared for by family members and reiterated the principle that "the child, for the full and harmonious development of his or her personality, should grow up in a family environment, in an atmosphere of happiness, love and understanding." It recommends a manageable transition period for states to phase out institutionalization but prohibits funding even to maintain existing institutions because "funding for institutions can exacerbate unnecessary family-child separation and the institutionalization of children."[24] It states, "No new institutions may be built, nor may old institutions be renovated beyond the most urgent measures necessary to safeguard residents' physical safety . . . new residents should not enter in place of those that leave." The adoption of the resolution was accompanied by the same kinds of absolutist statements that have long characterized public discourses on orphanages. For example, Hope and Homes for Children issued a statement confirming that "the adoption of the Resolution at the UN General Assembly underlines what we've known for a long time, that children never belong in orphanages, they always belong in a family."[25] Similarly, Save the Children applauded the resolution, reiterating their stance that "an orphanage is no place for children to grow up," and Bethany Christian Services' endorsement stated that "children need the kind of nurturing love of families not the four walls of orphanages."[26] In other words, the consensus continues that there is something inherent about orphanages that is harmful to children, rather than particular care practices or characteristics, and there is something inherent about families, regardless of the quality of care that they provide, that is automatically beneficial for children.

The COC now sits empty and silent. It's still lovely, with cheerfully painted buildings and lush plantings in a peaceful rural setting. We used to joke that the organization could support all its programs easily if they would just turn it into a resort, and the NGO now actually has plans to do just that. It's a valuable piece of property, and for now they are growing crops on it, but when the road from Siem Reap is finally improved, they will allow tourists to stay overnight and partake in wellness activities such as meditation, massage, bike rides through the countryside, dance and yoga in the pavilion, and healthy Cambodian meals in the dining hall. No doubt its history as a former orphanage will add to its appeal for foreign tourists. As one of the former residents said excitedly when I told him about this plan, "That will pay for everything from now on! All their projects!"

The UN resolution is likely to cause more countries to remove orphanages from the suite of child care options available, although in unsettled times orphanages are likely to arise and grow spontaneously, as they always have in humanitarian crises such as the massing of refugees in the 1980s along the Thai border, where the roots of many Cambodian orphanages lie.[27] If this book has to have a single take-home message, it is this: We need to move beyond the rigid and reflexive scandal-reform cycle when it comes to child care and child well-being, and seek solutions that are humane, practical, sustainable, and well regulated. Although the peculiar moment of the orphanage boom in Cambodia's history is over for now, "the particularities and vagaries" of history leave open the possibility that future events will again result in unmet needs for care of unparented children, and some reason to consider preparing for that possibility through remembering what we have learned about good orphanages, rather than being caught unexpectedly in circumstances that force us to rely on bad ones.[28]

ACKNOWLEDGMENTS

My biggest thank-you goes to the individuals I can't list by name—the young people from the COC who graciously shared their lives and their thoughts with me. I want to protect their privacy, but I owe so much to them! Thanks also especially to Nol Yourt, Ven. Lorm Loeurm, Path Soben, Somnieng Hoeurn, Sophea Chan, Tith Sreypich, Ratha Van, Sisotha Oeur, Chhany Sak-Humphrey, and Frank Smith, for all manner of help, support, advice, and information. I am indebted to Rachel Sanson and Scott Burnett for giving me the opportunity to visit Cambodia with them. I also wish to acknowledge my unceasing gratitude to Eve V. Clark, who supported and mentored me through graduate school and who must have been disappointed when I abandoned linguistics, but who might understand why if she sees this book.

This project could never have been completed without the generous support of a Senior Research Fellowship from the Center for Khmer Studies, and faculty research and travel grants from the University of Oregon's College of Arts and Sciences, Office for Research and Innovation, and Division of Global Engagement. The final production and indexing were made possible by an author subvention grant from the Oregon Humanities Center and the College of Arts and Sciences at the University of Oregon.

Thanks for logistical support, for helping me figure out my travel reimbursements, and for keeping the department functional, especially during my periods of absence and distraction are due to Melissa Bowers, Kenlei Cowell, Chelsey Fitzgerald, Hope Marston, Kaley McCarty, Alauna Perry, and David Schmunk.

Hearty thanks to Jasper Chang of the Rutgers University Press Editorial Department. From my initial inquiry through the final steps, he was a model of kindness, professionalism, and good ideas. I also thank Melody Negron, senior production editor at Westchester Publishing Services, for overseeing the vital, final stages of production, and Joseph Dahm, the copy editor who catches everything. Finally, I am grateful to Arc Indexing, Inc. for perceptively pulling it all together at the end with their creation of the index.

I've benefited enormously from the Writing Circles sponsored by Oregon's Division of Equity and Inclusion and the College of Arts and Sciences. Thanks to all my fellow participants, and especially the leaders—Lara Bovilsky, Gordon Hall, Nancy Cheng, Rachel de Nitto, Carol Stabile, and Harry Wonham. Your Writing Circles are the best!

For companionship and motivation, I thank my fellow hikers who joined me in exploring the ever-inspiring landscapes of Oregon, especially all the members of the Obsidians Outdoors Club of Eugene.

And, my family. Mom, Bill, Chip, Becky, Andy, Merany, and Xiao Delpha—I had all of you in mind as I wrote this. I hope that other readers will benefit from the fact that you are my real intended audience, and so motivated me to try to write accessibly and nontechnically. I wanted to write a book that my parents might actually want to read.

NOTES

CHAPTER 1   INTRODUCTION

1. An alias has been used here and in all mentions of people's names.

2. While many of these features are reported to be far more common among institutionalized children than among those in families, the existence of a discrete "institutionalization syndrome," characterized by a consistent profile of these features, has been called into question. See Mariunus van IJzendoorn, Jesus Palacios, Edmund J. S. Sonuga-Barke, Megan R. Gunnar, Panayiota Vorria, Robert B. McCall, Lucy LeMare, Marian J. Bakermans-Kranenburg, Natasha A. Dobrova-Krol, and Femmie Juffer, "Children in Institutional Care: Delayed Development and Resilience," *Monographs of the Society for Research in Child Development* 76, no. 4 (2011): 8–30.

3. Robin Mauney, "Cambodia Orphanage Survey" (Holt Children's Services/USAID, 2005), http://pdf.usaid.gov/pdf_docs/PNADI624.pdf.

4. Matthew Crenson, *Building the Invisible Orphanage* (Cambridge, MA: Harvard University Press, 1998).

5. It is interesting that even the word "orphanage" itself didn't mean "place where orphans reside" until 1865. Prior to that, the noun form "orphanage" meant "the state of being an orphan" (analogous with "dotage") and orphans resided in "orphan asylums."

6. Minnesota Department of Human Services Family and Children's Services Division, "Orphanages: An Historical Overview: A Discussion of the Role of Orphanages in Child Welfare Policy" (n.d.), https://www.leg.mn.gov/docs/pre2003/other/950265.pdf.

7. Chan Thul Prak, "Cambodia, U.N. Launch Plan to Tackle Fake Orphanages," Reuters, April 20, 2017, https://www.reuters.com/article/us-cambodia-orphanage/cambodia-u -n-launch-plan-to-tackle-fake-orphanages-idUSKBN17M0UD.

8. Margaret Sheridan, Stacy Drury, Kate McLaughlin, and Alisa Almas, "Early Institutionalization: Neurobiological Consequences and Genetic Modifiers," *Neuropsychology Review* 20, no. 4 (2010): 414–429; Nathan Fox, Alissa Almas, Kathryn Degnan, Charles A. Nelson, and Charles H. Zeanah, "The Effects of Severe Psychosocial Deprivation and Foster Care Intervention on Cognitive Development at 8 Years of Age: Findings for the Bucharest Early Intervention Project," *Journal of Child Psychology and Psychiatry* 52, no. 9 (2011): 919–928.

9. van IJzendoorn et al., "Children in Institutional Care."

10. Lara Dunston, "Why You Should Avoid Orphanage Visits in Cambodia," *Grantourismo*, June 17, 2014, https://grantourismotravels.com/2014/06/17/why-you-should-avoid-orpha nage-visits-in-cambodia/.

11. Waln Brown, "Foster Families or Orphanages: What Do Alumni Say?," *Chronicle of Social Change*, May 15, 2013, https://chronicleofsocialchange.org/featured/foster-families-or-orphanages-what-do-alumni-say.

12. John Bowlby, "Maternal Care and Mental Health: A Report Prepared on Behalf of the World Health Organization as a Contribution to the United Nations Program for the Welfare of Homeless Children" (World Health Organization, 1951).

13. Chris Walker and Morgon Hartley, "Cambodia's Orphan-industrial Complex," *Atlantic*, June 3, 2013, http://www.theatlantic.com/international/archive/2013/06/cambodias-orphan-industrial-complex/276472/.

14. Heidi Keller, "Universality Claim of Attachment Theory: Children's Socioemotional Development across Cultures," *Proceedings of the National Academy of Sciences* 115, no. 45 (2018): 11414–11419.

15. Jean Mercer, "Conventional and Unconventional Perspectives on Attachment and Attachment Problems: Comparisons and Implications, 2006–2016," *Child and Adolescent Social Work Journal* 36, no. 2 (2019): 81–95.

16. Kathie Carpenter, "A 'Nice, Knock-Down Argument' about Orphanage Tourism, Modern Slavery and the Power and Peril of Naming," in *Modern Day Slavery and Orphanage Tourism*, ed. Joseph M. Cheer, Leigh Mathews, Kathryn E. van Doore, and Karen Flanagan (Wallingford, UK: CABI, 2019), 128.

17. Leslie K. Wang, "Importing Western Childhoods into a Chinese State-Run Orphanage," *Qualitative Sociology* 33, no. 2 (2010): 137–159.

18. UNICEF, "Fact Sheet, Residential Care in Cambodia" (2009), https://www.unicef.org/cambodia/Fact_sheet_-_residential_care_Cambodia.pdf.

19. Hy V. Huynh, Susan Limber, Christin Gray, Martie Thompson, Augustine Wasonga, Vanroth Vann, Dafrosa Itemba, Misganaw Eticha, Ira Madan, and Kathryn Whetten, "Factors Affecting the Psychosocial Well-Being of Orphan and Separated Children in Five Low- and Middle-Income Countries: Which Is More Important, Quality of Care or Care Setting?," *PLOS ONE* 14 (2019): 6–12.

20. Richard B. McKenzie, "The American Dream Is Alive and Well—Among Orphanage Alumni!" (National Center for Policy Analysis Issue Brief No. 202, 2016); McKenzie, *The Home: A Memoir of Growing Up in an Orphanage* (New York: Basic Books, 1996).

21. Nancy G. Margie and Deborah A. Phillips, *Revisiting Home Visiting* (Washington, DC: National Academies Press, 1999).

22. David F. Bjorklund, Alyson J. Myers, and Ariel Bartolo-Kira, "Human Child Rearing and Family from an Evolutionary Perspective," in *Cross-Cultural Family Research and Practice*, ed. W. Kim Halford and Fons Van De Vijver (Cambridge, MA: Academic Press, 2020), 13–55.

23. Jill Lepore, "Baby Doe: A Political History of Tragedy," *New Yorker*, February 1, 2016.

24. Brigitte Zimmerman, "Orphan Living Situations in Malawi: A Comparison of Orphanages and Foster Homes" (master's thesis, Stanford University, 2005).

25. Jacqueline Gibbons, "Orphanages in Egypt," *Journal of Asian and African Studies* 40 (2005): 273.

26. Catherine Neimetz, "Navigating Family Roles within an Institutional Framework: An Exploratory Study in One Private Chinese Orphanage," *Journal of Child and Family Studies* 20, no. 5 (2011): 585–595.

27. Ruth Emond, "Caring as a Moral, Practical and Powerful Endeavor: Peer Care in a Cambodian Orphanage," *British Journal of Social Work* 40, no. 1 (2010): 63–81.

28. Kathryn Whetten, Jan Ostermann, Rachel A. Whetten, Brian W. Pence, Karen O'Donnell, Lynne C. Messer, Nathan M. Thielman, and the Positive Outcomes for Orphans (POFO) Research Team, "A Comparison of the Wellbeing of Orphans and Abandoned Children Ages 6–12 in Institutional and Community-Based Care Settings in 5 Less Wealthy Nations," *PLOS ONE* 4 (2009): e8169, https://doi.org/10.1371/journal.pone.0008169.

29. The significance of their findings has been questioned because of concerns that children in orphanages may be doing as well as those in family-based care only because all children in less wealthy societies are doing equally poorly. Nathan Fox and Charles H. Zeanah, "Comment on Whetten et al.," *PLOS ONE* 24 (December 2009).

30. Christine L. Gray, Sumedha Ariely, Brian W. Pence, and Kathryn Whetten, "Why Institutions Matter: Empirical Data from Five Low- and Middle-Income Countries Indicate the Critical Role of Institutions for Orphans," in *Child Maltreatment in Residential Care*, ed. Adrian V. Rus, Sheri R. Parris, and Ecaterina Stativa (Dordrecht: Springer, 2017), 379–400.

31. Joana Salifu Yendork and Nceba Z. Somhlaba, "Do Social Support, Self-Efficacy and Resilience Influence the Experience of Stress in Ghanaian Orphans? An Exploratory Study," *Child Care in Practice* 21, no. 2 (2015): 140–159, http://dx.doi.org/10.1080/13575279.2014.985286.

32. Allison Gayapersad, Caroline Ombok, Allan Kamanda, Carren Tarus, David Ayuku, and Paul Braitstein, "The Production and Reproduction of Kinship in Charitable Children's Institutions in Uasin Gishu County, Kenya," *Child and Youth Care Forum* 48 (2019): 797–828.

33. Kathryn Whetten, Jan Ostermann, Brian W. Pence, Rachel A. Whetten, Lynne C. Messer, Sumedha Ariely, Karen O'Donnell, Augustine I. Wasonga, Vanroth Vann, Dafrosa Itemba, Misganaw Eticha, Ira Madan, and Nathan M. Thielman, "Three-Year Change in the Wellbeing of Orphaned and Separated Children in Institutional and Family-Based Care Settings in Five Low- and Middle-Income Countries," *PLOS ONE*, August 27, 2014, https://doi.org/10.1371/journal.pone.0104872.

34. Christine L. Gray, Brian W. Pence, Jan Ostermann, Rachel A. Whetten, Karen O'Donnell, Nathan M. Thielman, and Kathryn Whetten, "Prevalence and Incidence of Traumatic Experiences among Orphans in Institutional and Family-Based Settings in 5 Low- and Middle-Income Countries: A Longitudinal Study," *Global Health: Science and Practice* 3, no. 3 (2015): 395–404.

35. Rachna Mishra and Vanita Sondhi, "Fostering Resilience among Orphaned Adolescents through Institutional Care in India," *Residential Treatment for Children and Youth* 36, no. 4 (2019): 314–337, https://doi.org/10.1080/0886571X.2018.1535286; Yan Hong, Xiaoming Li, Xiaoyi Fang, Guoxiang Zhao, Junfeng Zhao, Qun Zhao, Xiuyun Lin, Liying Zhang, and Bonita Stanton, "Care Arrangements of AIDS Orphans and Their Relationship with Children's Psychosocial Well-Being in Rural China," *Health Policy and Planning* 26 (2010): 115–123.

36. Lili Xia and Ching-Man Lam, "Where Is Home? The Lived Experiences of Chinese Children after Their Parents Have Been Incarcerated," *Journal of Social Work Practice* 34, no. 2 (2020): 191–203.

37. Richard B. McKenzie, *Miracle Mountain: A Hidden Sanctuary for Children, Horses, and Birds off a Road Less Traveled* (Irvine, CA: Dickens Press, 2013).

38. Linda Gordon, "The Perils of Innocence, or What's Wrong with Putting Children First?," *Journal of the History of Childhood and Youth* 1 (2008): 331–350.

39. NGO Coalition on the Rights of the Child, "UPR Submission on Cambodia Child Rights, 2009–2013," http://ngocrc.org/attachments/article/449UPRpercent20submissionpercent20onpercent20Childpercent20Rightspercent20inpercent20Cambodia.pdf.

40. Interestingly, in the heyday of orphanages in the United States, the proportion of children with no living parents was only around 10–20 percent, similar to the proportion in Cambodia during the height of the orphanage boom (Crenson, *Building the Invisible Orphanage*).

41. "Orphan," *Strong's Concordance* (n.d.), http://biblehub.com/greek/3737.htm.

42. "Orphan," *Oxford English Dictionary* (*OED*) (n.d.), http://OED.com.

43. UNICEF, "Orphans" (n.d.), https://www.unicef.org/media/orphans.

44. Eric Hartman, "Why UNICEF and Save the Children Are against Your Short-Term Service in Orphanages," *Campus Compact Global S.L. Blog* (n.d.), https://compact.org/why-unicef-and-save-the-children-are-against-you-caring-for-orphans/; Robert Carmichael, "UNICEF: Cambodia's Orphans not Really Orphans," *DW Asia*, March 24, 2011, https://www.dw.com/en/unicef-cambodias-orphans-not-really-orphans/a-6481673.

45. "Orphan," *OED*.

46. Philadelphia Courts, "Orphans' Court Division" (n.d.), https://www.courts.phila.gov/common-pleas/orphans/.

47. U.S. Citizenship and Immigration Services, "Orphan Process" (n.d.), https://www.uscis.gov/adoption/immigration-through-adoption/orphan-process; U.S. Citizenship and Immigration Services, "Orphan" (n.d.), https://www.uscis.gov/tools/glossary/orphan.

48. "Denotation" and "connotation" are both kinds of word meanings; "denotation" refers to the concrete dictionary definition, while "connotation" refers to the emotive or evaluative flavoring of the word.

49. Melanie Kimball, "From Folktales to Fiction: Orphan Characters in Children's Literature," *Library Trends* 47, no. 3 (1999): 558–578; Anne Hansen, "The Image of an Orphan: Cambodian Narrative Sites for Buddhist Ethical Reflection," *Journal of Asian Studies* 62, no. 3 (2003): 811–834.

50. "Harry Potter Was Inspired by Oliver Twist, Claims Academic," *Telegraph*, July 19, 2011, http://www.telegraph.co.uk/culture/harry-potter/8645593/Harry-Potter-was-inspired-by-Oliver-Twist-claims-academic.html.

51. Wikipedia, for instance, has an entire page devoted to "Orphan characters in video games." https://en.wikipedia.org/wiki/Category:Orphan_characters_in_video_games.

52. Luke has been orphaned by his father's turn to the dark side, a spiritual rather than physical death.

53. James Poniewozik, "'Everything's Gonna Be Okay' Review: Half-Siblings, Whole Family," *New York Times*, January 14, 2020.

54. Highlighted for example in the endings of *Lilo & Stitch*, *Harry Potter*, and *Despicable Me*, among others.

55. TV Tropes, "Orphanage of Fear" (n.d.), http://tvtropes.org/pmwiki/pmwiki.php/Main/OrphanageOfFear; TV Tropes, "Orphanage of Love" (n.d.), http://tvtropes.org/pmwiki/pmwiki.php/Main/OrphanageOfLove; TV Tropes, "Saving the Orphanage" (n.d.), http://tvtropes.org/pmwiki/pmwiki.php/Main/SavingTheOrphanage.

56. UNICEF, "Orphans" (n.d.), https://www.unicef.org/media/orphans.

57. Dale Keiger, "The Rise and Demise of the American Orphanage," *Johns Hopkins Magazine*, April 1996, http://pages.jh.edu/jhumag/496web/orphange.html; Crenson, *Building the Invisible Orphanage*.

58. Pamela Kruger, "Adopting from Abroad," *Child Magazine*, 2004, http://www.pamela kruger.com/articles/detail.asp?a=7.

59. David F. Lancy, "Accounting for Variability in Mother-Child Play," *American Anthropologist* 109, no. 2 (2007): 273; Lancy, *The Anthropology of Childhood: Cherubs, Chattel, Changelings* (Cambridge: Cambridge University Press, 2014).

60. Myra Bluebond-Langner and Jill E. Korbin, "Challenges and Opportunities in the Anthropology of Childhoods: An Introduction to 'Children, Childhoods and Childhood Studies,'" *American Anthropologist* 109, no. 2 (2007): 241–246.

61. Mimi Tatlow-Golden and Heather Montgomery, "Childhood Studies and Child Psychology: Disciplines in Dialogue?," *Children & Society* (2020), https://doi.org/10.1111/chso.12384.

62. Viviana Zelizer, *Pricing the Priceless Child: The Changing Social Value of Children* (Princeton, NJ: Princeton University Press, 1994).

63. Bluebond-Langner and Korbin, "Challenges and Opportunities," 242.

CHAPTER 2   HISTORY OF ORPHANAGES IN CAMBODIA

1. Maryanne Bylander, "Is Regular Migration Safer Migration? Insights from Thailand," *Journal on Migration and Human Security* 7, no. 1 (2019): 1–18.

2. May Mayko Ebihara, *Svay: A Khmer Village in Cambodia*, ed. Andrew Mertha (Ithaca, NY: Cornell University Press, 2018).

3. Theravada, rather than Mahayana, is the primary school of Buddhism practiced in Cambodia, Thailand, Burma, Laos, and Sri Lanka.

4. Ian Harris, *Cambodian Buddhism: History and Practice* (Honolulu: University of Hawai'i Press, 2005).

5. Milada Kalab, "Monastic Education, Village Structure and Social Mobility in Cambodia," in *The Anthropological Study of Education*, ed. Craig J. Calhoun and Francis A. Janni (The Hague: De Gruyter, 1976), 61–74.

6. David F. Lancy, "Adoption and the Circulation of Children," *Psychology Today*, January 13, 2017, https://www.psychologytoday.com/blog/benign-neglect/201701/adoption-and-the-circulation-children.

7. Toni Shapiro, *Dance and the Spirit of Cambodia* (Ithaca, NY: Cornell University Press, 1994), 94.

8. Paul Cravath, *Earth in Flower: The Divine Mystery of the Cambodian Dance Drama* (Holmes Beach, FL: Datasia, 2008), 56.

9. Cravath, *Earth in Flower*; Toni Shapiro-Phim, "Dance in Cambodia," *Asia Society*, 2019, https://asiasociety.org/dance-cambodia.

10. Cravath, *Earth in Flower*, 373–74.

11. Gregor Muller, *Colonial Cambodia's "Bad Frenchmen": The Rise of French Rule and the Life of Thomas Caraman, 1840–87* (London: Routledge, 2006); Charles Rollet, "The Story of Cambodia's Stolen Children," *Phnom Penh Post*, October 3, 2014; Christina Elizabeth Firpo, *The Uprooted: Race, Children, and Imperialism in French Indochina, 1890–1980* (Honolulu: University of Hawai'i Press, 2016).

12. Denise Heywood, *Cambodian Dance: Celebration of the Gods* (Bangkok: River Books, 2008), 83.

13. Toni Phim and Ashley Thompson, *Dance in Cambodia* (Oxford: Oxford University Press, 2000), 42.

14. Abby Seiff, "Cambodian Orphans Yearn for Answers 40 Years after Fleeing the Khmer Rouge," *Time*, April 14, 2015, https://time.com/3820620/cambodia-adoptees-khmer-rouge-orphans/.

15. Heywood *Cambodian Dance*, 83–84.

16. Canadian Broadcasting Corporation, "Khmer Rouge Victims Reunited 40 Years after Daring Rescue," *Radio West*, March 19, 2015, https://www.cbc.ca/news/canada/british-columbia/khmer-rouge-victims-reunited-40-years-after-daring-rescue-1.3002191.

17. The name "Khmers Rouges" was first used by King Sihanouk to refer to the various incarnations of Cambodian communism, and "Khmer Rouge" has become the term most widely used by English speakers to refer to the Cambodian regime of 1975–1979 and their military forces.

18. Leonie Kijewski, "Life Had No More Value Than the Smallest Atom Floating in Space in the Stars, Expert Says," *Cambodia Tribunal Monitor*, July 29, 2017, http://www.cambodiatribunal.org/2016/07/29/life-had-no-more-value-than-the-smallest-atom-floating-in-space-in-the-stars-expert-says/.

19. Gender Based Violence under the Khmer Rouge Information Platform (n.d.), http://gbvkr.org/gender-based-violence-under-khmer-rouge/facts-and-figures/forced-marriage/.

20. Kijewski, "Life Had No More Value."

21. Kijewski, "Life Had No More Value."

22. The forcible rupturing of families to place biracial children in French orphanages would also cast a pall on orphanages today, except that most people don't know about it.

23. Paul Cravath, "The Ritual Origins of the Classical Dance Drama of Cambodia," *Asian Theatre Journal* 3 (1986): 179.

24. Toni Shapiro-Phim, *The Dancer and Cambodian History* (Philadelphia: Pew Center for Arts and Heritage, 2007).

25. Shapiro, *Dance and the Spirit of Cambodia*, 282.

26. Samantha Bradley, "Domestic and Family Violence in Post-conflict Communities: International Human Rights Law and the State's Obligation to Protect Women and Children," *Health and Human Rights Journal*, December 4, 2018, https://www.hhrjournal.org/2018/12/domestic-and-family-violence-in-post-conflict-communities-international-human-rights-law-and-the-states-obligation-to-protect-women-and-children/; Melina Czymoniewicz-Klippel, "Parenting in the Context of Globalization and Acculturation: Perspectives of Mothers and Fathers in Siem Reap, Cambodia," *Childhood* 26, no. 4 (2019): 525–539.

27. At this time, Cambodia was referred to as Kampuchea. However, for the sake of narrative consistency, I use Cambodia as the default name.

28. As with the current orphanage boom, the children's centers in the refugee camps were referred to by a variety of terms, including "orphanage," "holding center," and "children's center." In general, I follow the lead of authors I am referencing in choosing which label to use, which will necessarily result in some inconsistency of usage.

29. Josephine Reynell, *Political Pawns: Refugees on the Thai-Kampuchean Border* (Oxford: Refugee Studies Program, 1989), 158.

30. Benoît Duchâteau-Arminjon, *Healing Cambodia One Child at a Time* (Singapore: Editions Didier Millet, 2013), 40, 412.

31. Neil Boothby, "Khmer Children: Alone at the Border," *Indochina Issues* 3, no. 2 (1982): 6.

32. Jan Williamson, "Centers for Unaccompanied Children in Khao I Dang Holding Center," *Disasters* 5, no. 2 (1981): 100–104.

33. Nuon Phaly, *My Name Is Phaly* (n.d.), http://www.eglobalfamily.org/phaly-story.html.

34. Duchâteau-Arminjon, *Healing Cambodia*, 57.

35. Duchâteau-Arminjon, *Healing Cambodia*, 47.

36. Reynell, *Political Pawns*, 106.

37. Fiona Terry, *Condemned to Repeat?* (Ithaca, NY: Cornell University Press, 2002), 145; Duchâteau-Arminjon, *Healing Cambodia*.

38. Stephen Wearing, *Volunteer Tourism: Experiences That Make a Difference* (Wallingford, UK: CABI, 2001); Shapiro, *Dance and the Spirit of Cambodia*, 42. In fact, "orphanage tourism" existed even earlier in Western child welfare systems, with many of today's tensions and ambivalences already present, although that label was not used. For example, signage at the Foundling Museum at Coram's Fields, London, established in the eighteenth century, reports that "the visiting public would often come to watch the children eat their Sunday lunch."

39. Yumiko Suenobo, *Management of Education Systems in Zones of Conflict-Relief Operations: A Case-Study in Thailand* (Bangkok: UNESCO, 1995).

40. Larry C. Thompson, *Refugee Workers in the Indochina Exodus, 1975–1982* (London: McFarland, 2010), 271, 225.

41. Joanna T. Pecore, "Sounding the Spirit of Cambodia: The Living Tradition of Khmer Music and Dance-Drama in a Washington, DC Community" (doctoral dissertation, University of Maryland, 2004), 122.

42. Anne Langford, "Working with Cambodian Refugees," *Journal of Transpersonal Psychology* 12 (1980): 122.

43. Duchâteau-Arminjon, *Healing Cambodia*, 73.

44. Duchâteau-Arminjon, *Healing Cambodia*, 121.

45. Duchâteau-Arminjon, *Healing Cambodia*.

46. Shapiro, *Dance and the Spirit of Cambodia*, 176.

47. Francois Bugnion, "Cambodia: Massive Aid Effort Planted Seeds of Recovery in Former 'Killing Fields'" (2009), https://www.icrc.org/eng/resources/documents/interview/cambodia-interview-011209.htm.

48. Toby Volkman, "Imagining Cambodia," *Cultural Survival Quarterly* 14 (September 1990), https://www.culturalsurvival.org/publications/cultural-survival-quarterly/imagining-cambodia.

49. Marita Eastmond, "Reconstruction and the Politics of Homecoming: Repatriation of Refugees in Cambodia" (Goteborg University, Department of Social Anthropology Working Paper no. 1, 2002), 6.

50. Janet McLellan, "Repatriation and Reintegration of Cambodian Refugees: Issues and Concerns," *Refuge* 13, no. 5 (1993): 15–17.

51. Catherine Geach, "Khmer Cultural Development Institute History" (2013), http://www.kcdi-cambodia.com/about-us/history/.

52. Rachel Scollay and Lon Nara, "Slum Children Dance for Their Supper," *Phnom Penh Post*, January 4, 2002. CLCA turned out to be a questionable organization that was shut down in 2003, but it was the corruption of this particular organization that

was targeted, not the use of dance performances to attract visitors and donations. The children were placed into a new orphanage, which continued its own dance program.

53. National AIDS Authority, "Monitoring Progress towards the 2011 UN Political Declaration on HIV and AIDS" (Cambodia Country Progress Report, 2015), https://www.unaids.org/sites/default/files/country/documents/KHM_narrative_report_2015.pdf.

54. Marie Charles, "HIV Epidemic in Cambodia, One of the Poorest Countries in Southeast Asia: A Success Story," *Expert Review of Anti-infective Therapy* 4 (2014): 1–4; Amber Dufus, "HIV/AIDS Rates in Cambodia Drop Down to Virtual Elimination," *Borgen Project Blog Latest News*, 2018, https://borgenproject.org/hiv-aids-rates-in-cambodia/.

55. Diny Van Bruggen, *Flowers on the Cactus: Aids and Orphan Care in Cambodia* (Phnom Penh: Don Bosco Technical School, 2005).

56. Schuster Institute for Investigative Journalism, "Capsule History of Adoption Issues in Cambodia," 2011, https://www.brandeis.edu/investigate/adoption/cambodia.html.

57. Schuster Institute, "Capsule History."

58. Bill Bainbridge and Lon Nara, "Few Babies 'Abandoned' since Moratorium: Orphanages," *Phnom Penh Post*, August 2, 2002; Robin Mauney, "Cambodia Orphanage Survey" (Holt Children's Services/USAID, 2005), http://pdf.usaid.gov/pdf_docs/PNADI624.pdf.

59. National Institute of Statistics, Directorate General for Health [Cambodia], and ORC Macro, "Cambodia Demographic and Health Survey 2000" (2001), https://dhsprogram.com/pubs/pdf/FR124/FR124.pdf; Mauney, "Cambodia Orphanage Survey."

60. Kathie Carpenter, "Continuity, Complexity and Reciprocity in a Cambodian Orphanage," *Children & Society* 29, no. 2 (2015): 85–94.

61. The terms "orphanage tourism" and "voluntourism" are both problematic since they combine negative connotations with complete lack of agreed-upon objective definitions. Wherever possible, therefore, I use the more neutral terms "visitor" and "volunteer." However, when summarizing or referencing the work or opinions of others, I follow their lead and use "orphanage tourism" and "voluntourism" for the sake of narrative consistency.

CHAPTER 3   ORPHANAGE TOURISM AND THE
ANTI-ORPHANAGE-TOURISM CAMPAIGN

1. Judith Ennew, "Prisoners of Childhood: Orphans and Economic Dependency," in *Studies in Modern Childhood*, ed. Jens Qvortrup (Basingstoke, UK: Palgrave Macmillan, 2005), 128.

2. Vannarith Chheang, "Tourism and Local Community Development in Siem Reap," *Ritsumeikan Journal of Asia Pacific Studies* 27 (2010): 85–101.

3. Although 7 million were predicted to visit in 2020, a catastrophic decline began in 2019 and continued through 2020 instead.

4. In neighboring Thailand orphanages remain the favored option for alternative care, and Thai people themselves support both state- and NGO-run orphanages through generous donations. Justin M. Rogers and Victor Karunan, "Is the Deinstitutionalisation of Alternative Care a 'Wicked Problem'? A Qualitative Study Exploring the Perceptions of Child Welfare Practitioners and Policy Actors in Thailand," *International Social Work* 63, no. 5 (2020): 626–639.

5. Stephen Wearing, *Volunteer Tourism: Experiences That Make a Difference* (Wallingford, UK: CABI, 2001).

6. Rachel Hughes, "Dutiful Tourism: Encountering the Cambodia Genocide," *Asia Pacific Viewpoint* 49, no. 3 (2008): 318–330.

7. Hughes, "Dutiful Tourism," 327.

8. Regina Scheyvens, *Tourism and Poverty* (New York: Routledge, 2010).

9. Elena Bogolyubova, Kathie Carpenter, and Valerii Mitrofanenko, "Re-thinking Civil Society in Russia through International and Intersectoral Collaboration in Youth Welfare in North Caucasus," *International Society for Third-Sector Research Working papers Series* 11, no. 1 (2019); Elena Bogolyubova, Kathie Carpenter, and Valerii Mitrofanenko, "The Peer-to-Peer Approach Works: Promoting and Understanding Unique Cultures of Volunteering in Russian and American Youth Social Services," *Professional Development* 2, no. 1 (forthcoming).

10. Mary Conran, "They Really Love Me! Intimacy in Volunteer Tourism," *Annals of Tourism Research* 38, no. 4 (2011): 1454–1473.

11. Al Jazeera, "Cambodia's Orphan Tourism," *101 East*, February 10, 2011, https://www.aljazeera.com/programmes/101east/2011/02/2011210123057338995.html.

12. Kristin Cheney and Karen Smith Rotabi, "Addicted to Orphans: How the Global Orphan Industrial Complex Jeopardizes Local Child Protection Systems," in *Conflict, Violence and Peace: Geographies of Children and Young People*, vol. 11, ed. T. Skelton, C. Harker, and K. Horschelmann (Singapore: Springer, 2017), 89–107

13. Stephen Wearing, Mary Mostafanezhad, Nha Nguyen, Truc Ha Thanh Nguyen, and Matthew McDonald, "'Poor Children on Tinder' and Their Barbie Saviours: Towards a Feminist Political Economy of Volunteer Tourism," *Leisure Studies* 37, no. 5 (2018): 500–514.

14. Sunrise Cambodia, "Visit Sunrise in Cambodia" (n.d.), http://sunrisecambodia.org.au/our-story/visit-sunrise-in-cambodia/.

15. Chan Thul Prak, "Official Accused of Extorting Orphan Dancers," *Cambodia Daily*, January 5, 2005.

16. Benoît Duchâteau-Arminjon, *Healing Cambodia One Child at a Time* (Singapore: Editions Didier Millet, 2013), 174. In 1992, Krousar Thmey dropped "orphanage" from their name. They have become Cambodia's most highly regarded educational center for children and youth who are deaf and blind.

17. Rachel Scollay and Lon Nara, "Slum Children Dance for Their Supper," *Phnom Penh Post*, January 4, 2002.

18. Geraldine Cox, *Home Is Where the Heart Is* (Sydney: Macmillan, 2000), 327.

19. Molly Ball, "Nightly Khmer Dance Back in Phnom Penh after 25 Years," *Cambodia Daily*, December 25, 2001.

20. Worldstrider, "Visit an Orphanage in Phnom Penh," Lonely Planet Thorn Tree Forum (2005), https://www.lonelyplanet.com/thorntree/forums/asia-south-east-asia-mainland/topics/visit-an-orphanage-in-phnom-penh.

21. AnnemarieJ5079BX, "Traditional Khmer Dance at ACODO Orphanage," *TripAdvisor*, January 19, 2014, https://www.tripadvisor.com/Attraction_Review-g297390-d1647060-Reviews-Traditional_Khmer_Dance_at_ACODO_Orphanage-Siem_Reap_Siem_Reap_Province.html.

22. Natanddrew, "Visit an Orphanage Near Siem Reap and Make the Highlight of Your Trip," Lonely Planet Thorn Tree Forum, 2008, https://www.lonelyplanet.com/thorntree/forums/responsible-travel/topics/visit-an-orphanage-near-siem-reap-and-make-the-highlight-of-your-trip.

23. Kompongthom, "Comments—Visit an Orphanage in Phnom Penh," Lonely Planet Thorn Tree Forum, 2010, https://www.lonelyplanet.com/thorntree/forums/asia-south-east -asia-mainland/topics/visit-an-orphanage-in-phnom-penh.

24. TripAdvisor, "Traditional Khmer Dance at ACODO Orphanage," https://www.tripadvisor .com/Attraction_Review-g297390-d1647060-Reviews-Traditional_Khmer_Dance_at _ACODO_Orphanage-Siem_Reap_Siem_Reap_Province.html.

25. Ben, "Comments—Cambodian Orphan Family Centre Organization Parts 1 and 2," *Travelpod*, 2011, https://web.archive.org/web/20110628050728/http://www.travelpod .com/travel-blog-entries/wendyworld/4/1261194608/tpod.html.

26. Tracey Shelton and Sam Rith, "Orphanage Tourism: A Questionable Industry," *Phnom Penh Post*, March 9, 2007.

27. Snookieboi, "Orphanages in Cambodia," *Travelfish Cambodia Forum*, 2013, https://www .travelfish.org/board/post/cambodia/12216_orphanages-in-cambodia.

28. Linda Richter and Amy Norman, "AIDS Orphan Tourism: A Threat to Young Children in Residential Care," *Vulnerable Children and Youth Studies* 5, no. 3 (2010): 217–229.

29. Tess Guiney and Mary Mostafanezhad, "The Political Economy of Orphanage Tourism in Cambodia," *Tourist Studies* 15, no. 2 (2014): 132–155.

30. P. Jane Reas, "'Boy, Have We Got a Vacation for You': Orphanage Tourism in Cambodia and the Commodification and Objectification of the Orphanaged Child," *Thammasat Review* 16 (2013): 121–140.

31. Proyrungroj is unusual in intentionally choosing the term "orphanage volunteer tourism" to avoid the value judgments that are inherent in the term "orphanage tourism." Raweewan Proyrungroj, "Orphan Volunteer Tourism in Thailand: Volunteer Tourists' Motivations and On-Site Experiences," *Journal of Hospitality and Tourism Research* 41, no. 5 (2017): 560–584.

32. Joni Verstraete, "The Impact of Orphanage Tourism on Residential Care Centres in Cambodia" (master's thesis, Leeds Metropolitan University, 2014).

33. Richter and Norman, "AIDS Orphan Tourism"; Tess Guiney, "'Hug-an-Orphan Vacations': 'Love' and Emotion in Orphanage Tourism," *Geographical Journal* 184, no. 2 (2018): 125–137.

34. Reas, "'Boy, Have We Got a Vacation for You,'" 126.

35. Liz Wilson, "Finding the Win-Win: Providing Supportive and Enriching Volunteer Tourism Experiences while Promoting Sustainable Social Change," *Worldwide Hospitality and Tourism Themes* 7, no. 2 (2015): 201–207.

36. Recall also from chapter 3 that the government's own minimum standards for alternative care use UNICEF's definition that explicitly states that an orphan is a child who has lost one or both parents; thus, by definition many orphans have a living parent.

37. Kathryn Burrington, "Justifiable Bad Press for Orphanage Tourism," *Travel with Kat*, 2014, https://travelwithkat.com/orphanage-tourism/.

38. Jjack, "Comments—Short-Term Volunteer Opportunity at Orphanage Phnom Penh," Lonely Planet Thorn Tree Forum, 2010, https://www.lonelyplanet.com/thorntree /forums/asia-south-east-asia-mainland/topics/short-term-volunteer-opportunity-at -orphanage-phnom-penh?page=11.

39. Friends International, "ChildSafe Movement" (n.d.), https://friends-international .org/childsafe-movement/.

40. Friends International, "ChildSafe International" (2007), http://www.childsafe-inter national.org.

41. Friends International, "Recommended Child Safe Tourist Information: Travel Tips" (2006), http://www.childsafe-cambodia.org:80/traveladvice.asp; Friends International, "ChildSafe Tips for Travelers and Foreign Residents" (2007), http//www.childsafe -internatinal.org/TFResidents.asp.

42. Sophal Ear, *Aid Dependence in Cambodia: How Foreign Assistance Undermines Democracy* (New York: Columbia University Press, 2012); Friends International, "Annual Report" (2009).

43. Robert Carmichael, "Cambodia's Orphanages Target the Wallets of Well-Meaning Tourists," *Independent,* March 25, 2011; Denise Hruby, "In Cambodia, Fake Orphanages Soak Up Donations by Duping Tourists," *Los Angeles Daily News,* July 21, 2014.

44. Although glowing, out-of-date reviews can still be found online; they almost always were posted prior to 2015.

45. Nicky Sullivan, "Apsara Dancing: A Bit of Tradition," Travelfish, November 29, 2016, https://www.travelfish.org/sight_profile/cambodia/western_cambodia/siem_reap /siem_reap/796.

46. Kathie Carpenter, "A 'Nice, Knock-Down Argument' about Orphanage Tourism, Modern Slavery and the Power and Peril of Naming," in *Modern Day Slavery and Orphanage Tourism,* ed. Joseph M. Cheer, Leigh Mathews, Kathryn E. van Doore, and Karen Flanagan (Wallingford, UK: CABI, 2019), 125–138.

47. Robin Mauney, "Cambodia Orphanage Survey" (Holt Children's Services/USAID, 2005), http://pdf.usaid.gov/pdf_docs/PNADI624.pdf.

48. MoSVY, "A Statistical Profile of Child Protection in Cambodia" (2018), https://urldefense .com/v3/__https://www.unicef.org/cambodia/media/711/file/Cambodia_Report_Final _web_ready_HIGH.pdf*20.pdf__;JQ!!C5qS4YX3!R31CsooA7_n5DBePcNnZnU4ob873y _SJ5HwDKGe38YAyJxdIFeXUiDL9dR3dhBJJxA$.

49. Touch Sokha and Erin Handley, "Over 35,000 Kids Still in Care," *Phnom Penh Post,* April 21, 2017, https://www.phnompenhpost.com/national/over-35000-kids-still-care; MoSVY, "Mapping of Residential Care Facilities in the Capital and 24 Provinces of the Kingdom of Cambodia" (2017), https://urldefense.com/v3/__https://www.unicef.org /cambodia/media/1301/file/*20Action*20Plan*20for*20improving*20child*20care _Eng.pdf__;JSUlJSUl!!C5qS4YX3!U-yPV9cjcZLWuUp_GCz7PAGPPjFjcZhyM61n1njePrTJ4 BmVgZZCN3GD3764YvSSJA$.

50. Suman Khadka and Buthdy Sem, "Caring for Children Left Behind in Residential Care during COVID-19" (UNICEF, 2020), https://www.unicef.org/cambodia/stories/caring -children-left-behind-residential-care-during-covid19.

51. Lindsay Stark, Beth L. Rubenstein, Kimchoeun Pak, and Sok Kosal, "National Estimation of Children in Residential Care Institutions in Cambodia: A Modelling Study," *BMJ Open 7,* no. 1 (2016), http://dx.doi.org/10.1136/bmjopen-2016-013888.

52. Kong Meta, and Daphne Chenhen, "Government to Miss Orphan Goal," *Phnom Penh Post,* December 29, 2017, https://www.phnompenhpost.com/national/government-miss -orphan-goal.

53. Patricia Fronek, Robert Common, Karen Smith Rotabi, and Johnny Statham, "Identifying and Addressing Risk in the Implementation of Alternative Care Policies in Cambodia," *Journal of Human Rights and Social Work* 4 (2019): 140–144.

54. Morgan Hartley and Chris Walker, "Cambodia's Booming New Industry: Orphanage Tourism," *Forbes*, May 24, 2013, https://www.forbes.com/sites/morganhartley/2013/05/24/cambodias-booming-new-industry-orphanage-tourism/#45592744794a; Kong Meta and Cristina Maza, "Government Shutters 56 Shelters," *Phnom Penh Post*, February 16, 2017, https://www.phnompenhpost.com/national/government-shutters-56-shelters.

55. Meta and Maza, "Government Shutters 56 Shelters"; Audrey Wilson and Vandy Muong, "Homeward Bound? How to Fix a Damaged System," *Phnom Penh Post*, September 30, 2016, https://www.phnompenhpost.com/post-weekend/homeward-bound-how-fix-damaged-system.

56. UNICEF, "Cambodia Launches the 'Strong Family Campaign' Aiming to End Violence Against Children and Unnecessary Family Separation" (2020), https://urldefense.com/v3/__https://www.unicef.org/cambodia/press-releases/cambodia-launches-strong-family-campaign-aiming-end-violence-against-children-and__;!!C5qS4YX3!QViSA8LwOGTZQUDIKTTr_cUFeTAXthoVKMC5TT58O_ir_q2W-xw75ozTRXlkvZm4ow$.

57. Similar pressures and complications surrounding deinstitutionalization have recently been reported elsewhere in Southeast Asia as well as in South Asia and the Caucasus. Helen McLaren and Nismah Qonita, "Indonesia's Orphanage Trade: Islamic Philanthropy's Good Intentions, Some Not So Good Outcomes," *Religions* 11, no. 1 (2020), https://doi.org/10.3390/rel11010001; Sheila Ramaswamy and Shekhar Seshadri, "The Deinstitutionalisation Debate in India: Throwing the Baby Out with the Bathwater?," *Scottish Journal of Residential Child Care* 19, no. 1 (2020): 8–31; Olga Ulybina, "Transnational Agency and Domestic Policies: The Case of Childcare Deinstitutionalization in Georgia," *Global Social Policy* (2020), https://doi.org/10.1177/1468018120926888.

58. Kathie Carpenter, "Volunteer Tourism in Cambodian Orphanages: Is There Such a Thing as Best Practices?," in *Proceedings of Greenlines Institute for Sustainable Development International Conference on Global Tourism and Sustainability* (Lagos, Portugal, 2016), 105–113, http://greenlines-institute.org/proceedings/Tourism2016/TOURISM_2016_EBOOK.pdf.

59. Carpenter, "'Nice, Knock-Down Argument'"; Commonwealth of Australia, "Orphanage Trafficking" (2017), https://www.aph.gov.au/Parliamentary_Business/Committees/Joint/Foreign_Affairs_Defence_and_Trade/ModernSlavery/Final_report/section?id=committees%2Freportjnt%2F024102%2F25036.

60. Stahili Foundation, "Families, Not Orphanages" (2018), https://www.stahili.org/orphanages/.

61. This criticism has been levied against the entire field of childhood studies by Canosa and Graham, who document and critique "the gap between policy rhetoric and children's everyday lived experiences." Antonia Canosa and Anne Graham, "Tracing the Contribution of Childhood Studies: Maintaining Momentum while Navigating Tensions," *Childhood* 27, no. 1 (2020): 41.

CHAPTER 4   METHODS

1. Kathie Carpenter, "Continuity, Complexity and Reciprocity in a Cambodian Orphanage," *Children & Society* 29, no. 2 (2015): 85–94.

2. For more information on the sampling and analysis of texts, see Kathie Carpenter, "Childhood Studies and Orphanage Tourism in Cambodia," *Annals of Tourism Research* 55 (2015): 15–27.

3. Although I had originally planned to interview only former residents who had attained the legal age of consent for participation, which is sixteen in Cambodia, the NGO encouraged me to also speak with three former residents who were below that age. The NGO director is their legal guardian and gave consent for me to do so.

4. As of April 2019, 46.7 percent of Cambodians were on Facebook. NapoleonCat, "Facebook Users in Cambodia" (April 2019), https://napoleoncat.com/stats/facebook-users -in-cambodia/2019/04.

5. Kathie Carpenter, "The Child as Method? Paradigm Shifts, Positionality and Participatory Methods for Researching Children in Asia," in *Methods and Moments: Ethnographic Research in Asia*, ed. Nayantara Sheoran Appleton and Caroline Bennett (London: Rowman & Littlefield, forthcoming).

6. It's important to make clear that the traumatic memories in both cases were of adverse events that had occurred before placement, not of their placement or life in the orphanage itself. In both cases, participants explained that life in the orphanage had brought them considerable relief after these traumatic events.

7. Since educational indicators for Cambodia continue to rise, the attainment levels for their age cohorts would actually be even lower. OpenDevelopment Cambodia, "Education and Training" (2018), https://opendevelopmentcambodia.net/topics/educa tion-and-training/.

8. Because of the large number of unregistered marriages, however, the median ages are actually lower.

9. Ashley D. Jordana, "Situational Analysis on Child, Early and Forced Marriage in Vietnam, Laos, Myanmar and Cambodia" (World Vision, 2016), https://www.wvi.org/sites /default/files/report_SituationalanalysisCEFMVietnamLaosMyanmarandCambodia -FINAL.docx-2.pdf.

10. UNICEF even explicitly defines child marriage prevalence as "the percentage of women 20–24 years old who were married or in union before they were 18 years old" (UNICEF, "State of the World's Children 2017" [2017], https://www.unicef.org/sowc2017). Although early marriage is often not forced in Cambodia, early marriage and marriage at a young age are often confounded in the literature. Jordana, for example, writes, "At its heart, CEFM [child, early, and forced marriage] is driven by beliefs about the rights and status of girls who are seen as having little value outside the traditional role of being a wife and mother." Jordana, "Situational Analysis," 6.

11. Joseph Schatz, "Cambodia's Child Grooms," *Al Jazeera America* May 6, 2015.

12. H. F. Hsieh and S. E. Shannon, "Three Approaches to Qualitative Content Analysis," *Qualitative Health Research* 15, no. 9 (2005): 1277–1288.

CHAPTER 5   THE RHYTHMS OF DAILY LIFE IN THE ORPHANAGE

1. At the time, Cambodia was second only to Rwanda. Helena Domashneva, "NGOs in Cambodia: It's Complicated," *Diplomat*, December 3, 2013. https://thediplomat.com /2013/12/ngos-in-cambodia-its-complicated.

2. Burca Munyas, "Genocide in the Minds of Cambodian Youth: Transmitting (Hi)stories of Genocide to Second and Third Generations in Cambodia," *Journal of Genocide Research* 10, no. 3 (2008): 413–439, https://doi.org/10.1080/14623520802305768; United Nations, "World Statistics Pocketbook" (2016), http://data.un.org/CountryProfile.aspx ?crName=Cambodia#Social.

3. Although at the time of my original fieldwork it was a house for school-age boys, it later served as a library for residents and the neighboring community, and the original library became a storage and meeting room.

4. Over the years, there have been changes in the wake-up hour, and at times it was four thirty.

5. The morning glory is a nontoxic variety, also known as water convolvulus (*Ipomoea aquatica*).

6. Other days they might walk or bike, or up to five of them at a time might crowd onto the orphanage motorcycle, to be ferried by one of the housemothers to school.

7. Some ages are approximate and not known precisely.

8. I relied on my fourteen-year-old daughter's intuitions about the children's games. While to me it looked like a chaotic jumble of hopping and tagging, she caught on immediately and without missing a beat remarked, "Wow, there are a lot of people on base." In this and other situations, her interpretation of the children's activities was essential.

9. This number has decreased over the years. While demand in terms of children whose families or communities recommend them for placement is still high, the government has tightened restrictions on residential care and made it more difficult to place children in orphanages.

10. Orphanage directors in Kenya, Ethiopia, and India, as well as Cambodia, similarly express a preference for caregivers who are loving, service-minded, and patient, regardless of whether they have formal degrees. Blen M. Biru, Rae Jean Proeschold-Bell, Bonnie N. Kaiser, Heather E. Parnell, Venkata Gopala, Krishna Kaza, Ira Madan, Misganaw Eticha Dubie, Vanroth Vann, Cyrilla Amanya, and Kathryn Whetten, "Residential Care Directors' Perceptions of Desirable Characteristics of Caregivers for Orphaned and Separated Children," *International Journal of Applied Positive Psychology* (2020), https://doi.org/10.1007/s41042-020-00041-9.

11. May Mayko Ebihara, *Svay: A Khmer Village in Cambodia*, ed. Andrew Mertha (Ithaca, NY: Cornell University Press, 2018).

12. Will Brehm, "Historical Memory and Educational Privatisation: A Portrait from Cambodia," *Ethnography and Education* 14, no. 1 (2019): 34-50.

13. This enthusiasm for school attendance lessened in later years as more residents entered their teens and started junior high school, as will be discussed in the interviews presented in chapter 7.

14. In 2017, the NGO proudly announced Rathana's university graduation. Because of his experience and English skills, he had progressed from dancing to working for NGOs to support his studies.

15. For example, biking with lollipops in their mouths, stick fighting, kissing the unvaccinated dogs and free-roaming chickens, and perching on the roofs of the houses all left me torn between my desire to remain professionally detached and my desire to keep them safe.

16. Kunthea Mom, "Curb Physical Discipline: Charity," *Khmer Times*, June 1, 2017.

17. Leonie Kijewski, "Study Explores Cambodia's Use of Corporal Punishment," *Phnom Penh Post*, March 1, 2017.

18. This changed, however, in later years as staff came to focus more on conflict resolution strategies and mediation.

19. The reasons for children's admission to the COC are mirrored by those reported for children in Philippine orphanages, who "embrace their entry" into residential care after experiencing maltreatment, harm, and educational deprivation, in addition to poverty. Steven Roche, "Conceptualising Children's Life Histories and Reasons for Entry into Residential Care in the Philippines: Social Contexts, Instabilities and Safeguarding," *Children and Youth Services Review* 110 (2020): 104820.

20. Interestingly, the average age of placement of just under eight years coincides with the age at which Smith-Hefner reported Khmer parents recognize that their children are becoming capable of reason, and when parents therefore intensify their efforts to *bradav*, or teach (literally discipline), children the responsibilities they will assume in early adulthood. Nancy Smith-Hefner, *Khmer-American: Identity and Moral Education in a Diasporic Community* (Berkeley: University of California Press, 1999).

21. Only two of the orphanages I visited had toddlers in residence, and one of those planned to return the younger children to their communities after their medical conditions had been treated and stabilized. While they referred to themselves as an "orphanage," they might be more accurately labeled an acute care center or convalescent center.

22. Hope and Homes for Children, "National Survey of Institutions for Children in Rwanda" (2013), http://www.socialserviceworkforce.org/system/files/resource/files/NATIONAL%20SURVEY%20OF%20INSTITUTIONS%20FOR%20CHILDREN%20IN%20RWANDA_FINAL.pdf.

23. Yuko Nonoyama-Tarumi and Kurt Bredenberg, "Impact of School Readiness Program Interventions on Children's Learning in Cambodia," *International Journal of Educational Development* 29 (2009): 39–45.

24. Judy Ledgerwood, "Education in Cambodia" (2002), http://www.seasite.niu.edu/khmer/ledgerwood/education.htm.

25. *Pinpeat* is a traditional Khmer orchestra; at the orphanage, it consisted of circular gong chimes and wooden xylophones.

26. This observation is corroborated by others, such as Robin Mauney, "Cambodia Orphanage Survey" (Holt Children's Services/USAID, 2005), http://pdf.usaid.gov/pdf_docs/PNADI624.pdf, and Kathryn Whetten, Jan Ostermann, Rachel A. Whetten, Brian W. Pence, Karen O'Donnell, Lynne C. Messer, Nathan M. Thielman, and the Positive Outcomes for Orphans (POFO) Research Team, "A Comparison of the Wellbeing of Orphans and Abandoned Children Ages 6–12 in Institutional and Community-Based Care Settings in 5 Less Wealthy Nations," *PLOS ONE* 4 (2009): e8169, https://doi.org/10.1371/journal.pone.0008169.

27. Julia Karpati, Chris de Neubourg, Arnaud Laillou, and Etienne Poirot, "Improving Children's Nutritional Status in Cambodia: Multidimensional Poverty and Early Integrated Interventions," *Maternal & Child Nutrition* 16, no. S2 (2020): e12731.

28. *Most* of the children, that is. One of the teenage boys complained privately to us that he didn't like traditional dance and found it hard. Eight years later when I interviewed him he again told me how much he disliked it.

29. See also Ruth Emond, "Caring as a Moral, Practical and Powerful Endeavor: Peer Care in a Cambodian Orphanage," *British Journal of Social Work* 40, no. 1 (2010): 63–81.

30. Combating stigma can be important in and of itself, as a way to counter internalized negative judgments about children's status as orphans, but also can pragmatically affect interactions and opportunities for socialization and network building. Stigma

is a bigger problem for orphanages located in town, as the rural-urban divide in Cambodia is large and there are more wealthy people in the cities. Two urban orphanages reported to me that children attending the neighborhood school had been teased or bullied by other children or slighted by teachers and other school staff, and as a result they had enrolled the children in a private school, which had actually raised their prestige in the community.

31. My first inkling of this came the very first time I visited Cambodia, when I made arrangements to visit one of the oldest and most respected of Siem Reap's orphanages. I was welcome, they told me, to view the facilities, but the children were not there. When I got there, the place was indeed homey and attractive but completely deserted because the children had "all gone to visit their families for the water festival."

32. In fact, two residential centers in Egypt that are run by the same international organization, also very well resourced and with a reputation for keeping to themselves, were invaded and looted, and some staff assaulted, during the 2011 unrest there.

33. This became evident when I volunteered to be a guest English teacher at the junior high school.

34. Mindful of Western obsessions with toileting, staff at two different newly opened orphanages proudly showed me the new Western-style toilets that had been built even before the living quarters of the children had been completed, and even before the children had been enrolled in the local school.

35. My experiences with them were based on observation and interaction, and while it is true that I didn't run any formal assessments on them, I nonetheless have extensive experience with children as a parent, an older sibling, a volunteer in a special ed class, a preschool professional, a babysitter, and a researcher.

CHAPTER 6   THE ORPHANAGE REMEMBERED

1. I use the terms "Mom" and "Dad" to refer to the housemother and the head monk because residents and staff used kinship terms to refer to each other. The use of kinship terms with non–family members is usual in Cambodia, and in addition staff and residents were encouraged to regard the COC as a family. When referring to children's families of origin, the same terms are used.

2. He used the English word "god"; even among Buddhist Cambodians, this phrasing is used.

3. Morning glory happens to be a very easy crop to grow in home vegetable gardens, and as the children and staff were establishing the organic vegetable garden, it was their most successful crop. I too remember a lot of morning glory soup! The cook was expected by management to prepare separate meals for foreign visitors that were intended to appeal to their taste preferences. The visitors' meals were usually vegetarian and had more choices, including more stir-fried dishes. At my request, the cook happily gave up preparing special meals for me, and so I was able to experience the same food that the children were served.

4. Sheina Lew-Levy, Stephen M. Kissler, Adam H. Boyette, Alyssa N. Crittenden, Ibrahim A. Mabulla, and Barry S. Hewle, "Who Teaches Children to Forage? Exploring the Primacy of Child-to-Child Teaching among Hadza and BaYaka Hunter-Gatherers of Tanzania and Congo," *Evolution and Human Behavior* 41 (2020): 12–22; Maria Mammen, Bahar Köymen, and Michael Tomasello, "Children's Reasoning with Peers and Parents about Moral Dilemmas," *Developmental Psychology* 55, no. 11 (2019): 2324–2335;

David F. Lancy, "Playing with Knives: The Socialization of Self-Initiated Learners," *Child Development* 87 (2016): 654–665.

5. "Two-headed fish" means two-faced, insincere.

6. This could have been a matter of tactfulness on their part, not wanting to criticize foreigners in front of a foreigner. However, this interpretation is outweighed by the many spontaneous expressions of enjoyment and the fact that they did find some things to criticize.

7. It's a little hard to know how to interpret this since these two also laughed about how they cried while watching love stories on television and when they were hungry but the cook had made food they didn't like.

8. Kathie Carpenter, "Childhood Studies and Orphanage Tourism in Cambodia," *Annals of Tourism Research* 55 (2015): 15–27.

9. I often see this when I go to restaurants and notice the entire staff huddled in the kitchen doorway, all but drawing straws to decide who has to go take the order from the foreigner who just sat down.

10. Corporal punishment is common in Cambodian schools, although technically it is not legal.

11. I made the decision not to ask about abuse because the public settings and short-term nature of the interviews would have made it impossible to provide the kind of support required by such a traumatic disclosure, and I believed that it was the participants' prerogative to maintain control of such a sensitive topic.

12. Tess Guiney and Mary Mostafanezhad, "The Political Economy of Orphanage Tourism in Cambodia," *Tourist Studies* 15, no. 2 (2014): 132–155; Tess Guiney, "'Hug-an-Orphan Vacations': 'Love' and Emotion in Orphanage Tourism," *Geographical Journal* 184, no. 2 (2018): 125–137; P. Jane Reas, "'Children That Are Cute Enough to Eat': The Commodification of Children in Volunteering Vacations to Orphanages and Childcare Establishments in Siem Reap, Cambodia," *Tourism Culture & Communication* 20, nos. 2–3 (2020): 83–93.

13. By way of context for this comment, however, it's important to recognize that he was speaking as an adult visitor about living arrangements that had been designed for children.

CHAPTER 7   REFLECTING BACK AND LOOKING AHEAD

1. Fillers are utterances such as "um" and "hmmm."

2. By the time I started visiting the COC regularly, dance performances for donors were infrequent and the facility didn't feature the regular dance shows for tourists that some other orphanages did. Performances were mostly for local festivals or events at the pagoda in town.

3. In France, "Restaurant work is not seen as a low-paid, thankless job for those unable to find employment elsewhere, but as an endeavour worthy of recognition." Rhiannon L. Coslett, "French Waiters Aren't Rude, They Merely Demand Respect," *Guardian* June 12, 2015, https://www.theguardian.com/commentisfree/2015/jun/12/french-waiters -rude-respect-service.

4. Phan Soumy and Danielle Keeton-Olsen, "Minister: School Quality Improving, Dropout Rate Still High," *Cambodia Daily*, March 22, 2017, https://english.cambodiadaily .com/news/minister-school-quality-improving-dropout-rate-still-high-126857/.

5. I took 90 percent to mean "a whole lot" because certainly it was not literally true.

6. Charlotte Knaub, *A Memoir: Delivering Health Care in Cambodian Refugee Camps, 1979–1980* (Bloomington, IN: Balboa Press, 2014), 58.

7. We didn't ask the two youngest participants since they had only just left and were still desolate.

8. Most family farmers in Cambodia are functioning at a subsistence level, an arduous and precarious livelihood currently made more tenuous by climate change, drought, and widespread debt. None of the participants romanticized this possible outcome.

9. Sothy is referring to tensions between herself, the daughter from her father's previous marriage, and her new stepmother.

10. Cambodia's Center for Alliance of Labor and Human Rights estimates that some 1.7 to 2 million Cambodians are currently working in Thailand, with large numbers also in Malaysia and South Korea. Savi Korn, "Cambodian Workers 'Vulnerable' in Thailand," *Phnom Penh Post*, January 29, 2019. Only one so far has gone to work in Thailand, to my knowledge. He was unfortunately one of the former residents I was unable to interview, although NGO staff reported to me that they had heard he was back from Thailand and living somewhere in southern Cambodia.

11. "Do good receive good" is a reference to the Buddhist principle of karma; the entire proverb is, "Do good, receive good; do bad, receive bad."

12. Jintao Zhang, Guoxiang Zhao, Xiaoming Li, Yan Hong, Xiaoyi Fang, Douglas Barnett, Xiuyun Lin, Junfeng Zhao, and Liying Zhang, "Positive Future Orientation as a Mediator between Traumatic Events and Mental Health among Children Affected by HIV/AIDS in Rural China," *AIDS Care* 21, no. 12 (2009): 1508–1516.

13. Vichet Sam, "Impacts of Educational Mismatches in Developing Countries with a Focus on Cambodia" (doctoral dissertation, Université Grenoble Alpes, 2018).

14. Ruth Emond, "'I Am All about the Future World': Cambodian Children's Views on Their Status as Orphans," *Children and Society* 23 (2009): 407–417.

15. Emond, "'I Am All about the Future World,'" 412.

16. Virginia Morrow, "Rethinking Childhood Dependency: Children's Contribution to the Domestic Economy," *Sociological Review* 44 (1996): 58–77.

17. She is referring to herself as "Mom."

CHAPTER 8   DISCUSSION AND CONCLUSIONS

1. Melina Czymoniewicz-Klippel, "Parenting in the Context of Globalization and Acculturation: Perspectives of Mothers and Fathers in Siem Reap, Cambodia," *Childhood* 26, no. 4 (2019): 525–539.

2. Children living with HIV/AIDS in institutions have been reported to have significantly better oral health than similar children living with biological parents, a finding attributed to "the regulation of children's mealtimes and routines in institutions." Kimiyo Kikuchi, Yusuke Furukawa, Sovannary Tout, Khuondyla Pal, Chantheany Huot, and Siyan Yi, "'Who Cares' Is Key: Factors Associated with Oral Health Status in Children Living with HIV in Phnom Penh, Cambodia," *AIDS Care* 32, no. 4 (2020): 468.

3. Leslie K. Wang, *Outsourced Children: Orphanage Care and Adoption in Globalizing China* (Stanford, CA: Stanford University Press, 2016), 78.

4. Hope and Homes for Children, "National Survey of Institutions for Children in Rwanda" (2013), http://www.socialserviceworkforce.org/system/files/resource/files

/NATIONAL%20SURVEY%20OF%20INSTITUTIONS%20FOR%20CHILDREN%20IN%20
RWANDA_FINAL.pdf.

5. Although foster care is often preferred over orphanages because it is family based, it
    often results in undesirably high turnover, even in countries with well-developed
    social services such as Denmark. See Christian Christrup Kjeldsen and Marianne
    Bruhn Kjeldsen, "When Family Becomes the Job," *Adoption and Fostering Volume* 34,
    no. 1 (2010): 52–64. In my own home state of Oregon, the foster care system is so under-
    funded and overwhelmed that foster children are being housed in hotels, state
    offices, and juvenile detention centers rather than with families. It is possible that
    intentionally planned orphanages might not be worse than ad hoc detention centers.
    Hillary Borrud, "Oregon Sends Hundreds of Foster Kids to Former Jails, Institutions,
    Not Families," *OregonLive*, March 15, 2019, https://www.oregonlive.com/politics/2019/03
    /oregon-sends-hundreds-of-foster-kids-to-former-jails-institutions-not-families.html.

6. Marie K. Cohen, "Needed: A New Vision of Foster Care," *Chronicle of Social Change*,
    December 21, 2016, https://chronicleofsocialchange.org/blogger-co-op/needed-new
    -vision-foster-care/23425.

7. Richard B. McKenzie, *Rethinking Orphanages for the 21st Century* (Thousand Oaks,
    CA: Sage, 1998).

8. Kathie Carpenter, "Childhood Studies and Orphanage Tourism in Cambodia," *Annals
    of Tourism Research* 55 (2015): 15–27.

9. Kathie Carpenter, "A 'Nice, Knock-Down Argument' about Orphanage Tourism, Mod-
    ern Slavery and the Power and Peril of Naming," in *Modern Day Slavery and Orphanage
    Tourism*, ed. Joseph M. Cheer, Leigh Mathews, Kathryn E. van Doore, and Karen Fla-
    nagan (Wallingford, UK: CABI, 2019), 4; David F. Lancy, *Child Helpers: A Multidisciplinary
    Perspective* (Cambridge: Cambridge University Press, 2019),14.

10. Viviana Zelizer, *The Purchase of Intimacy* (Princeton, NJ: Princeton University Press,
    2009), 34.

11. Kathryn van Doore, "Orphanages as Sites of Modern Slavery," in Cheer et al., *Modern
    Day Slavery and Orphanage Tourism*, 19–30.

12. In fact, in one program evaluation I wrote for them, I made the recommendation that
    they should be *less* forthcoming about the children's actual family circumstances
    because I believed that making that information available was an unnecessary viola-
    tion of children's privacy. In any case, nobody could accuse them of being less than
    forthcoming about the actual circumstances of the children in their care, and they
    never claimed that none of the children had living parents.

13. Wayne Cornish, "The World Must Wake to the Dangers of Orphanages," *New States-
    man*, 2017, https://www.newstatesman.com/world/2017/03/world-must-wake-dangers
    -orphanages.

14. Lerato Constance Moalosi, "Focusing on Caregivers: The Experiences of Women Care-
    givers Caring for Orphans and Vulnerable Children at Crossroads Child and Youth
    Care Center, Matatiele" (master's thesis, University of Kwazulu-Natal, 2019); Xiaoqian
    Liu, Kathryn Whetten, Neil Prose, David Eagle, Heather Parnell, Cyrilla Amanya, Van-
    roth Vann, Misganaw Eticha Dubie, Venkata Gopala Krishna Kaza, Senti Tzudir, and
    Rae Jean Proeschold-Bell, "Enjoyment and Meaning in Daily Activities among Caregiv-
    ers of Orphaned and Separated Children in Four Countries," *Children and Youth Services
    Review* 116 (2020): 1–10; Rae Jean Proeschold-Bell, Nneka Jebose Molokwu, Corey L. M.
    Keyes, Malik Muhammad Sohail, David E. Eagle, Heather E. Parnell, Warren A.

Kinghorn, Cyrilla Amanya, Vanroth Vann, Ira Madan, Blen M. Biru, Dean Lewis, Misganaw Eticha Dubie, and Kathryn Whetten, "Caring and Thriving: An International Qualitative Study of Caregivers of Orphaned and Vulnerable Children and Strategies to Sustain Positive Mental Health," *Children and Youth Services Review* 98 (2019): 143–153.

15. Janelle Retka, "When an Orphanage Can Provide What a Parent Cannot," *Bright Magazine*, April 24, 2018, 1–11.

16. Hannah Hawkins and Khy Sovuthy, "NGOs Scramble to Care for Children as Orphanages Close," *Cambodia Daily*, February 17, 2017, https://english.cambodiadaily.com/news/ngos-scramble-to-care-for-children-as-orphanages-close-125325/.

17. Often the dismissiveness toward children's games and songs stems from an inadequate understanding of how complex their language often is. "If you're happy and you know it," for example, models appropriate usage of conditional constructions, complex syntax that can be hard to master without practice. Jasmin Alić, "Conditionals: An English Learner's Worst Nightmare," *Speechling*, September 21, 2017, https://speechling.com/blog/conditionals-an-english-learners-worst-nightmare/; P. Jane Reas, "'So, Child Protection, I'll Make a Quick Point of It Now': Broadening the Notion of Child Abuse in Volunteering Vacations in Siem Reap, Cambodia," *Tourism Review International* 18, no. 4 (2015): 295–309.

18. In an analysis of a volunteer visit to a Kenyan orphanage by British young people, Cheung Judge proposes that "playful, friendly interactions between British and African youth disrupted relations of charitable pity and signalled desires for solidarity and equality," suggesting that "just" playing and having fun with orphanage residents can have political as well as affective consequence. Ruth Cheung Judge, "Refusing Reform, Reworking Pity, or Reinforcing Privilege? The Multivalent Politics of Young People's Fun and Friendship within a Volunteering Encounter," *Antipode* (2020), https://doi.org/10.1111/anti.12635.

19. Will Brehm, "Historical Memory and Educational Privatisation: A Portrait from Cambodia," *Ethnography and Education* 14, no. 1 (2019): 34–50. Most of my friends say explicitly that they won't enroll their kids in a public school but rather will do whatever is necessary for them to attend one of the many private schools that are popping up in urban areas all over Cambodia.

20. Adrian Rus, Ecaterina Stativa, Sheri R. Parris, Jacquelyn S. Pennings, Max E. Butterfield, Wesley C. Lee, and Ovidu Gavrilovici, "Punishment, Peer Exploitation and Sexual Abuse in Long-Term Romanian Residential Centers," 61–86, and Shalhevet Attar-Schwartz, "Experience of Victimization by Peers and Staff in Residential Care for Children at Risk in Israel from an Ecological Perspective," 269–300, both in *Child Maltreatment in Residential Care*, ed. Adrian V. Rus, Sheri R. Parris, and Ecaterina Stativa (Dordrecht: Springer, 2017).

21. Reported also in Czymoniewicz-Klippel, "Parenting in the Context of Globalization."

22. Linda Gordon, "The Perils of Innocence, or What's Wrong with Putting Children First?," *Journal of the History of Childhood and Youth* 1 (2008): 332.

23. As everywhere, in Cambodia the boundary between childhood and adulthood is actually quite complicated. For example, the age of consent is fifteen; the age of civil majority is sixteen; marriage with parental permission is legal at sixteen, although parental permission is still required for marriage until age eighteen; motorcycles may be driven at sixteen and automobiles at eighteen; the voting age is also eighteen; and the drinking age is twenty-one. Furthermore, rarely are any of these legal age limits

enforced consistently, reflecting the tension between local beliefs and legal statutes that are often constructed with foreign influence.

24. United Nations General Assembly, "Rights of the Child" (resolution, December 17, 2015), https://www.un.org/en/development/desa/population/migration/generalassembly/docs/globalcompact/A_RES_70_137.pdf.

25. Hope and Homes for Children, "Landmark Moment as the UN Calls for the End of Orphanages" (December 18, 2019), https://www.hopeandhomes.org/news-article/unga/.

26. Save the Children, "Governments Now Have an Opportunity to Stop Supporting the Unnecessary Separation of Children from Parents" (December 18, 2019), https://www.savethechildren.org/us/about-us/media-and-news/2019-press-releases/unnecessary-child-separation-resolution-passes; Bethany Children's Services, "UN General Assembly Makes Landmark Decision for Children: Prioritizes Family Preservation Just in Time for Christmas" (December 20, 2019), https://bethany.org/news-room/icymi-un-general-assembly-makes-landmark-decision-for-children-prioritizes-family-preservation-just-in-time-for-christmas.

27. Beth L. Rubenstein, Matthew MacFarlane, Celina Jensen, and Lindsay Stark, "Measuring Movement into Residential Care Institutions in Haiti after Hurricane Matthew: A Pilot Study," *PLOS ONE* 13, no. 4 (2018), https://doi.org/10.1371/journal.pone.0195515.

28. John Twyning, *Forms of English History in Literature, Landscape and Architecture* (Basingstoke, UK: Palgrave Macmillan, 2012), 133.

BIBLIOGRAPHY

Alić, Jasmin. "Conditionals: An English Learner's Worst Nightmare." *Speechling*, September 21, 2017. https://speechling.com/blog/conditionals-an-english-learners-worst -nightmare/.

Al Jazeera. "Cambodia's Orphan Business." *People and Power*, June 27, 2012. https://www .youtube.com/watch?v=-hf_snNO9X8.

———. "Cambodia's Orphan Tourism." *101 East*, February 10, 2011. https://www.aljazeera.com /programmes/101east/2011/02/2011210123057338995.html.

AnnemarieJ5079BX. "Traditional Khmer Dance at ACODO Orphanage." *TripAdvisor*, January 19, 2014. https://www.tripadvisor.com/Attraction_Review-g297390-d1647060 -Reviews-Traditional_Khmer_Dance_at_ACODO_Orphanage-Siem_Reap_Siem _Reap_Province.html.

Aquino, Michael. "Orphanages in Cambodia Are Not Tourist Attractions." *TripSavvy*, October 14, 2017. https://www.tripsavvy.com/orphanages-in-cambodia-1629144.

Attar-Schwartz, Shalhevet. "Experience of Victimization by Peers and Staff in Residential Care for Children at Risk in Israel from an Ecological Perspective." In *Child Maltreatment in Residential Care*, edited by Adrian V. Rus, Sheri R. Parris, and Ecaterina Stativa, 269–300. Dordrecht: Springer, 2017.

Bainbridge, Bill, and Lon Nara. "Few Babies 'Abandoned' since Moratorium: Orphanages." *Phnom Penh Post*, August 2, 2002.

Bakermans-Kranenburg, Marian J., Marinus H. Van IJzendoorn, and Femmie Juffer. "Earlier Is Better: A Meta-analysis of 70 Years of Intervention Improving Cognitive Development in Institutionalized Children." *Monographs of the Society for Research in Child Development* 73 (2008): 279–293.

Ball, Molly. "Nightly Khmer Dance Back in Phnom Penh after 25 Years." *Cambodia Daily*, December 25, 2001.

Basic Education and Teacher Training. "Education Structure in Cambodia." 2008. http:// bookbridge.org/en/the-education-system-in-cambodia/.

Ben. "Comments—Cambodian Orphan Family Centre Organization Parts 1 and 2." *Travelpod*, 2011. https://web.archive.org/web/20110628050728/http://www.travelpod.com/travel -blog-entries/wendyworld/4/1261194608/tpod.html.

Bethany Children's Services. "UN General Assembly Makes Landmark Decision for Children: Prioritizes Family Preservation Just in Time for Christmas." December 20, 2019. https:// bethany.org/news-room/icymi-un-general-assembly-makes-landmark-decision-for -children-prioritizes-family-preservation-just-in-time-for-christmas.

Biru, Blen M., Rae Jean Proeschold-Bell, Bonnie N. Kaiser, Heather E. Parnell, Venkata Gopala, Krishna Kaza, Ira Madan, Misganaw Eticha Dubie, Vanroth Vann, Cyrilla Amanya, and

Kathryn Whetten. "Residential Care Directors' Perceptions of Desirable Characteristics of Caregivers for Orphaned and Separated Children." *International Journal of Applied Positive Psychology* (2020). https://doi.org/10.1007/s41042-020-00041-9.

Bjorklund, David F., Alyson J. Myers, and Ariel Bartolo-Kira. "Human Child Rearing and Family from an Evolutionary Perspective." In *Cross-Cultural Family Research and Practice*, edited by W. Kim Halford and Fons Van De Vijver, 13–55. Cambridge, MA: Academic Press, 2020.

Bluebond-Langner, Myra, and Jill E. Korbin. "Challenges and Opportunities in the Anthropology of Childhoods: An Introduction to 'Children, Childhoods and Childhood Studies.'" *American Anthropologist* 109, no. 2 (2007): 241–246.

Bogolyubova, Elena, Kathie Carpenter, and Valerii Mitrofanenko. "The Peer-to-Peer Approach Works: Promoting and Understanding Unique Cultures of Volunteering in Russian and American Youth Social Services." *Professional Development* 2, no. 1 (forthcoming).

———. "Re-thinking Civil Society in Russia through International and Intersectoral Collaboration in Youth Welfare in North Caucasus." *International Society for Third-Sector Research Working papers Series* 11, no. 1 (2019).

Boothby, Neil. "Khmer Children: Alone at the Border." *Indochina Issues* 3, no. 2 (1982): 1–7.

Borrud, Hillary. "Oregon Sends Hundreds of Foster Kids to Former Jails, Institutions, Not Families." *OregonLive*, March 15, 2019. https://www.oregonlive.com/politics/2019/03/oregon-sends-hundreds-of-foster-kids-to-former-jails-institutions-not-families.html.

Bowlby, John. "Maternal Care and Mental Health: A Report Prepared on Behalf of the World Health Organization as a Contribution to the United Nations Program for the Welfare of Homeless Children." World Health Organization, 1951.

Bradley, Samantha. "Domestic and Family Violence in Post-conflict Communities: International Human Rights Law and the State's Obligation to Protect Women and Children." *Health and Human Rights Journal*, December 4, 2018. https://www.hhrjournal.org/2018/12/domestic-and-family-violence-in-post-conflict-communities-international-human-rights-law-and-the-states-obligation-to-protect-women-and-children/.

Brehm, Will. "Historical Memory and Educational Privatisation: A Portrait from Cambodia." *Ethnography and Education* 14, no. 1 (2019): 34–50.

Brown, Waln. "Foster Families or Orphanages: What Do Alumni Say?" *Chronicle of Social Change*, May 15, 2013. https://chronicleofsocialchange.org/featured/foster-families-or-orphanages-what-do-alumni-say.

Bugnion, Francois. "Cambodia: Massive Aid Effort Planted Seeds of Recovery in Former 'Killing Fields.'" 2009. https://www.icrc.org/eng/resources/documents/interview/cambodia-interview-011209.htm.

Burrington, Kathryn. "Justifiable Bad Press for Orphanage Tourism." *Travel with Kat*, 2014. https://travelwithkat.com/orphanage-tourism/.

Bylander, Maryanne. "Is Regular Migration Safer Migration? Insights from Thailand." *Journal on Migration and Human Security* 7, no. 1 (2019): 1–18.

"Cambodia, U.N. Launch Plan to Tackle Fake Orphanages." Reuters, April 20, 2017. https://www.reuters.com/article/us-cambodia-orphanage/cambodia-u-n-launch-plan-to-tackle-fake-orphanages-idUSKBN17MoUD.

Canadian Broadcasting Corporation. "Khmer Rouge Victims Reunited 40 Years after Daring Rescue." *Radio West*, March 19, 2015. https://www.cbc.ca/news/canada/british-columbia/khmer-rouge-victims-reunited-40-years-after-daring-rescue-1.3002191.

Canosa, Antonia, and Anne Graham. "Tracing the Contribution of Childhood Studies: Maintaining Momentum while Navigating Tensions." *Childhood* 27, no. 1 (2020): 25–47.

Carmichael, Robert. "Cambodia's Orphanages Target the Wallets of Well-Meaning Tourists." *Independent,* March 25, 2011.

——. "UNICEF: Cambodia's Orphans Not Really Orphans." *DW Asia,* March 24, 2011. https://www.dw.com/en/unicef-cambodias-orphans-not-really-orphans/a-6481673.

Carpenter, Kathie. "The Child as Method? Paradigm Shifts, Positionality and Participatory Methods for Researching Children in Asia." In *Methods and Moments: Ethnographic Research in Asia,* edited by Nayantara Sheoran Appleton and Caroline Bennett. London: Rowman & Littlefield, forthcoming.

——. "Childhood Studies and Orphanage Tourism in Cambodia." *Annals of Tourism Research* 55 (2015): 15–27.

——. "Continuity, Complexity and Reciprocity in a Cambodian Orphanage." *Children & Society* 29, no. 2 (2015): 85–94.

——. "A 'Nice, Knock-Down Argument' about Orphanage Tourism, Modern Slavery and the Power and Peril of Naming." In *Modern Day Slavery and Orphanage Tourism,* edited by Joseph M. Cheer, Leigh Mathews, Kathryn E. van Doore, and Karen Flanagan, 125–138. Wallingford, UK: CABI, 2019.

——. "Volunteer Tourism in Cambodian Orphanages: Is There Such a Thing as Best Practices?" In *Proceedings of Greenlines Institute for Sustainable Development International Conference on Global Tourism and Sustainability,* 105–113. Lagos, Portugal, 2016. http://greenlines-institute.org/proceedings/Tourism2016/TOURISM_2016_EBOOK.pdf.

Charles, Marie. "HIV Epidemic in Cambodia, One of the Poorest Countries in Southeast Asia: A Success Story." *Expert Review of Anti-infective Therapy* 4 (2014): 1–4.

Cheer, Joseph M., Leigh Mathews, Kathryn E. van Doore, and Karen Flanagan, eds. *Modern Day Slavery and Orphanage Tourism.* Wallingford, UK: CABI, 2019.

Cheney, Kristin, and Karen Smith Rotabi. "Addicted to Orphans: How the Global Orphan Industrial Complex Jeopardizes Local Child Protection Systems." In *Conflict, Violence and Peace: Geographies of Children and Young People,* vol. 11, edited by T. Skelton, C. Harker, and K. Horschelmann, 89–107. Singapore: Springer, 2017.

Cheung Judge, Ruth. "Refusing Reform, Reworking Pity, or Reinforcing Privilege? The Multivalent Politics of Young People's Fun and Friendship within a Volunteering Encounter." *Antipode* (2020). https://doi.org/10.1111/anti.12635.

Chheang, Vannarith. "Tourism and Local Community Development in Siem Reap." *Ritsumeikan Journal of Asia Pacific Studies* 27 (2010): 85–101.

Cohen, Marie K. "Needed: A New Vision of Foster Care." *Chronicle of Social Change,* December 21, 2016. https://chronicleofsocialchange.org/blogger-co-op/needed-new-vision-foster-care/23425.

Commonwealth of Australia. "Orphanage Trafficking." 2017. https://www.aph.gov.au/Parliamentary_Business/Committees/Joint/Foreign_Affairs_Defence_and_Trade/ModernSlavery/Final_report/section?id=committees%2Freportjnt%2F024102%2F25036.

ConCERT. "Responsible Volunteering." n.d. http://concertcambodia.org/responsible-volunteering/.

Conran, Mary. "They Really Love Me! Intimacy in Volunteer Tourism." *Annals of Tourism Research* 38, no. 4 (2011): 1454–1473.

Cornish, Wayne. "The World Must Wake to the Dangers of Orphanages." *New Statesman,* 2017. https://www.newstatesman.com/world/2017/03/world-must-wake-dangers-orphanages.

Coslett, Rhiannon L. "French Waiters Aren't Rude, They Merely Demand Respect." *Guardian,* June 12, 2015. https://www.theguardian.com/commentisfree/2015/jun/12/french-waiters-rude-respect-service.

Cox, Geraldine. *Home Is Where the Heart Is.* Sydney: Macmillan, 2000.

Cravath, Paul. *Earth in Flower: The Divine Mystery of the Cambodian Dance Drama*. Holmes Beach, FL: Datasia, 2008.

———. "The Ritual Origins of the Classical Dance Drama of Cambodia." *Asian Theatre Journal* 3 (1986): 179–203.

Crenson, Matthew. *Building the Invisible Orphanage*. Cambridge, MA: Harvard University Press, 1998.

Czymoniewicz-Klippel, Melina. "Parenting in the Context of Globalization and Acculturation: Perspectives of Mothers and Fathers in Siem Reap, Cambodia." *Childhood* 26, no. 4 (2019): 525–539.

D'Hoore, Alain, Matt Davies, Sodeth Ly, Robert Hagemann, Pokar Khemani, Dennis Botman, and Bikas Joshi. "Cambodia: Selected Issues and Statistical Appendix." International Monetary Fund Country Report No. 06/26, 2006. https://www.imf.org/external /pubs/ft/scr/2006/cro6265.pdf.

Domashneva, Helen. "NGOs in Cambodia: It's Complicated." *Diplomat*, December 3, 2013. https://thediplomat.com/2013/12/ngos-in-cambodia-its-complicated.

Duchâteau-Arminjon, Benoît. *Healing Cambodia: One Child at a Time*. Singapore: Editions Didier Millet, 2013.

Dufus, Amber. "HIV/AIDS Rates in Cambodia Drop Down to Virtual Elimination." *Borgen Project Blog Latest News*, 2018. https://borgenproject.org/hiv-aids-rates-in-cambodia/.

Dunston, Lara. "Why You Should Avoid Orphanage Visits in Cambodia." *Grantourismo*, June 17, 2014. https://grantourismotravels.com/2014/06/17/why-you-should-avoid -orphanage-visits-in-cambodia/.

Ear, Sophal. *Aid Dependence in Cambodia: How Foreign Assistance Undermines Democracy*. New York: Columbia University Press, 2012.

Eastmond, Marita. "Reconstruction and the Politics of Homecoming: Repatriation of Refugees in Cambodia." Goteborg University, Department of Social Anthropology Working Paper no. 1, 2002.

Ebihara, May Mayko. *Svay: A Khmer Village in Cambodia*. Edited by Andrew Mertha. Ithaca, NY: Cornell University Press, 2018.

Emond, Ruth. "Caring as a Moral, Practical and Powerful Endeavor: Peer Care in a Cambodian Orphanage." *British Journal of Social Work* 40, no. 1 (2010): 63–81.

———. "'I Am All about the Future World': Cambodian Children's Views on Their Status as Orphans." *Children and Society* 23 (2009): 407–417.

Ennew, Judith. "Prisoners of Childhood: Orphans and Economic Dependency." In *Studies in Modern Childhood*, edited by Jens Qvortrup, 128–146. Basingstoke, UK: Palgrave Macmillan, 2005.

Firpo, Christina Elizabeth. *The Uprooted: Race, Children, and Imperialism in French Indochina, 1890–1980*. Honolulu: University of Hawai'i Press, 2016.

Fox, Nathan, Alissa Almas, Kathryn Degnan, Charles A. Nelson, and Charles H. Zeanah. "The Effects of Severe Psychosocial Deprivation and Foster Care Intervention on Cognitive Development at 8 Years of Age: Findings for the Bucharest Early Intervention Project." *Journal of Child Psychology and Psychiatry* 52, no. 9 (2011): 919–928.

Fox, Nathan, and Charles H. Zeanah. "Comment on Whetten et al." *PLOS ONE* 24 (December 2009).

Friends International. "Annual Report." 2009. https://urldefense.com/v3/__https://www .yumpu.com/en/document/view/47417542/annual-report-2009-friends-international __;!!C5qS4YX3!VgrnlPetx5d5LeGPoi9Ldog3j4JYFbtOO6-ibm7PaOZI9SXuPipLCSP7kC4y NccCPmzzOaI$.

———. "ChildSafe International." 2007. http://www.childsafe-international.org.

———. "ChildSafe Movement." n.d. https://friends-international.org/childsafe-movement/.

———. "ChildSafe Tips for Travelers and Foreign Residents." 2007. http//www.childsafe -internatinal.org/TFResidents.asp.

———. "Recommended Child Safe Tourist Information: Travel Tips." 2006. http://www .childsafe-cambodia.org:80/traveladvice.asp.

Fronek, Patricia, Robert Common, Karen Smith Rotabi, and Johnny Statham. "Identifying and Addressing Risk in the Implementation of Alternative Care Policies in Cambodia." *Journal of Human Rights and Social Work* 4 (2019): 140–144.

Gayapersad, Allison, Caroline Ombok, Allan Kamanda, Carren Tarus, David Ayuku, and Paul Braitstein. "The Production and Reproduction of Kinship in Charitable Children's Institutions in Uasin Gishu County, Kenya." *Child and Youth Care Forum* 48 (2019): 797–828.

Geach, Catherine. "Khmer Cultural Development Institute History." 2013. http://www.kcdi -cambodia.com/about-us/history/.

Gender Based Violence under the Khmer Rouge Information Platform. n.d. http://gbvkr.org /gender-based-violence-under-khmer-rouge/facts-and-figures/forced-marriage/.

Gibbons, Jacqueline. "Orphanages in Egypt." *Journal of Asian and African Studies* 40 (2005): 261–285.

Gordon, Linda. "The Perils of Innocence, or What's Wrong with Putting Children First?" *Journal of the History of Childhood and Youth* 1 (2008): 331–350.

Gray, Christine L., Sumedha Ariely, Brian W. Pence, and Kathryn Whetten. "Why Institutions Matter: Empirical Data from Five Low- and Middle-Income Countries Indicate the Critical Role of Institutions for Orphans." In *Child Maltreatment in Residential Care*, edited by Adrian V. Rus, Sheri R. Parris, and Ecaterina Stativa, 379–400. Dordrecht: Springer, 2017.

Gray, Christine L., Brian W. Pence, Jan Ostermann, Rachel A. Whetten, Karen O'Donnell, Nathan M. Thielman, and Kathryn Whetten. "Prevalence and Incidence of Traumatic Experiences among Orphans in Institutional and Family-Based Settings in 5 Low- and Middle-Income Countries: A Longitudinal Study." *Global Health: Science and Practice* 3, no. 3 (2015): 395–404.

Guiney, Tess. "'Hug-an-Orphan Vacations': 'Love' and Emotion in Orphanage Tourism." *Geographical Journal* 184, no. 2 (2018): 125–137.

Guiney, Tess, and Mary Mostafanezhad. "The Political Economy of Orphanage Tourism in Cambodia." *Tourist Studies* 15, no. 2 (2014): 132–155.

Hansen, Anne. "The Image of an Orphan: Cambodian Narrative Sites for Buddhist Ethical Reflection." *Journal of Asian Studies* 62, no. 3 (2003): 811–834.

Harris, Ian. *Cambodian Buddhism: History and Practice.* Honolulu: University of Hawai'i Press, 2005.

"Harry Potter Was Inspired by Oliver Twist, Claims Academic." *Telegraph*, July 19, 2011. http:// www.telegraph.co.uk/culture/harry-potter/8645593/Harry-Potter-was-inspired-by -Oliver-Twist-claims-academic.html.

Hartley, Morgan, and Chris Walker. "Cambodia's Booming New Industry: Orphanage Tourism." *Forbes*, May 24, 2013. https://www.forbes.com/sites/morganhartley/2013/05/24 /cambodias-booming-new-industry-orphanage-tourism/#45592744794a.

Hartman, Eric. "Why UNICEF and Save the Children Are Against Your Short-Term Service in Orphanages." *Campus Compact Global S.L. Blog*, n.d. https://compact.org/why-unicef -and-save-the-children-are-against-you-caring-for-orphans/.

Hawkins, Hannah, and Khy Sovuthy. "NGOs Scramble to Care for Children as Orphanages Close." *Cambodia Daily*, February 17, 2017. https://english.cambodiadaily.com/news /ngos-scramble-to-care-for-children-as-orphanages-close-125325/.

Heywood, Denise. *Cambodian Dance: Celebration of the Gods*. Bangkok: River Books, 2008.

Hong, Yan, Xiaoming Li, Xiaoyi Fang, Guoxiang Zhao, Junfeng Zhao, Qun Zhao, Xiuyun Lin, Liying Zhang, and Bonita Stanton. "Care Arrangements of AIDS Orphans and Their Relationship with Children's Psychosocial Well-Being in Rural China." *Health Policy and Planning* 26 (2010): 115–123.

Hope and Homes for Children. "Landmark Moment as the UN Calls for the End of Orphanages." December 18, 2019. https://www.hopeandhomes.org/news-article/unga/.

———. "National Survey of Institutions for Children in Rwanda." 2013. http://www.social serviceworkforce.org/system/files/resource/files/NATIONAL%20SURVEY%20OF%20 INSTITUTIONS%20FOR%20CHILDREN%20IN%20RWANDA_FINAL.pdf.

Hruby, Denise. "In Cambodia, Fake Orphanages Soak Up Donations by Duping Tourists." *Los Angeles Daily News*, July 21, 2014.

Hsieh, H. F. and S. E. Shannon. "Three Approaches to Qualitative Content Analysis." *Qualitative Health Research* 15, no. 9 (2005): 1277–1288.

Hughes, Rachel. "Dutiful Tourism: Encountering the Cambodia Genocide." *Asia Pacific Viewpoint* 49, no. 3 (2008): 318–330.

Huynh, Hy V., Susan Limber, Christin Gray, Martie Thompson, Augustine Wasonga, Vanroth Vann, Dafrosa Itemba, Misganaw Eticha, Ira Madan, and Kathryn Whetten. "Factors Affecting the Psychosocial Well-Being of Orphan and Separated Children in Five Low- and Middle-Income Countries: Which Is More Important, Quality of Care or Care Setting?" *PLOS ONE* 14 (2019): 6–12.

Jenks, Chris. "Childhood and Transgression." In *Studies in Modern Childhood: Society, Agency and Culture*, edited by Jens Qvortrup, 115–127. Basingstoke, UK: Palgrave Macmillan, 2005.

Jjack. "Comments—Short-Term Volunteer Opportunity at Orphanage Phnom Penh." Lonely Planet Thorn Tree Forum, 2010. https://www.lonelyplanet.com/thorntree/forums/asia -south-east-asia-mainland/topics/short-term-volunteer-opportunity-at-orphanage -phnom-penh?page=11.

Jordana, Ashley D. "Situational Analysis on Child, Early and Forced Marriage in Vietnam, Laos, Myanmar and Cambodia." World Vision, 2016. https://www.wvi.org/sites/default /files/report_SituationalanalysisCEFMVietnamLaosMyanmarandCambodia-FINAL .docx-2.pdf.

Kalab, Milada. "Monastic Education, Village Structure and Social Mobility in Cambodia." In *The Anthropological Study of Education*, edited by Craig J. Calhoun and Francis A. Janni, 61–74. The Hague: De Gruyter, 1976.

Karpati, Julia, Chris de Neubourg, Arnaud Laillou, and Etienne Poirot. "Improving Children's Nutritional Status in Cambodia: Multidimensional Poverty and Early Integrated Interventions." *Maternal & Child Nutrition* 16, no. S2 (2020): e12731.

Keiger, Dale. "The Rise and Demise of the American Orphanage." *Johns Hopkins Magazine*, April 1996. http://pages.jh.edu/jhumag/496web/orphange.html.

Keller, Heidi. "Universality Claim of Attachment Theory: Children's Socioemotional Development across Cultures." *Proceedings of the National Academy of Sciences* 115, no. 45 (2018): 11414–11419.

Khadka, Suman, and Buthdy Sem. "Caring for Children Left Behind in Residential Care during COVID-19." UNICEF, 2020. https://www.unicef.org/cambodia/stories/caring -children-left-behind-residential-care-during-covid19.

Kijewski, Leonie. "Life Had No More Value Than the Smallest Atom Floating in Space in the Stars, Expert Says." *Cambodia Tribunal Monitor*, July 29, 2017. http://www.cambodia

tribunal.org/2016/07/29/life-had-no-more-value-than-the-smallest-atom-floating-in
-space-in-the-stars-expert-says/.

———. "Study Explores Cambodia's Use of Corporal Punishment." *Phnom Penh Post*, March 1, 2017.

Kikuchi, Kimiyo, Yusuke Furukawa, Sovannary Tout, Khuondyla Pal, Chantheany Huot, and Siyan Yi. "'Who Cares' Is Key: Factors Associated with Oral Health Status in Children Living with HIV in Phnom Penh, Cambodia." *AIDS Care* 32, no. 4 (2020): 462–470.

Kimball, Melanie. "From Folktales to Fiction: Orphan Characters in Children's Literature." *Library Trends* 47, no. 3 (1999): 558–578.

Kjeldsen, Christian Christrup, and Marianne Bruhn Kjeldsen. "When Family Becomes the Job." *Adoption and Fostering Volume* 34, no. 1 (2010): 52–64.

Knaub, Charlotte. *A Memoir: Delivering Health Care in Cambodian Refugee Camps, 1979–1980.* Bloomington, IN: Balboa Press, 2014.

Kompongthom. "Comments—Visit an Orphanage in Phnom Penh." Lonely Planet Thorn Tree Forum, 2010. https://www.lonelyplanet.com/thorntree/forums/asia-south-east -asia-mainland/topics/visit-an-orphanage-in-phnom-penh.

Korn, Savi. "Cambodian Workers 'Vulnerable' in Thailand." *Phnom Penh Post*, January 29, 2019.

Kruger, Pamela. "Adopting from Abroad." *Child Magazine*, 2004. http://www.pamelakruger .com/articles/detail.asp?a=7.

Lancy, David F. "Accounting for Variability in Mother-Child Play." *American Anthropologist* 109, no. 2 (2007): 273–284.

———. "Adoption and the Circulation of Children." *Psychology Today*, January 13, 2017. https:// www.psychologytoday.com/blog/benign-neglect/201701/adoption-and-the-circulation -children.

———. *The Anthropology of Childhood: Cherubs, Chattel, Changelings.* Cambridge: Cambridge University Press, 2014.

———. *Child Helpers: A Multidisciplinary Perspective.* Cambridge: Cambridge University Press, 2019.

———. "Playing with Knives: The Socialization of Self-Initiated Learners." *Child Development* 87 (2016): 654–665.

Langford, Anne. "Working with Cambodian Refugees." *Journal of Transpersonal Psychology* 12 (1980): 122.

Ledgerwood, Judy. "Education in Cambodia." 2002. http://www.seasite.niu.edu/khmer /ledgerwood/education.htm.

Lepore, Jill. "Baby Doe: A Political History of Tragedy." *New Yorker*, February 1, 2016.

Lew-Levy, Sheina, Stephen M. Kissler, Adam H. Boyette, Alyssa N. Crittenden, Ibrahim A. Mabulla, and Barry S. Hewle. "Who Teaches Children to Forage? Exploring the Primacy of Child-to-Child Teaching among Hadza and BaYaka Hunter-Gatherers of Tanzania and Congo." *Evolution and Human Behavior* 41 (2020): 12–22.

Liu, Xiaoqian, Kathryn Whetten, Neil Prose, David Eagle, Heather Parnell, Cyrilla Amanya, Vanroth Vann, Misganaw Eticha Dubie, Venkata Gopala Krishna Kaza, Senti Tzudir, and Rae Jean Proeschold-Bell. "Enjoyment and Meaning in Daily Activities among Caregivers of Orphaned and Separated Children in Four Countries." *Children and Youth Services Review* 116 (2020): 1–10.

Mammen, Maria, Bahar Köymen, and Michael Tomasello. "Children's Reasoning with Peers and Parents about Moral Dilemmas." *Developmental Psychology* 55, no. 11 (2019): 2324–2335. https://doi.org/10.1037/dev0000807.

Margie, Nancy G., and Deborah A. Phillips. *Revisiting Home Visiting.* Washington, DC: National Academies Press, 1999.

Mauney, Robin. "Cambodia Orphanage Survey." Holt Children's Services/USAID, 2005. http://pdf.usaid.gov/pdf_docs/PNADI624.pdf.

McGehee, Nancy G. "Oppression, Emancipation and Volunteer Tourism." *Annals of Tourism Research* 39, no. 1 (2012): 84–107.

McKenzie, Richard B. "The American Dream Is Alive and Well—Among Orphanage Alumni!" National Center for Policy Analysis Issue Brief No. 202 (2016).

———. *The Home: A Memoir of Growing Up in an Orphanage.* New York: Basic Books, 1996.

———. *Miracle Mountain: A Hidden Sanctuary for Children, Horses, and Birds off a Road Less Traveled.* Irvine, CA: Dickens Press, 2013.

———. *Rethinking Orphanages for the 21st Century.* Thousand Oaks, CA: Sage, 1998.

McLaren, Helen, and Nismah Qonita. "Indonesia's Orphanage Trade: Islamic Philanthropy's Good Intentions, Some Not So Good Outcomes." *Religions* 11, no. 1 (2020). https://doi.org/10.3390/rel11010001.

McLellan, Janet. "Repatriation and Reintegration of Cambodian Refugees: Issues and Concerns." *Refuge* 13, no. 5 (1993): 15–17.

Mercer, Jean. "Conventional and Unconventional Perspectives on Attachment and Attachment Problems: Comparisons and Implications, 2006–2016." *Child and Adolescent Social Work Journal* 36, no. 2 (2019): 81–95.

Meta, Kong, and Daphne Chenhen. "Government to Miss Orphan Goal." *Phnom Penh Post*, December 29, 2017. https://www.phnompenhpost.com/national/government-miss-orphan-goal.

Meta, Kong, and Cristina Maza. "Government Shutters 56 Shelters." *Phnom Penh Post*, February 16, 2017. https://www.phnompenhpost.com/national/government-shutters-56-shelters.

Ministry of Social Affairs, Veterans and Youth Rehabilitation. "Minimum Standards on Alternative Care for Children." Phnom Penh: Ministry of Social Affairs, Veterans and Youth Rehabilitation, 2008.

———. "With the Best of Intentions: A Study of Attitudes towards Residential Care in Cambodia." Phnom Penh: Ministry of Social Affairs, Veterans and Youth Rehabilitation, 2011. http://www.crin.org/docs/Study_Attitudes_towards_RC.pdf.

Minnesota Department of Human Services Family and Children's Services Division. "Orphanages: An Historical Overview: A Discussion of the Role of Orphanages in Child Welfare Policy." N.d. https://www.leg.mn.gov/docs/pre2003/other/950265.pdf.

Mishra, Rachna, and Vanita Sondhi. "Fostering Resilience among Orphaned Adolescents through Institutional Care in India." *Residential Treatment for Children and Youth* 36, no. 4 (2019): 314–337. https://doi.org/10.1080/0886571X.2018.1535286.

Moalosi, Lerato Constance. "Focusing on Caregivers: The Experiences of Women Caregivers Caring for Orphans and Vulnerable Children at Crossroads Child and Youth Care Center, Matatiele." Master's thesis, University of Kwazulu-Natal, 2019.

Mom, Kunthea. "Curb Physical Discipline: Charity." *Khmer Times*, June 1, 2017.

Morrow, Virginia. "Rethinking Childhood Dependency: Children's Contribution to the Domestic Economy." *Sociological Review* 44 (1996): 58–77.

Mostafanezhad, Mary. *Volunteer Tourism: Popular Humanitarianism in Neoliberal Times.* Farnham: Ashgate, 2016.

MoSVY. "Mapping of Residential Care Facilities in the Capital and 24 Provinces of the Kingdom of Cambodia." 2017. https://urldefense.com/v3/__https://www.unicef.org/cambodia/media/1301/file/*20Action*20Plan*20for*20improving*20child*20care_Eng.pdf_

_;JSUlJSUl!!C5qS4YX3!U-yPV9cjcZLWuUp_GCz7PAGPPjFjcZhyM6In1njePrTJ4BmVgZZC
N3GD3764YvSSJA$.

———. "A Statistical Profile of Child Protection in Cambodia." 2018. https://urldefense.com
/v3/__https://www.unicef.org/cambodia/media/711/file/Cambodia_Report_Final
_web_ready_HIGH.pdf*20.pdf__;JQ!!C5qS4YX3!R3ICsooA7_n5DBePcNnZnU4ob873y
_SJ5HwDKGe38YAyJxdIFeXUiDL9dR3dhBJJxA$.

Muller, Gregor. *Colonial Cambodia's "Bad Frenchmen": The Rise of French Rule and the Life of
Thomas Caraman, 1840–87.* London: Routledge, 2006.

Munyas, Burca. "Genocide in the Minds of Cambodian Youth: Transmitting (Hi)stories of
Genocide to Second and Third Generations in Cambodia." *Journal of Genocide Research*
10, no. 3 (2008): 413–439. https://doi.org/10.1080/14623520802305768.

NapoleonCat. "Facebook Users in Cambodia." April 2019. https://napoleoncat.com/stats
/facebook-users-in-cambodia/2019/04.

Natanddrew. "Visit an Orphanage Near Siem Reap and Make the Highlight of Your Trip."
Lonely Planet Thorn Tree Forum, 2008. https://www.lonelyplanet.com/thorntree
/forums/responsible-travel/topics/visit-an-orphanage-near-siem-reap-and-make-the
-highlight-of-your-trip.

National AIDS Authority. "Monitoring Progress towards the 2011 UN Political Declaration
on HIV and AIDS." Cambodia Country Progress Report, 2015. https://www.unaids.org
/sites/default/files/country/documents/KHM_narrative_report_2015.pdf.

National Institute of Statistics, Directorate General for Health [Cambodia], and ORC Macro.
"Cambodia Demographic and Health Survey 2000." 2001. https://dhsprogram.com
/pubs/pdf/FR124/FR124.pdf.

Neimetz, Catherine. "Navigating Family Roles within an Institutional Framework: An
Exploratory Study in One Private Chinese Orphanage." *Journal of Child and Family Studies*
20, no. 5 (2011): 585–595.

NGO Coalition on the Rights of the Child. "UPR Submission on Cambodia Child Rights,
2009–2013." http://ngocrc.org/attachments/article/449UPRpercent20submissionperce
nt20onpercent20Childpercent20Rightspercent20inpercent20Cambodia.pdf.

Nonoyama-Tarumi, Yuko, and Kurt Bredenberg. "Impact of School Readiness Program
Interventions on Children's Learning in Cambodia." *International Journal of Educational
Development* 29 (2009): 39–45.

OpenDevelopment Cambodia. "Education and Training." 2018. https://opendevelopment
cambodia.net/topics/education-and-training/.

"Orphan." *Oxford English Dictionary*, n.d. http://OED.com.

"Orphan." *Strong's Concordance*, n.d. http://biblehub.com/greek/3737.htm.

Pecore, Joanna T. "Sounding the Spirit of Cambodia: The Living Tradition of Khmer Music
and Dance-Drama in a Washington, DC Community." Doctoral dissertation, University of Maryland, 2004.

Phaly, Nuon. *My Name Is Phaly.* n.d. http://www.eglobalfamily.org/phaly-story.html.

Philadelphia Courts. "Orphans' Court Division." n.d. https://www.courts.phila.gov/common
-pleas/orphans/.

Phim, Toni, and Ashley Thompson. *Dance in Cambodia.* Oxford: Oxford University Press, 2000.

Poniewozik, James. "'Everything's Gonna Be Okay' Review: Half-Siblings, Whole Family."
New York Times, January 14, 2020.

Prak, Chan Thul. "Cambodia, U.N. Launch Plan to Tackle Fake Orphanages." Reuters,
April 20, 2017. https://www.reuters.com/article/us-cambodia-orphanage/cambodia-u
-n-launch-plan-to-tackle-fake-orphanages-idUSKBN17M0UD.

———. "Official Accused of Extorting Orphan Dancers." *Cambodia Daily*, January 5, 2005.

Proeschold-Bell, Rae Jean, Nneka Jebose Molokwu, Corey L. M. Keyes, Malik Muhammad Sohail, David E. Eagle, Heather E. Parnell, Warren A. Kinghorn, Cyrilla Amanya, Vanroth Vann, Ira Madan, Blen M. Biru, Dean Lewis, Misganaw Eticha Dubie, and Kathryn Whetten. "Caring and Thriving: An International Qualitative Study of Caregivers of Orphaned and Vulnerable Children and Strategies to Sustain Positive Mental Health." *Children and Youth Services Review* 98 (2019): 143–153.

Proyrungroj, Raweewan. "Orphan Volunteer Tourism in Thailand: Volunteer Tourists' Motivations and On-Site Experiences." *Journal of Hospitality and Tourism Research* 41, no. 5 (2017): 560–584.

Ramaswamy, Sheila, and Shekhar Seshadri. "The Deinstitutionalisation Debate in India: Throwing the Baby Out with the Bathwater?" *Scottish Journal of Residential Child Care* 19, no. 1 (2020): 8–31.

Reas, P. Jane. "'Boy, Have We Got a Vacation for You': Orphanage Tourism in Cambodia and the Commodification and Objectification of the Orphanaged Child." *Thammasat Review* 16 (2013): 121–140.

———. "'Children That Are Cute Enough to Eat': The Commodification of Children in Volunteering Vacations to Orphanages and Childcare Establishments in Siem Reap, Cambodia." *Tourism Culture & Communication* 20, nos. 2–3 (2020): 83–93.

———. "'So, Child Protection, I'll Make a Quick Point of It Now': Broadening the Notion of Child Abuse in Volunteering Vacations in Siem Reap, Cambodia." *Tourism Review International* 18, no. 4 (2015): 295–309.

Retka, Janelle. "When an Orphanage Can Provide What a Parent Cannot." *Bright Magazine*, April 24, 2018, 1–11.

Reynell, Josephine. *Political Pawns: Refugees on the Thai-Kampuchean Border.* Oxford: Refugee Studies Program, 1989.

Richter, Linda, and Amy Norman. "AIDS Orphan Tourism: A Threat to Young Children in Residential Care." *Vulnerable Children and Youth Studies* 5, no. 3 (2010): 217–229.

Roche, Steven. "Conceptualising Children's Life Histories and Reasons for Entry into Residential Care in the Philippines: Social Contexts, Instabilities and Safeguarding." *Children and Youth Services Review* 110 (2020): 104820.

Rogers, Justin M., and Victor Karunan. "Is the Deinstitutionalisation of Alternative Care a 'Wicked Problem'? A Qualitative Study Exploring the Perceptions of Child Welfare Practitioners and Policy Actors in Thailand." *International Social Work* 63, no. 5 (2020): 626–639.

Rollet, Charles. "The Story of Cambodia's Stolen Children." *Phnom Penh Post*, October 3, 2014.

Rubenstein, Beth L., Matthew MacFarlane, Celina Jensen, and Lindsay Stark. "Measuring Movement into Residential Care Institutions in Haiti after Hurricane Matthew: A Pilot Study." *PLOS ONE* 13, no. 4 (2018). https://doi.org/10.1371/journal.pone.0195515.

Rus, Adrian V., Sheri R. Parris, and Ecaterina Stativa, eds. *Child Maltreatment in Residential Care.* Dordrecht: Springer, 2017.

Rus, Adrian V., Ecaterina Stativa, Sheri R. Parris, Jacquelyn S. Pennings, Max E. Butterfield, Wesley C. Lee, and Ovidu Gavrilovici. "Punishment, Peer Exploitation and Sexual Abuse in Long-Term Romanian Residential Centers." In *Child Maltreatment in Residential Care*, edited by Adrian V. Rus, Sheri R. Parris, and Ecaterina Stativa, 61–86. Dordrecht: Springer, 2017.

Sam, Vichet. "Impacts of Educational Mismatches in Developing Countries with a Focus on Cambodia." Doctoral dissertation, Université Grenoble Alpes, 2018.

Save the Children. "Governments Now Have an Opportunity to Stop Supporting the Unnecessary Separation of Children from Parents." December 18, 2019. https://www.savethe

children.org/us/about-us/media-and-news/2019-press-releases/unnecessary-child
-separation-resolution-passes.

Schatz, Joseph. "Cambodia's Child Grooms." *Al Jazeera America*, May 6, 2015.

Scheyvens, Regina. *Tourism and Poverty*. New York: Routledge, 2010.

Schuster Institute for Investigative Journalism. "Capsule History of Adoption Issues in Cambodia." 2011. https://www.brandeis.edu/investigate/adoption/cambodia.html.

Scollay, Rachel, and Lon Nara. "Slum Children Dance for Their Supper." *Phnom Penh Post*, January 4, 2002.

Seiff, Abby. "Cambodian Orphans Yearn for Answers 40 Years after Fleeing the Khmer Rouge." *Time*, April 14, 2015. https://time.com/3820620/cambodia-adoptees-khmer -rouge-orphans/.

Shapiro, Toni. *Dance and the Spirit of Cambodia*. Ithaca, NY: Cornell University Press, 1994.

Shapiro-Phim, Toni. "Dance in Cambodia." *Asia Society*, 2019. https://asiasociety.org/dance -cambodia.

——. *The Dancer and Cambodian History*. Philadelphia: Pew Center for Arts and Heritage, 2007.

Shelton, Tracey, and Sam Rith. "Orphanage Tourism: A Questionable Industry." *Phnom Penh Post*, March 9, 2007.

Sheridan, Margaret, Stacy Drury, Kate McLaughlin, and Alisa Almas. "Early Institutionalization: Neurobiological Consequences and Genetic Modifiers." *Neuropsychology Review* 20, no. 4 (2010): 414–429.

Smith-Hefner, Nancy. *Khmer-American: Identity and Moral Education in a Diasporic Community*. Berkeley: University of California Press, 1999.

Snookieboi. "Orphanages in Cambodia." *Travelfish Cambodia Forum*, 2013. https://www .travelfish.org/board/post/cambodia/12216_orphanages-in-cambodia.

Sokha, Touch, and Erin Handley. "Over 35,000 Kids Still in Care." *Phnom Penh Post*, April 21, 2017. https://www.phnompenhpost.com/national/over-35000-kids-still-care.

Soumy, Phan, and Danielle Keeton-Olsen. "Minister: School Quality Improving, Dropout Rate Still High." *Cambodia Daily*, March 22, 2017. https://english.cambodiadaily.com /news/minister-school-quality-improving-dropout-rate-still-high-126857/.

Stahili Foundation. "Families, Not Orphanages." 2018. https://www.stahili.org/orphanages/.

Stark, Lindsay, Beth L. Rubenstein, Kimchoeun Pak, and Sok Kosal. "National Estimation of Children in Residential Care Institutions in Cambodia: A Modelling Study." *BMJ Open* 7, no. 1 (2016). http://dx.doi.org/10.1136/bmjopen-2016-013888.

Suenobo, Yumiko. *Management of Education Systems in Zones of Conflict-Relief Operations: A Case-Study in Thailand*. Bangkok: UNESCO, 1995.

Sullivan, Nicky. "Apsara Dancing: A Bit of Tradition." Travelfish, November 29, 2016. https:// www.travelfish.org/sight_profile/cambodia/western_cambodia/siem_reap/siem _reap/796.

Sunrise Cambodia. "Visit Sunrise in Cambodia." n.d. http://sunrisecambodia.org.au/our -story/visit-sunrise-in-cambodia/.

Tatlow-Golden, Mimi, and Heather Montgomery. "Childhood Studies and Child Psychology: Disciplines in Dialogue?" *Children & Society* (2020). https://doi.org/10.1111/chso.12384.

Terry, Fiona. *Condemned to Repeat?* Ithaca, NY: Cornell University Press, 2002.

Thompson, Larry C. *Refugee Workers in the Indochina Exodus, 1975–1982*. London: McFarland, 2010.

TripAdvisor. "Traditional Khmer Dance at ACODO Orphanage." https://www.tripadvisor .com/Attraction_Review-g297390-d1647060-Reviews-Traditional_Khmer_Dance_at _ACODO_Orphanage-Siem_Reap_Siem_Reap_Province.html.

TV Tropes. "Orphanage of Fear." n.d. http://tvtropes.org/pmwiki/pmwiki.php/Main/Orpha nageOfFear.

———. "Orphanage of Love." n.d. http://tvtropes.org/pmwiki/pmwiki.php/Main/Orphan ageOfLove.

———. "Saving the Orphanage." n.d. http://tvtropes.org/pmwiki/pmwiki.php/Main/Saving TheOrphanage.

Twyning, John. *Forms of English History in Literature, Landscape and Architecture.* Basingstoke, UK: Palgrave Macmillan, 2012.

Ulybina, Olga. "Transnational Agency and Domestic Policies: The Case of Childcare Dein-stitutionalization in Georgia." *Global Social Policy* (2020). https://doi.org/10.1177 /1468018120926888.

UNICEF. "Cambodia Launches the 'Strong Family Campaign' Aiming to End Violence Against Children and Unnecessary Family Separation" (2020), https://urldefense.com /v3/__https://www.unicef.org/cambodia/press-releases/cambodia-launches-strong -family-campaign-aiming-end-violence-against-children-and__;!!C5qS4YX3!QViSA8L wOGTZQUDIKTTr_cUFeTAXthoVKMC5TT58O_ir_q2W-xw75ozTRXlkvZm4ow$.

———. "Fact Sheet, Residential Care in Cambodia." 2009. https://www.unicef.org/cambodia /Fact_sheet_-_residential_care_Cambodia.pdf.

———. "Orphans." n.d. https://www.unicef.org/media/orphans.

———. "State of the World's Children 2008." 2008. http://www.unicef.org/sowc08/docs /sowc08_table_4.pdf.

———. "State of the World's Children 2012." 2012. http://www.unicef.org/sowc/files/SOWC _2012-Main_Report_EN_21Dec2011.pdf.

———. "State of the World's Children 2017." 2017. https://www.unicef.org/sowc2017/.

United Nations. "World Statistics Pocketbook." 2016. http://data.un.org/CountryProfile.aspx ?crName=Cambodia#Social.

United Nations General Assembly. "Rights of the Child." Resolution, December 17, 2015. https://www.un.org/en/development/desa/population/migration/generalassembly /docs/globalcompact/A_RES_70_137.pdf.

U.S. Citizenship and Immigration Services. "Orphan." n.d. https://www.uscis.gov/tools /glossary/orphan.

———. "Orphan Process." n.d. https://www.uscis.gov/adoption/immigration-through-adop tion/orphan-process.

Van Bruggen, Diny. *Flowers on the Cactus: Aids and Orphan Care in Cambodia.* Phnom Penh: Don Bosco Technical School, 2005.

van Doore, Kathryn. "Orphanages as Sites of Modern Slavery." In *Modern Day Slavery and Orphanage Tourism*, edited by Joseph M. Cheer, Leigh Mathews, Kathryn E. van Doore, and Karen Flanagan, 19–30. Wallingford, UK: CABI, 2019.

van IJzendoorn, Mariunus, Jesus Palacios, Edmund J. S. Sonuga-Barke, Megan R. Gunnar, Panayiota Vorria, Robert B. McCall, Lucy LeMare, Marian J. Bakermans-Kranenburg, Natasha A. Dobrova-Krol, and Femmie Juffer. "Children in Institutional Care: Delayed Development and Resilience." *Monographs of the Society for Research in Child Develop-ment* 76, no. 4 (2011): 8–30.

Verstraete, Joni. "The Impact of Orphanage Tourism on Residential Care Centres in Cam-bodia." Master's thesis, Leeds Metropolitan University, 2014.

Volkman, Toby. "Imagining Cambodia." *Cultural Survival Quarterly* 14 (September 1990). https://www.culturalsurvival.org/publications/cultural-survival-quarterly/imagining -cambodia.

Walker, Chris, and Morgon Hartley. "Cambodia's Orphan-Industrial Complex." *Atlantic*, June 3, 2013. http://www.theatlantic.com/international/archive/2013/06/cambodias -orphan-industrial-complex/276472/.

Wang, Leslie K. "Importing Western Childhoods into a Chinese State-Run Orphanage." *Qualitative Sociology* 33, no. 2 (2010): 137–159.

———. *Outsourced Children: Orphanage Care and Adoption in Globalizing China.* Stanford, CA: Stanford University Press, 2016.

Wearing, Stephen. *Volunteer Tourism: Experiences That Make a Difference.* Wallingford, UK: CABI, 2001.

Wearing, Stephen, Mary Mostafanezhad, Nha Nguyen, Truc Ha Thanh Nguyen, and Matthew McDonald. "'Poor Children on Tinder' and Their Barbie Saviours: Towards a Feminist Political Economy of Volunteer Tourism." *Leisure Studies* 37, no. 5 (2018): 500–514. https://doi.org/10.1080/02614367.2018.1504979.

Wendyworld. "Cambodian Orphan Family Centre Organization Parts 1 and 2." *Travelpod*, 2009. https://web.archive.org/web/20110628050728/http://www.travelpod.com/travel -blog-entries/wendyworld/4/1261194608/tpod.html.

Whetten, Kathryn, Jan Ostermann, Brian W. Pence, Rachel A. Whetten, Lynne C. Messer, Sumedha Ariely, Karen O'Donnell, Augustine I. Wasonga, Vanroth Vann, Dafrosa Itemba, Misganaw Eticha, Ira Madan, and Nathan M. Thielman. "Three-Year Change in the Wellbeing of Orphaned and Separated Children in Institutional and Family-Based Care Settings in Five Low- and Middle-Income Countries." *PLOS ONE*, August 27, 2014. https://doi.org/10.1371/journal.pone.0104872.

Whetten, Kathryn, Jan Ostermann, Rachel A. Whetten, Brian W. Pence, Karen O'Donnell, Lynne C. Messer, Nathan M. Thielman, and the Positive Outcomes for Orphans (POFO) Research Team. "A Comparison of the Wellbeing of Orphans and Abandoned Children Ages 6–12 in Institutional and Community-Based Care Settings in 5 Less Wealthy Nations." *PLOS ONE* 4 (2009): e8169. https://doi.org/10.1371/journal.pone.0008169.

Williamson, Jan. "Centers for Unaccompanied Children in Khao I Dang Holding Center." *Disasters* 5, no. 2 (1981): 100–104.

Wilson, Audrey, and Vandy Muong. "Homeward Bound? How to Fix a Damaged System." *Phnom Penh Post*, September 30, 2016. https://www.phnompenhpost.com/post-weekend /homeward-bound-how-fix-damaged-system.

Wilson, Liz. "Finding the Win-Win: Providing Supportive and Enriching Volunteer Tourism Experiences while Promoting Sustainable Social Change." *Worldwide Hospitality and Tourism Themes* 7, no. 2 (2015): 201–207.

Worldstrider. "Visit an Orphanage in Phnom Penh." Lonely Planet Thorn Tree Forum, 2005. https://www.lonelyplanet.com/thorntree/forums/asia-south-east-asia-mainland /topics/visit-an-orphanage-in-phnom-penh.

Xia, Lili, and Ching-Man Lam. "Where Is Home? The Lived Experiences of Chinese Children after Their Parents Have Been Incarcerated." *Journal of Social Work Practice* 34, no. 2 (2020): 191–203.

Yendork, Joana Salifu, and Nceba Z. Somhlaba. "Do Social Support, Self-Efficacy and Resilience Influence the Experience of Stress in Ghanaian Orphans? An Exploratory Study." *Child Care in Practice* 21, no. 2 (2015): 140–159. http://dx.doi.org/10.1080/13575279.2014 .985286.

Zelizer, Viviana. *Pricing the Priceless Child: The Changing Social Value of Children.* Princeton, NJ: Princeton University Press, 1994.

———. *The Purchase of Intimacy.* Princeton, NJ: Princeton University Press, 2009.

Zhang, Jintao, Guoxiang Zhao, Xiaoming Li, Yan Hong, Xiaoyi Fang, Douglas Barnett, Xiuyun
    Lin, Junfeng Zhao, and Liying Zhang. "Positive Future Orientation as a Mediator
    between Traumatic Events and Mental Health among Children Affected by HIV/AIDS
    in Rural China." *AIDS Care* 21, no. 12 (2009): 1508–1516.
Zimmerman, Brigitte. "Orphan Living Situations in Malawi: A Comparison of Orphanages
    and Foster Homes." Master's thesis, Stanford University, 2005.

INDEX

abuse, 181n11; child exploitation, 45–46; domestic violence, 26–27, 78, 101, 104, 126, 140–141; in orphanages, concerns about, 9, 12; in orphanages and family-based care, 12; orphanage tourism and, 44–46; in refugee camps, 26–27; sexual, 26, 44–46; by stepparent, 80; by volunteers, concern about, 115–116

addiction. *See* substance abuse

adoption: corruption in, 31, 82; criteria for, 15; United States suspending Cambodian, 31, 34

adulthood, childhood and, 158, 184n23

adults, at Children's Opportunity Center, 68–70, 75

adverse experiences: impact of earlier, 134, 177n6; pre-orphanage issues, 12, 57, 134, 153–154, 177n6

age: of Children's Opportunity Center residents, 80–81; of junior high school students, 65, 75, 145; marriage, 58, 177n10, 184n23

agency, 18; individual, gratitude and, 124, 136–141, 156; self-efficacy and, orphanages cultivating, 156–157

alcohol abuse, 79–80, 104, 126, 152

Angka, 24

Angkor Thom, 22

Angkor Wat, 62, 104

anti-orphanage-tourism campaign, 45–47, 49, 160

antiretroviral (ARV) treatment, 31, 34, 80

attachment, 8–9, 44, 147

Australia: Modern Slavery Act, 34, 49; Stolen Generation in, 144

Baez, Joan, 29

bathrooms, 94, 180n34.

best interests, of child, 3–4, 7, 145

Bowlby, John, 8

breakfast, 64–65

Buddhism, 22, 180n2; Children's Opportunity Center, founding of, and, 31–32, 71; Children's Opportunity Center NGO and, 21, 68, 137; Children's Opportunity Center residents and, 70, 91, 102, 133, 137; dharma class, 102; karma in, 133, 137, 182n11; merit

in, 21, 137; temple boys, 21, 73, 96; Theravada, 21, 169n3

Burrington, Kathryn, 44

Cambodia: domestic violence in, 26, 78; educational attainment in, 58, 128, 177n7; legal marriage age in, 184n23; NGOs in, high number of, 62, 177n1; Siem Reap, 35, 37–38, 52, 55, 61–64, 93; stigma and culture of, 91; Thai border with, 1, 161; tourism industry of, 34–36, 38–39, 45, 160, 172n3; transnational adoption from, 31, 34; United States war in, 20, 23–24, 34. *See also* government, Cambodian; orphanages, Cambodian

Cambodian Light Children Association (CLCA), 30, 171n52

care: adults as caretakers, 76; children giving, 86–90, 102, 108–110, 137–138, 156; quality of, measuring, 151–152

caregivers: criteria for, 69, 178n10; ratio of, 68

cell phones, disputes over, 153, 159

Charet, Eloise, 24

Cheung Judge, Ruth, 184n18

Chheng Phon, 23–24

child circulation, 21–23, 91–92

child exploitation, 45–46

childhood: with adulthood, boundary of, 158, 184n23; norms, changing, of, 157–159; subjective beliefs about, 10, 145; Western beliefs about, 49

childhood studies, 18–19, 176n61

child labor, 27, 106–107, 123, 147–148

child protection: foreign volunteers and, concerns about, 115–116; policies of, 44, 84, 115–116

children are not tourist attractions campaign, 46–47

Children's Council, 78, 84, 140

Children's Opportunity Center (COC), 3, 178n9, 178n15, 180n35; adults at, 68–70, 75; in afternoon, 71, 73–76; age of residents, 80–81; arrival at, interviews on, 97–98, 101, 103–107, 126; bathrooms at, 94; Buddhism and, 21, 31–32, 68, 70–71, 91, 102, 133, 137; Cambodian orphanages, history of, and, 31–33; as caretakers,

ABOUT THE AUTHOR

KATHIE CARPENTER is associate professor of global studies at the University of Oregon. She received her doctorate in linguistics from Stanford University, with a focus on Thai linguistics and children's psycholinguistics. She has conducted research on children's lived experiences and the idea of childhood in Thailand, Indonesia, and Cambodia and on youth volunteerism in Russia as well as in Asia. She also researches and publishes on childhood representations and best practices for inclusivity in children's museums in Europe, North America, and Asia. She lives in Eugene, Oregon.